The Italian Colony of São Paulo

Critical Studies in Italian Migrations

Nancy C. Carnevale and Laura E. Ruberto, *series editors*

This series publishes scholarship on Italian migrations, mobilities, and other related transnational concerns. Authors include both emerging and established scholars with differing theoretical and methodological approaches, all rooted in humanities and social science disciplines. Books in the series seek to engage and extend questions of identity and community pertinent to the fields of ethnic studies, gender studies, and migration studies, among others.

The Italian Colony of São Paulo

Race, Class, and Cultural Capital in Brazil

Giulia Riccò

FORDHAM UNIVERSITY PRESS
NEW YORK 2025

Image credit: Edifício Martinelli (named in honor of Italian industrialist Giuseppe Martinelli), the first skyscraper in Brazil and, at the time of its opening, the tallest building in South America, circa 1928. Autoria não identificada/Acervo Instituto Moreira Salles.

This book is freely available in an open-access edition thanks to TOME (Toward an Open Monograph Ecosystem)—a collaboration of the Association of American Universities, the Association of University Presses, and the Association of Research Libraries—and the generous support of the University of Michigan's College of Literature, Science & the Arts and the Office of the Vice President for Research. Learn more at the TOME website, available at: openmonographs.org.

Fordham University Press also publishes its books in a variety of electronic formats. Some content that appears in print may not be available in electronic books.

Visit us online at www.fordhampress.com.

Library of Congress Cataloging-in-Publication Data available online at https://catalog.loc.gov.

Printed in the United States of America

27 26 25 5 4 3 2 1

First edition

To Justin

CONTENTS

The Italian Colony of São Paulo

SÃO PAULO PREDIO MARTINELLI

NOVA YORK DA SUL-AMERICA

INTRODUCTION

São Paulo, Nova York da Sul America

Italian Immigrants in São Paulo and the Making of Modern Brazilian Culture

A visitor to São Paulo in 1928 had the unique chance to witness the unfolding in real time of what would become the first skyscraper in the city, and, at that time, the tallest building in South America. If they were lucky enough, they could even have snatched a postcard of this brand-new construction to remember their visit. The building in question is the well-known Predio Martinelli, or Martinelli Building, located on Rua São Bento. Funded by Italian entrepreneur Giuseppe Martinelli, who made his fortune as a supplier, the ongoing construction pictured on the postcard (reproduced to the left and on the cover of this book) would go on to become, once completed, a staple of São Paulo's architecture. The postcard shows the building still wrapped in scaffolding but with at least two promotional signs clearly visible to the naked eye. The largest one, on the building's left side, is an advertisement for the internationally known Italian liqueur Fernet-Branca; the second one, in the center and right above what would become the entrance, is an advertisement for the *Saturnia*, the famous record-breaking motor ship designed by Niccolò Costanzi and constructed for the Cosulich Line of Trieste.

Nothing less than a skyscraper could have symbolized the fast-paced industrialization that the city had experienced in the span of just two decades. After all, the caption on the postcard proudly reads, "New York of South America." But perhaps the person who created the postcard was alluding not only to the built environment of the cityscape but also to the presence of European immigrants among the workers that populated the city itself. São Paulo and New York become in the postcard inextricably bound together by their modern architecture, as well as by the presence in the urban fabric of immigrants actively making these cities, through their labor, into symbols of American modernity. And yet, the postcard also marks a clear difference in the way certain immigrant groups, Italians in particular, were able to directly shape and take part in the modernization of São Paulo vis-à-vis the role they played in New York.

What stands out the most when viewing the postcard are the unquestionably Italian-sounding name of the building and the presence of not one but two Italian companies among the sponsors. First, the fact that it was an Italian immigrant who made his fortune in São Paulo that financed the building challenges a commonplace narrative about the poverty and misery that accompanied the Italian diaspora in the Americas. Second, the presence of the advertisement for Fernet-Branca makes visible the intense commercial trade that Italian companies engaged in with South America due to the large presence of Italians in the region, highlighting a very peculiar (post)colonial relationship between, in this instance, Italy and Brazil. Third, the image of the motor ship *Saturnia*, one of the fastest and most massive motor ships to cross the Atlantic, reveals the fraught nature of the Italian national project which, since its inception, was marked by transnational crossings and imperialist desires (one need only consider how the *Saturnia*, commissioned to connect the ports of Italy to La Plata, was later deployed in the Abyssinian campaign of 1935). In other words, *italianità* (Italianness) permeates and marks all that is modern and urban about this New York of South America. The aim of this book is to understand how the representation of Italianness in this postcard came to be and what that process can teach us about modern and contemporary Italian culture.

In the late nineteenth century, Brazilian elites implemented an aggressive plan to dilute their country's Black population. They did so by subsidizing the migration of white people from Europe. As a direct result of this whitening project, São Paulo—today the most populous city in the Americas—became home to the largest concentration of people of Italian descent outside of Italy. The emergence of what I call a "New World Italian discourse" enabled Italians to become the unlikely standard bearers of white racial identity in modern-day Brazil, a country with the largest number of people of African descent outside of Nigeria. *The Italian Colony of São Paulo* reconstructs the cultural and political discourse surrounding the mass migration and integration of Italians into the city of São Paulo, which evolved and changed over the course of the twentieth century. In so doing, this book reveals how these overlooked experiences of Italians in Brazil complicate conventional narratives: first, about the racial ambiguity and oppression of Italians in the Americas, and second, about the conflation of Italians with cultural and economic backwardness in Europe. Moreover, by examining how Brazilian racial theorists, writers, and the mainstream press viewed Italians as vectors of whiteness—elevating them above both other immigrant groups and Black Brazilians—*The Italian Colony of São Paulo* offers a novel angle from which to further challenge the myth of Brazilian racial democracy.

In the first part of this introduction, I explain how Italians have been constructed as racially ambiguous in the United States and in Italy. I also show how this ambiguity has, in turn, frequently prevented Italians from fully acknowledging their own complicity in institutional racism and white supremacy. In the second part, I show how the Italian experience in São Paulo tells a different story from the one in the United States, which is often seen as paradigmatic. In this alternative, less well-known story, Italians played not a bit part, but, instead, a leading role in constructing and mediating notions of white racial and cultural superiority. Here I reveal how, in São Paulo, overlapping discourses about race, modernization, and civilization led to the popular image of Italians as paragons of whiteness. These discursive practices represent important antecedents to the racial nationalism that reared its ugly head in the Italian nation-state throughout the twentieth century, and which remains central to contemporary debates about national identity in the Italian public sphere.

1. Are All Italians White in the Same Way?

"Are Italians White?" So asked scholars of Italian American Studies Jennifer Guglielmo and Salvatore Salerno in an edited collection published in 2003. Their goal with this provocative question was to analyze a persistent and, at times, unspoken, anxiety over Italians' racial ambiguity (or what literary critic Tatiana Petrovich Njegosh has called Italians' "racial double status"). This racial ambiguity, as Guglielmo points out in her contribution to the collection, makes for a troubling paradox. On the one hand, racially inflected discrimination against Italians, particularly in America, allows Italians to claim victim status alongside people of color. On the other hand, focusing on discrimination against Italians tends to obscure their access—sometimes fragile but nonetheless real—to the white racial privileges that enabled their social mobility, particularly compared to Black and Latinx populations. Such obfuscation allows Italians to downplay the persistence of racism and structural inequalities that afflict other groups and cast themselves as members of a model minority.[1]

Drawing on W.E.B. Dubois's 1935 analysis of cross-racial working class solidarity, or the lack thereof, historian David R. Roediger explains how notions of whiteness in the United States have been entangled with specific ideas about work. Working-class whites—whether native-born or foreigners—became especially attached to their whiteness. This was because, despite their exploitative working conditions, they understood whiteness as a "wage," whereby they could claim to be above those formerly enslaved. Roediger expanded his argument in a later book to include the immigrants arriving from Southern and Eastern Europe to the United States, namely Italians, but also Poles, Slavs, and European Jews. They too, he explained, despite their initial status as "in-between" peoples, gradually became white and embraced the same values of the native-born white working class. The "messiness" (to use his own word) through which this operation happened depended upon how willing these immigrants were to distance themselves from their Black counterparts, as well as how US laws, such as the Immigration Act of 1924, and institutions shaped the very contours of their whiteness.[2]

And it is true that Italians, despite being officially categorized as "white" upon their arrival in the United States, became targets of xenophobic attacks that had deeply racist undercurrents.[3] The infamous 1891 lynching of eleven Italians in New Orleans, after all, is the largest recorded mass lynching in US history.[4] "In the eyes of native-born Americans," notes historian Gary Gerstle, "southern Italians were seen as a group that, of all the European immigrants, most closely resembled blacks." Similarly, political scientist Adolph L. Reed Jr. recollects how, living in the US South under Jim Crow, "the dark-complexioned Sicilians shaded phenotypically into indistinguishability from the black Creole population."[5] And yet, by the end of the twentieth century, Italian Americans had become closely associated with anti-Black violence. One need only think of the brutal killing of Yussuf Hawkins in 1989—a young African American male who ventured into Bensonhurst, a predominantly Italian American enclave in Brooklyn, to look at a used car—as well as that community's racist response to a peaceful protest held in Hawkins's honor.[6] The history of Italians in America reveals a process whereby Italians went from having a tenuous grasp on whiteness to becoming gatekeepers of Black-white racial boundaries. If what made Italians racially ambiguous had partly to do with the fact that, as historian Matthew Frye Jacobson has pointed out, Italians did not *act* white, then one way Italians in America learned to assert their whiteness was by perpetrating acts of anti-Black racism.[7]

The discrepancy between how Italians were categorized on paper in the United States and how they were treated in everyday life offers perhaps one of the best illustrations of the social construction of race. Here race is what Pierre Bourdieu would call a "symbolic" category, as opposed to a biological or scientific reality. Using Bourdieu's notion of the symbolic to account for race (intended as a category) and racialization (intended as the discourse which informs that category) illuminates the social production of "a system of perceived differences . . . that is, a distribution of symbolic capital . . . whose objective truth is misrecognized."[8] Thus, in this book, I understand whiteness and blackness as artificial categories constructed through a series of historical, economic, and social relations. Moreover, these categories do not stay fixed; instead, they change according to the exigencies of a particular moment and politico-economic structures. Rather than treat race and racial categories as axiomatic or stable, I understand them as products of contingent processes that unfold largely in the realm of cultural production, where they then acquire the patina of commonsense.

In addition to their failure to act in accord with the cultural dictates of whiteness as defined by America's Anglo-Protestant elites, Italians' protracted proximity—in terms of color, class, and geography to Black and Brown peoples in the United States—also threatened to undermine their whiteness.[9] This explains why Italian Americans worked so hard to distance themselves from these spaces, once they had the means to do so; and why, when they lacked such means, they sometimes resorted to violence to prevent Black and Brown encroachment on what they perceived as their rightful racial and ethnic territory.[10] Back in Italy, a similar racial anxiety and pressure to assert a specific white identity animated political and cultural life, since the country was near, in both geographical and historical terms, to Africa. Thus, Italians both in the United States and Italy constructed their whiteness by fanatically disavowing their affinities—real and imagined—with Blackness and Africanness.

In fact, the tendency to view Italians as an inferior subrace of white people in the United States had its roots in the racial debates that raged in Italy at the turn of the twentieth century, as millions of Italians, largely from Central and Southern Italy, fled their homeland not only for the United States, but also Canada, Argentina, and, as discussed here, Brazil. The theoretical underpinning of these later debates was an 1853 treatise, *An Essay on the Inequality of Human Races*, which laid the groundwork for scientific racism. This work, by French author Arthur De Gobineau, declared the Aryan race as superior to others. Moreover, it relegated Italians, along with other Southern European groups, to an inferior race, on account of their geographical proximity to Africa and their longer historical tradition of ethnic mixing.

Shortly after the unification of Northern and Southern Italy in 1871, homegrown pseudoscientists like Cesare Lombroso and Alfredo Niceforo, following in De Gobineau's footsteps, devised different theories to demonstrate the superiority of the Italian race over the African one.[11] Both Lombroso and Niceforo attributed the racial inferiority of Italians to Southern Italians. After all, they argued, it was those in Southern Italy who had most likely come into contact with African populations; by this logic, Italian racial inferiority was in fact concentrated in the South. This line of thinking echoed the colonial undertones that accompanied the annexation of the Italian southern territories to the Savoy Crown.[12] Some scholars have described what has taken place in Italy, with regard to its so-called Southern Question, as "orientalism in one country": Northern Italian elites stigmatized Southern Italians as primitive and degenerate in order to project an image of themselves as authentic, civilized, and, by extension, thoroughly white Europeans.[13]

Already at the very inception of the modern Italian nation-state, Italian elites sought desperately to invoke notions of whiteness and racial purity. And these notions hinged on disarticulating Italianness from Africanness, although, in this case, an Africanness embodied not by immigrants, but by native-born Italian citizens.[14] Also, Italian elites sought to exorcise their fears of racial contamination and inferiority by joining the rush for colonies, and by establishing imperial dominion over Africa. Eager to expand their colonial possessions—which at that point included a series of protectorates on the Red Sea—and further demonstrate their claims to white racial superiority, Italian elites launched a foolhardy and disorganized campaign to annex Ethiopia. The troops of Emperor Menelik II ably defended the country against the Italian army, officially defeating the Europeans at Adwa in 1896.[15] This humiliating defeat reinforced the racial ambiguity of Italians. Their failure to subjugate Africans seemed to confirm their inferiority to the supposedly stronger and purer peoples of Northern Europe. The crushing blow that Italians experienced at Adwa would haunt them for decades, on both sides of the Atlantic.

With the rise of Mussolini, racial ideas about the role of Italians in the Mediterranean began to change. However, they had less to do with racial purity and more to do with the supremacy of Italians as a *razza mediterranea*.[16] This theory celebrated Italians as the strongest race to emerge from centuries of mixing along the shores of the Mediterranean. In other words, Mussolini tried to transform Italians' racial ambiguity into a virtue, one directly linked to the legacy of the Roman Empire. And, in fact, it was precisely at the service of his imperialist agenda that he deployed these notions of Italy's exemplary *mediterraneità*. Since Italians were the prime subjects to emerge from the Mediterranean melting pot, it follows that (at least, according to the Mediterranean racial theory) they should settle the more putatively primitive spaces within the Mediterranean.[17] The violence with which Mussolini occupied Ethiopia in 1935 and the segregationist laws that he enforced, both in the colonies and the metropole, soon contrasted starkly with his earlier ideas about *meticciato* and Italians' role within it.[18] Such actions revealed, with brutal force, the racial anxiety that has dogged the Italian nation-state since its inception.

This mixture of scientific racism, imperial failure, and *mediterraneità* helped to create the mythology of Italians' racial ambiguity or "double racial status." Thus, even in Italy, Italians have had to grapple with racialized anxieties about their place within the European order.[19] And, as with Italian Americans, Italians in Italy often use their perceived subaltern status in relation to Northern Europe, as well as their comparatively modest history of colonialism, to downplay or deflect attention away from the nation's crimes and shortcomings, particularly on the question of race.[20] For Italian Americans in the United States, their perceived racial ambiguity often leads many of them to embrace a model minority myth; similarly, for Italians in Italy, such notions often lead many to embrace the myth of Italian color blindness.

The problem with Italian color blindness, as both Alessandro Portelli and Cristina Lombardi-Diop have pointed out, is that it equates whiteness with "normal." As literary critic Marzia Milazzo has shown, color blindness is actually a constitutive "tool" of white supremacy because it camouflages practices that are actually deeply racist. Indeed, in response to claims that racism, particularly directed toward those of African descent, permeates Italian society, the common response is simple: "race" does not exist in Italy. To be sure, as an official category or notion of personhood, this indeed holds true. And yet, ideas of white racial nationalism have profoundly shaped Italian political history and widespread cultural assumptions about who or what qualifies as authentically Italian.[21]

Drawing on literary scholars Charles Burdett and Loredana Polezzi, *The Italian Colony of São Paulo* participates in the process of "opening up Italian Studies to cultural phenomena which emerge and circulate not only in other spaces but also in different languages" and of "stressing the dynamic tension between the national and transnational." It contributes to the "transnational turn" in Italian Studies advanced by Emma Bond and, more recently,

Teresa Fiore. Through the conceptual category of "pre-occupied spaces," Fiore shows how emigration, immigration, and (post)colonial experiences cannot be disentangled from one another when discussing the making of Italy and Italian identity.[22] This book similarly insists on the connection of these phenomena by drawing attention to the peculiar (post)colonial relationship between Italy and São Paulo.

But *The Italian Colony of São Paulo* also adopts a different approach to transnational Italian Studies from these previous studies. Instead of remapping transnational formations of Italy across multiple locations, my book zeroes in on one specific locality, the city of São Paulo, and the discourses that accompanied the arrivals of Italians in Brazil. At the same time, I situate my book in the larger body of works that have studied what historian Pamela Ballinger has called "the multiple natures of Italy and Italianness" from the point of view of diaspora studies, mobility studies, and border studies. It is within this cross-disciplinary and transnational panorama that I focus my analysis of Italians in São Paulo.[23]

That same racial ambiguity which prompted Guglielmo and Salerno to ask their provocative question takes on a completely different meaning when we look at the relationship between Brazilians and Italians at the end of the nineteenth century.[24] *The Italian Colony of São Paulo* proposes that we understand São Paulo as a kind of laboratory or workshop for the racialization of Italians as white. In this sense, *The Italian Colony of São Paulo* is also in conversation with the research pioneered by Cristina Lombardi-Diop, who, in a 2015 essay, hints at the possibility that "the study of Italian American racial models of italianità may illuminate aspects of colonial and postcolonial racial culture that might otherwise remain muted."[25] At the same time, the paradigm advanced by the Black Mediterranean Collective (an interdisciplinary group of scholars working on race and racial capitalism in Southern Europe) has become a crucial point of reference for thinking about the anti-Blackness inherent in the Italian national project. I am interested in looking at the ways in which that same anti-Blackness informs the largest Italian diasporic community in South America, and how it can operate differently, albeit no less deleteriously, in a society that prizes *mestiçagem* (racial mixing). Just as geographer Camilla Hawthorne has acknowledged the limits of the US race model for understanding the kind of racist forces operating in Italy—and intuited that, instead, Caribbean theories of creolization work better for theorizing the Black Mediterranean—I too suggest that perhaps another racial paradigm, one that paradoxically prizes both whiteness and *mestiçagem*, is needed to study race and racism in the Italian context.[26] By focusing my inquiry on the racialization of Italians in Brazil, I reveal how the Brazilian racial imaginary tells an alternative story about the imbrications between whiteness and Italianness. In many aspects, the discourse of Italian racial, economic, and cultural superiority that I trace in this book—a discourse that I have called "New World Italian"—anticipates the ways in which Italians have come to understand themselves in the later part of the twentieth century.[27] Turning to these discursive strategies, through which Italians entered the fraught racial dynamics of a nation like Brazil, allows me to shed new light on what Tatiana Njegosh has described as the "tight, and yet obscure and potent link" between Italian national identity and whiteness.[28]

2. "*White on Arrival*" in Brazil

Numerically fewer Italians arrived in Brazil than in the United States and Argentina.[29] According to the Instituto Brasileiro de Geografia e Estatística (IBGE), a total of 1,401,335 Italians arrived in Brazil between 1884 and 1933. They counted as the most populous national group, followed by the Portuguese with 1,145,737 recorded entries; the Spanish with 142,457; the Germans with 154,397; the Japanese with 142,457; and the Syrian and "Turks" (a term sometimes used to describe immigrants from Lebanon) with 97,914. In other words, 36.7 percent of the immigrants who arrived in Brazil at the turn of the twentieth century were Italians.[30]

While their large numbers alone give prima facie indication of Italians' privileged status in turn-of-the-century Brazil, one should not assume that Italians emerged as the only model minority among this hodgepodge of immigrant groups. In fact, Syrian and Lebanese immigrants followed a similar trajectory. As recent studies by historians John Karam and Oswaldo Truzzi have shown, these groups' economic mobility not only helped them get rid of the pariah status to which Brazilian elites relegated them, but it also distanced them from racially ambiguous groups (such as Black Brazilians and poor, working-class, mixed-race families).[31] That said, the sheer volume of Italian immigrants probably goes a long way toward explaining why Italians, rather than, say, "Turks," have become what is arguably Brazil's model minority par excellence.

The city of São Paulo in particular stands out because of the massive density of Italian settlement there. Italian scientist and travel writer Gina Lombroso Ferrero, whose travel writing about Brazil is the subject of this book's first chapter, notes how at the turn of the century "one hears more Italian spoken in São Paulo than in Turin, Milan, Naples." In fact, more than a half of the Italian arrivals in Brazil went to the city of São Paulo. What Gina Lombroso Ferrero defined as an overwhelming Italianness, sociologist Lúcia Lippi Oliveira describes as a "phenomenon that one can observe with a naked eye." Despite somewhat scarce and at times conflicting data, Oliveira informs us that, in the case of São Paulo, Italians constituted the most populous group: 41 percent of the total arrivals in the city.[32] When we consider how this data articulates with the modernization of São Paulo—whose population nearly doubled between 1893 and 1900—we can begin to appreciate the importance of placing São Paulo squarely at the center of an investigation into the links between race and nationality in Italian Studies. It is perhaps the only city in the Americas—if not the world—where Italianness became synonymous primarily with the salutary effects of modernity.

It makes sense, then, that given the massive presence of Italians in Brazil, numerous sociological and historical works, for the most part written in Portuguese or Italian, have been dedicated to this topic.[33] Works by historians Angelo Trento, Franco Cenni, Chiara Vangelista, Emilio Franzina, and Zuleika Alvim have greatly informed the thinking behind this book.[34] However, without discounting the precious sociological and historical insights they offer, *The Italian Colony of São Paulo* approaches this rich subject from a literary and cultural studies perspective. Rather than offering yet another account of the social and material conditions of Italians in São Paulo, this book traces the discourse that has framed their arrival and subsequent integration in the city, which remains the cultural and economic capital of Brazil. The questions that have guided this book and that set it apart from more traditional sociological and historical studies of Italian migration to Brazil, can be summarized as follows: What literary forms did Italian and Brazilian authors use to (re)construct Italian identity in Brazil and to render the multifaceted relationship between Italians and the city of São Paulo? How do the works of these authors register the Brazilian racial hierarchy that links Italianness with whiteness? In what ways have their discursive practices worked either to maintain or subvert Italians' claims to racial, economic, and cultural superiority in São Paulo?

Upon arriving en masse in Brazil, Italians promptly fulfilled one of their primary functions: to flood the Brazilian free market with cheap labor and, as a result, crush the negotiating power of recently emancipated slaves. For almost two decades, from the 1870s until 1895, the *fazendeiros*, or landowners, completely controlled São Paulo's immigration programs and policies. These elite families stood at the top of the social hierarchy of São Paulo and masterminded the mass migration of Italians and other Southern Europeans. In fact, they formed the Association to Aid Colonization and Immigration, which later became known in 1886 as the Sociedade Promotora da Imigração; at its helm was Martinho Prado Junior, who historian Thomas Holloway describes as "a slave-owning coffee planter of republican political sympathies, representing the booming and labor-hungry Mogiana zone [a region in the northeastern part of São Paulo State, bordering Minas Gerais]." Prado was an influential figure in aiding the passing of several laws facilitating the introduction of immigrants to offset the use of slaves. One law in particular "created an annual tax of one mil reais per slave employed in agriculture, and twice that amount for slaves not employed in agriculture, with the proceeds to be used for the immigration service."[35]

From the point of view of the planters, of course, the Sociedade was extremely successful. The coffee crop harvested in 1888, in the months immediately after the promulgation of the Golden Law—which sanctioned the formal abolition of slavery in Brazil—was larger than the preceding or following crop for western São Paulo. With the promulgation of the Brazilian Federal Constitution in 1891, the Sociedade slowly transitioned into a control-regulated agency, operating under the São Paulo Department of Agriculture; officially, it ended its operations in 1895. When looking at the numbers of immigrants who entered through the Sociedade first and the Department of Agriculture later, Italians comprised the largest nationality group. And Italians predominated precisely during the transition to free labor and the ensuing coffee boom, during which period (from 1887 through 1900) they supplied 73 percent of all arrivals.

The second, perhaps less visible, function of Italian mass migration to Brazil was to fulfill a eugenic project on a national scale, one that aimed to repopulate the country with putatively superior Europeans and thereby whiten the Brazilian people. Early twentieth-century Brazilian racial theorists championed the whitening of the population through racial miscegenation, a process known as *branqueamento*.[36] While they regarded people with darker skin as inferior, intellectuals such as Silvio Romero, Alberto Torres, and Oliveira Vianna nonetheless rejected the idea of race that equated superiority with purity of blood. Over and against De Gobineau, who declared Brazil a lost cause due to its "completely mulatto population," these thinkers identified race mixing as the source of their country's strength. What was needed, in their view, was an influx of European blood that would assimilate and supersede the other components, bringing about a new, modern Brazilian man.[37]

Italians thus arrived in Brazil at an opportune moment. While American elites tended to see Italians as potentially dangerous harbingers of an attenuated whiteness, Brazilian policymakers viewed them as uniquely suited to diluting the Blackness of Brazil through miscegenation—indeed, even more so than supposedly "whiter" groups. In her study on national censuses and racial categories in Latina America, sociologist Mara Loveman reveals that "in Brazil when 'Whites' mixed with 'non-Whites,' the result was not the pollution and degeneration of whiteness, but the improvement, regeneration, and eventual dissipation of non-whiteness." She explains how Brazil might be the only case in which "*mestizaje* was explicitly described as a demographic process that would eventually yield a whitened population." This belief, of course, directly contrasts with the one-drop rule of the United States, which posited any form of racial mixing as mongrelization. Likewise, Brazil's unique stance with regard to whiteness also sets it apart from Argentina—which often appears alongside the United States in comparative studies on the Italian diaspora to the Americas—whose government, instead, when "presenting racial statistics departed from the assumption that

Argentina was always-already white." Thus, Argentina and Brazil's racial imaginaries could not differ more.[38]

Paradoxically, then, Italians' newfound honorific status as "white," and the attendant privileges thereof, depended largely on their willingness to embrace the very racial ambiguity that, in the United States and Italy, threatened to sabotage their claims to whiteness, particularly in the first half of the twentieth century. Under these circumstances, Italian whiteness is not only uncontested, but numerically and culturally hegemonic. In Brazil, as elsewhere, Italians had to define themselves in relation to people of African descent but on terms far more flattering to their self-image than those they have ever encountered in the United States, and with an intimacy that did not even become conceivable in domestic Italian politics until the late twentieth century.

In this sense, then, tracing the discourse that racializes Italians as white in São Paulo fundamentally upends the narrative of victimhood that accompanies popular and scholarly discussions of the racial status of Italians in Italian and Italian American studies. Such a discourse reveals the dynamics that have emerged when whiteness has articulated with Italianness in an explicit and uncompromising way. Furthermore, unmasking the racialization of Italians as white in São Paulo allows us to see more clearly the lie that has sustained the notion of Brazil's exceptional racial inclusiveness, also known as the myth of Brazilian racial democracy. Sociologist Patricia de Santana Pinho has written extensively about the tacit ways in which not all "mestiço types" carry the same value within Brazilian racial democracy, and how "whiteness has silently become hegemonic through discourses of mestiçagem/mestizaje."[39] Such hegemony is better understood when framed as the analytical category of *branquitude*. Sociologist Lilia Moritz Schwarcz finds the theoretical framework of *branquitude*—instead of *brancura*, or whiteness—more apt to think about the ways in which people who are racialized as white partake in "a series of values and costumes that are first lived than assumed" as markers of social identity.[40] In other words, people who are white tend to negate their association to it. Through the critical lenses of *branquitude*, Schwarcz reveals a complex strategic system of representations that has allowed white Brazilians to naturalize their social status, while also establishing the neutrality of a category that, as her subtitle deftly points to, is "absently present" throughout the making of Brazil. To understand not only how Italians first became unambiguously white but also how they first came to play a crucial role in forging a supposedly multiracial democracy, *The Italian Colony of São Paulo* looks closely at the discourse that accompanied their integration in São Paulo.

But Brazilian racial theories alone did not give rise to the New World Italian discourse that I trace in this book. As I mentioned before, we should understand race as a process, one that depends on multiple variables at any given point. Italians' arrival in São Paulo coincided with a period of overwhelming economic growth: the recent abolition of slavery in 1888 initiated the transition to a market economy organized around free labor. At the same time, a parallel discursive practice conflated the presence of Italians in São Paulo with modernization; this, in turn, reinforced the ideas put forth by Brazilian racial theorists and helped solidify the image of Italians as model immigrants.

At the end of the nineteenth century, Italians—specifically, those who ventured to Brazil with financial capital—found themselves in an environment friendly to foreign entrepreneurial investment. Not coincidentally, some of the wealthiest industrialist in the first half of the twentieth century in São Paulo were Italians. Francesco Matarazzo, who historian Warren Dean calls "the most successful and loquacious of the immigrant industrialists," embodies the best example of this commercial Italian elite.[41] Even though the local elite, in the form of the *fazendeiros* behind the migration policies, held on to their social and economic privileges, they soon had to make deals with these same Italians who they welcomed into their country as cheap labor. Alas, not all Italian migrants were able to attain the same level of success as Matarazzo.

In her study on the lives of working-class people in São Paulo, historian Molly C. Ball explains that the key opportunity for achieving success and establishing oneself as part of an emerging middle class was to secure what she calls "good jobs," or jobs in the growing industries like transportation, cement, and cars.[42] Coincidentally, it is precisely in these jobs that we find Italian immigrants.[43] Relying more heavily than other groups on family connections and national ties to secure employment allowed Italians access not only to better job opportunities, but to more opportunities for work. In turn, this explains why Italians, more so than other immigrant groups, were more likely to participate in the labor movement. In fact, one should bear in mind that if the nascent São Paulo's industrial economy was dominated by Italians, so too was its labor movement. The Italian workers of São Paulo actively unsettled the capitalist push spearheaded by their own compatriots. Brazilian mainstream media, consequently, labeled these attitudes as undesirable and began to represent Italians as problematic political agitators. This, in turn, tainted Italians' image. To some extent, Italians' racial privilege depended on their complicity in making São Paulo the wealthiest city in Brazil. And yet, as historian João Fábio Bertonha has shown, these contrasting narratives of the Italian presence in São Paulo have not fundamentally altered the image that Italians have maintained in the Brazilian national imaginary.[44] As it turns out, the adjective "Italian" can simultaneously conjure a multiplicity of meanings that, at times, mingle in dialectical tension with one another. It is this polyvalency that, on the one hand, makes the New World Italian discourse so rich and complex and, on the other hand, allows its oppressive and exclusionary scope to go largely unnoticed.

As Italians gained a foothold in local industries both large and small—often directly at the expense of Black Brazilians and recently freed captives—they became active agents in the technological and economic modernization of what would ultimately become the largest city in the Americas. Historian Barbara Weinstein sheds light on the discourses that have allowed São Paulo to become the symbol of a racialized modernization vis-à-vis the rest of Brazil. She explains how "the economic success of São Paulo has cemented the widely assumed association between whiteness and civilization, between whiteness and modernization, between whiteness and productivity." The problem, however, is that "this association can be expressed in regional terms rather than explicitly racial ones," thus perpetuating the myth of a Brazilian racial democracy.[45] Writers and social observers began to equate the presence of Italians in São Paulo with modernization, reinforcing the ideas espoused by Brazilian racial theorists and helping to solidify the image of Italians as model immigrants. In this way, these thinkers further differentiated Italians in Brazil from their counterparts not only across the Atlantic Ocean but also across the Americas. Thus, while the Italian peninsula and its islands, perhaps specifically its islands and its southern territories, continued to occupy a space widely regarded as economically, geographically, and racially marginal to modern Europe and while Italians in other parts of the world found themselves "working toward whiteness," to use David Roediger's phrase, Italians in São Paulo were truly white on arrival.[46] Indeed, they embodied the very quintessence of whiteness. The process by which they did so depended on two factors: their contributions to Brazil's whitening project, and their position within the modern, post-abolition economic system. But what would happen once these two contingencies ceased to determine Italians' racial status?

If we take the Brazilian racial theorists at their word, the Italian component of the new modern Brazil would seamlessly blend in with the other groups. This would result in what historian Jeffrey Lesser has called the "hidden" hyphenated identities of Brazil. Lesser rightly points out that, despite the fact that immigrant communities in Brazil did not adopt a hyphenated identity—like Japanese-Brazilian, for example, or Italo-Brazilian—it does not mean that they existed as equal in the Brazilian imaginary.[47]

What I want to suggest is that the twofold discourse on race and modernization that brought about the construction of Italian whiteness in São Paulo also took advantage of the civilizationist discourse associated with Italy, also known as *civiltà italiana*. In her foundational work on Italian diaspora, historian Donna Gabaccia highlights how, despite Italy's economic stagnation, "the term 'Italian' signified something quite concrete and positive in the west. Italian was not yet a noun for a human identity, people or nation. But it was an adjective that described a distinctive range of cultural products—both secular and religious—that the rest of the world found valuable."[48] If Italy's position within the Mediterranean meant a more ambiguous racial status as well as a less developed industrial economy, it nonetheless allowed Italy to champion a celebratory narrative about its cultural heritage. Italian commercial elites, having acquired a uniquely privileged status in São Paulo, quickly understood that promulgating these ideas of Italy's cultural greatness would naturalize their superior status in the public sphere and thus help to prevent them from losing their privileges within Brazil's racial-democratic regime. Ironically, this Italian entrepreneurial class was aided in this endeavor by local Brazilian elites. A cursory look at the essays published in the *Revista da Academia Paulista de Letras* in the first half of the twentieth century, for example, reveals a staggering number of references to Italian writers, mostly from the Renaissance.[49] Hence whitening was both a racial and a cultural project. By demonstrating their knowledge and mastery of the Italian literary canon, these largely native-born Brazilian writers sought to lay claim to a Western, classical heritage, in the hopes that this would redound to their honor.

Thus, the New World Italian discourse I trace in this book emerged through a transatlantic exchange between Italy and Brazil at the turn of the twentieth century. It circulated through Italian and Portuguese-language travelogues, newspapers, political pamphlets, fiction, memoirs, school curricula, and, later, film and television shows. This discourse enabled Italians to epitomize whiteness in São Paulo by stressing their European roots, their pivotal role in the technological and economic modernization of Brazil, and their association with various civilizationist projects in both the history of the Mediterranean and the New World. This discourse not only shows how Italians have played a crucial yet covert role in propping up white racial and cultural supremacy in Brazil; it also complicates overly totalizing narratives about the oppression, marginalization, and racial ambiguity of Italians in the Americas and Europe.

3. Overview of Chapters

This book comprises five chapters. Each chapter explores key texts that have contributed to the emergence of the New World Italian discourse. These chapters follow a chronological arc. At the same time, they also exist in a dialectical relationship with one another, meaning that they alternate between positive and negative narratives associated with the Italian presence of São Paulo.

In Chapter One, I show how scientist Gina Lombroso Ferrero—daughter of Cesare Lombroso, the father of criminology and racial profiling—refracts ongoing debates about the Italian race through the lens of Brazilian racial dynamics. In the aftermath of the Italian military defeat at Adwa, Ethiopia in 1896, a deep racial anxiety emerged in Italian travel writing about Brazil. Although Italian imperialists praised São Paulo as a model Italian *colonia* (colony), they nonetheless condemned the work done by Italian *colonos*, the indentured workers on the coffee plantations who had replaced enslaved Africans. Thus, travel accounts of Brazil after 1896 tended to liken Italian laborers in the coffee fields to African slaves. I argue that Lombroso Ferrero's travelogue *Nell'America Meridionale* (1908) proposes a solution to the racial anxiety provoked by these circumstances.[50] Specifically, she rehabilitates the image of Italians in Brazil by depicting them as modern, white, settlers.

In Chapter Two, I reveal how Brazilian modernist writer Antônio de Alcântara Machado, in his short story cycle *Brás, Bexiga, Barra Funda* (1927), crystallizes the New World Italian discourse that Lombroso Ferrero had cultivated in her travel writing.[51] Alcântara Machado views the Italians of São Paulo as the *raça alegre* (jovial race): that is, as the people primed to bring the city into the future. By choosing to make second-generation characters the protagonists of his stories, Alcântara Machado implies that the *raça alegre* not only revivified the spirit of São Paulo but also established lasting spheres of influence within the city's socioeconomic order. The short story form, which in Machado's hands becomes a "newspaper" à la Dos Passos, asks us to focus on the totality of the stories rather than their fragmentary nature. It also echoes the fundamental role that the Italian press played in São Paulo. On the one hand, Alcântara Machado wants to incorporate these Italo-Paulistanos into a coherent whole, all the while keeping them fragmented. On the other hand, he absorbs and embellishes the ethnic newspaper so as to align it more fully with an overarching Paulistano discourse. Both in its contents and its form, *Brás, Bexiga e Barra Funda* materializes the tension of simultaneously assimilating and othering that lies at the heart of the encounter between Italians and São Paulo. Alcântara Machado's canonical work thus consecrates the Italian culture of São Paulo as one of the mainstreams in the lifeblood of Brazilian literary modernism and, by extension, national identity.

Chapter Three analyzes the 1924 satirical columns of Black Brazilian political activist José Correia Leite, who grew up working for and living with an Italian family in São Paulo.[52] Leite's columns were written under the pseudonym Juó P. Carretta, a fictitious Italian parvenu who speaks the Italo-Portuguese *patois* that Leite learned as his first language. Much like the films of African American director Spike Lee, Leite's satirical columns simultaneously lionized and mocked the modern, white Italian identity celebrated by modernists and nationalists. I argue that Leite "talks back" to that Italian identity by reclaiming it not only for himself, but for Black Brazilians in São Paulo more broadly. For example, the collective strategies that Italian immigrants used to foster solidarity and to claim their space in the city are translated, partially, by Leite for use by the Afro-Brazilian community of São Paulo. By adapting notions of Italian economic, cultural, and racial nationalism to fit the needs of the city's Black community, Leite exposes and challenges the New World Italian discourse that elevates Italians as avatars of white racial superiority.

Chapter Four examines the political essays (1934; 1964) and the autobiography (1987) of a prominent Brazilian nationalist of Italian origins: Miguel Reale.[53] Reale was a Brazilian politician who cofounded the Brazilian fascist party *Ação Integralista Brasileira* (AIB) in 1932 and openly supported the twenty-one-year-long military dictatorship instituted in 1964. Throughout his autobiography, Reale not only frequently uses Italian colloquial expressions but even asserts his Italian heritage by directly comparing himself to the pillar of Italian letters, Dante Alighieri. Reale weaponized the New World Italian discourse by weaving it with authoritarian political projects, namely, fascism and militarism. The Italian cultural nationalism that had shaped Reale's emotional, social, and intellectual formation greatly informs his version of Brazilian nationalism. Such a dual sense of national loyalty aligns with the meaning produced by the New World Italian discourse, which established the association of Italians with whiteness and modernity upon their arrival in Brazil. Foregrounding the political and literary writings of Reale illuminates the most conservative aspects of the New World Italian discourse.

By contrast, in Chapter Five, I conclude by turning to Zelia Gattai's best-selling memoir *Anarquistas, graças a Deus* (1979).[54] Gattai, wife of famed Brazilian novelist Jorge Amado, chronicles the exploits of her anarchist Italian family in São Paulo, including those of her grandfather, who participated in the anarchist commune Colônia Cecília. The enthusiastic reception of *Anarquistas* in both the Brazilian and Italian literary market, and its later adaptation into a TV series, suggests that the Italian anarchist, more so than the Italian settler or parvenu, has become the paradigmatic symbol of the Italian experience in São Paulo. Meanwhile, a similar story of Italian radicalism—that of Brazilian Communist author Carlos Marighella, the child of an Italian man and a Black Brazilian woman—has not received the same fanfare. I argue that the transnational success of stories like *Anarquistas* shows how, despite their radicalism, even self-identified Italian leftists in Brazil often benefit from the conservative values of the New World Italian discourse.

The world in which the New World Italian discourse took shape is an important laboratory for exploring Italian identity as it develops within a self-consciously multiracial and multiethnic society. Italo-Brazilians, after all, rapidly ascended to the top of the racial hierarchy that undergirds Brazil's purportedly color-blind regime. And this rise in Brazil actually prefigures the conditions of Italians in contemporary Italy: where multiracial democracy remains a fledgling and uncertain project, hampered by the state's steadfast refusal to combat the racialization of citizenship.

One indication of the unique, enduring affinity between Italian citizens in Brazil and Italy lies in the fact that *both* voted, in large numbers, to elect far-right Prime Minister Giorgia Meloni, who has promised to restore the economic, cultural, and racial primacy of Italy by imposing harsh restrictions on immigration. Likewise, Brazil's ultraconservative former president Jair Bolsonaro—who frequently boasts of his Italian heritage—has won broad support among Italo-Brazilians. Hence, Italians on both sides of the Atlantic have played crucial, at times overlapping roles in the resurgence of the global far right. *The Italian Colony of São Paulo* offers the first account of one of the key discourses that has facilitated this process.

And yet, *The Italian Colony of São Paulo* also emphasizes the lability of this discourse. Drawing on travel narratives, autobiographies, fiction, political pamphlets, and newspapers, this book shows that while the New World Italian discourse emerged through transatlantic exchanges between elites in Italy and Brazil at the turn of the twentieth century, this discourse has subsequently evolved to serve different constituencies and inform competing nationalist projects, including those of Black Brazilians. *The Italian Colony of São Paulo* thus advances a transnational, transracial, and translinguistic framework for understanding Italian cultural identity, and thereby proposes an alternative to the nation-centered methodology that has defined the field of Modern Languages and Literatures up to the present.

ONE

Tutto è italiano

Gina Lombroso Ferrero and the Cultivation of Italian São Paulo

In 1908 Gina Lombroso Ferrero—daughter and English-language translator of the founder of criminology Cesare Lombroso—published a travelogue dedicated to the time she spent in South America. The city of São Paulo, a burgeoning metropolis in the southeastern part of Brazil, left an indelible impression on her, especially its pronounced Italian contours. For Lombroso Ferrero, the emergence of a coherent pan-Italian identity in an American city, particularly a modern one like São Paulo, seemed altogether natural. She writes:

> Wine, bread, cars, clothes, fabric, books, advertisements, *everything is Italian*. In markets you see mountains of boxes of Sicilian tomatoes, of Neapolitan pastries: in clothing stores you find all of our Lombard cottons, our silks from Como, our Florentine and Alexandrian hats.[1]

Across the ocean, Italians had not only flooded this South American city with their labor; they had also inundated its booming market with signature

Italian products. When we read it today, Lombroso Ferrero's description seems almost prescient, as if her fin-de-siècle Italian São Paulo prefigured postwar Italy. The very products she singles out as distinctly Italian would, of course, become staples of Italy's economic boom decades later: food, automobiles, and fashion. At the same time, this litany of products—some from Northern Italy, others from the South—implies the existence of an Italian identity fundamentally different from anything that existed back in the old country. Here, across the ocean, is an Italy that is allegedly unburdened by the Southern Question and that, in its unique heterogeneity, finds the strength of national unity. São Paulo becomes a symbol for all that Italians can accomplish, a source of nationalist pride located outside of the geographical constraints of the nation. In this sense, Lombroso Ferrero's travel writing stands out as a transnational nationalist narrative. Her 1908 *Nell'America Meridionale (Brasile-Uruguay-Argentina): note e impressioni di Gina Lombroso Ferrero* (henceforth *Nell'America Meridionale*) is a work of literature that recasts the formation of a specific national identity outside of its intended geographical confines, and, consequently, makes certain claims of superiority that would not be sustainable inside the Italian nation-state.

Paradoxically, for Italian travelers like Lombroso Ferrero, no other place seemed to adduce more abundant evidence of Italian national and cultural superiority. Far from the Mediterranean, industrious Italians had solidified their presence in industries large and small.[2] In so doing, they became highly visible agents in the modernization of what would ultimately become the largest city in the Americas. The same could not be said for Italians back in Italy. Within Europe, Italians occupied—both geographically and symbolically—a space that was marginalized and liminal.[3] In the writings of visitors such as Lombroso Ferrero, then, São Paulo becomes the model *colonia*—literally "colony"—but used here to mean a *voluntary* Italian settlement outside of Italy. Italian travel writers left São Paulo enthusiastic about what they witnessed, especially when juxtaposed with the misery that had notoriously bedeviled the first waves of immigrants to the city.

Even so, São Paulo's success as a colonia of Italy could not completely overshadow the racial anxiety emerging from the status of Italian *colonos*. After all, many Italians remained concentrated in the state of São Paulo's rural interior, where they had gone to serve as indentured workers on Brazilian coffee plantations, replacing the previous workforce of enslaved Black people. In 1886, a group of private investors—most of them plantation owners—started a subsidized migration program aimed at importing cheap labor from Europe. They wanted to oversaturate the labor market and, consequently, diminish the bargaining power of the recently emancipated captives. In response to this program, Italians migrated en masse, constituting the initiative's single largest group of beneficiaries. Yet the similarities between the exploitative working conditions of enslaved Black laborers and Italian colonos carried racial implications that troubled observers from Italy. Even as they praised São Paulo as a paragon of urban modernity, these visitors ultimately condemned Brazil as primitive and backward. Beginning in the late 1880s and continuing through the rest of the nineteenth century, Italian accounts about the conditions of colonos aroused the indignation of the Italian government. In 1902, an emissary of the Italian government, Adolfo Rossi, published an unflinching report on the miserable conditions of Italians in the coffee plantations, known as *fazendas*. His testimony instigated the infamous Prinetti Decree of the same year, which thereafter banned subsidized migration to Brazil for Italians.

Not surprisingly, Brazilian elites fretted over the incessant international reporting on the abusive treatment meted out to colonos in the coffee plantations. What was needed, it seemed, was a public relations campaign to rehabilitate Brazil's international image. This was precisely why the Brazilian Foreign Minister, Baron Rio Branco, invited the Lombroso Ferrero family to the country. The invitation to tour Brazil had originally been extended to Italian historian Guglielmo Ferrero, and Gina Lombroso Ferrero elected to accompany her husband. It was the chair of the Brazilian Academy of Letters, famed Brazilian writer Machado de Assis, who, under the pressure of Rio Branco, sent the letter inviting Ferrero.[4] Having discovered that Emilio Mitre, owner of the newspaper *La Nación*, had recently invited Guglielmo Ferrero to Argentina, Rio Branco thought he might be able to entice the family to visit Brazil during their sojourn in South America. In addition to a stipend of five thousand francs, the Brazilian Academy of Letters and the Brazilian Foreign Ministry offered to cover the costs of lodgings and transportation within Brazil for Ferrero, his wife Gina, their child Leo, and the latter's nanny.[5] Given how the invitation was framed, however, it seems that what Rio Branco had not entertained was the idea that it might be Ferrero's *wife* who would take the most serious and sustained interest in addressing Brazil's public relations problem.

Published immediately after the visit, Lombroso Ferrero's *Nell'America Meridionale* speaks simultaneously to two national projects: on the one hand, the travel account celebrates the magnitude and scope of Italian achievements in São Paulo, implying that the city's success stemmed directly from the presence of Italians; on the other hand, it glorifies Brazil's distinctive racial politics of miscegenation—according to which racial mixing does not attenuate one's race but, instead, strengthens it—allowing Lombroso Ferrero to portray Brazil as a modern, progressive country. In her travel writing, there is no mention of how Italian colonos suffered under miserable conditions. In her view, they are not exploited indentured laborers but rather settlers who, by triumphing over adversity, have brought glory to the motherland. Indeed, in the labor of the colonos Lombroso Ferrero locates the making of an Italian empire. Colonos cultivate the land by clearing out the frontier, preparing it for farming, and, most importantly, imparting a distinctly Italian character to it. Their work reshapes the Brazilian land, that is, to make it look like an Italian imperial outpost. Without them and their work, she implies, there could not be a city like São Paulo: the model colonia, where "everything is Italian." At the same time, Lombroso Ferrero justifies the presence of the colonos by placing Italians in the longer history of Brazil's colonization, revealing a crucial but often overlooked overlap between the two meanings of the Italian word colonia delineated by historian Mark Choate—that of spontaneous settlements of Italian emigrants on the one hand, and that of colonies of direct dominion on the other.[6]

Land was not the only thing colonos cultivated, though. Unlike other Italian travelers, Lombroso Ferrero was well acquainted with Brazilian racial theories of the time. Such theories saw in miscegenation the only way to redeem Brazil in the eyes of the international public. According to prominent Brazilian intellectuals such as Graça Aranha—who accompanied the Lombroso Ferrero family on their Brazilian tour—miscegenation would ensure the erasure of the Black race from Brazil, and, in turn, launch Brazil into modernity. Italians, perhaps unconsciously, played a major role in this biopolitical experiment: they became the purveyors of that coveted whiteness.

Italian bodies—while physically cultivating the Brazilian landscape and transforming Brazil into an Italy *d'oltremare*—also eugenically cultivated a new, whitened, Brazilian subject of Italian descent.

By informing readers of the economic and racial transformations taking place in Brazil at the turn of the twentieth century, Lombroso Ferrero cultivates an image of New World Italians—as modern settlers and harbingers of a superior race—that ramifies back to Italy and sets the tone for later cultural developments in Brazil. Indeed, as we shall see, in Lombroso Ferrero's travel account a series of key tropes—the racialization of Italian subjects as white, the lionization of Italian immigrants as catalysts for the modernization of São Paulo, and the chauvinistic appeal to the superiority of Italian civilization vis á vis the New World and other parts of Europe—converge and coalesce to form a uniquely lucid iteration of the emergent New World Italian discourse.

1. In the Name of the Father: The Lombroso Legacy

In Brazil, Lombroso Ferrero received the warmest accolades from her fellow Italian nationals.[7] The "screaming crowd" Lombroso Ferrero encountered when in São Paulo "cheered . . . the patriotic heroes [and] the dearest name to them [was] above all Cesare Lombroso's name."[8] Cesare Lombroso, Gina's father, founded the field known as criminal anthropology and was famous among Italians overseas. Lombroso's theories linked the tendency to commit criminal acts to biology, suggesting that the roots of social deviance lay in genetics. Not coincidentally, such a tendency, according to his studies, prevailed among subjects who live in hotter climates, suffer from malnutrition, and indulge in alcohol consumption. Lombroso's theories lent scientific credibility to the internal racism that governed the relationship between Northern and Southern Italians. In fact, his first case study, Giuseppe Villella, was a man from Italy's poor, underdeveloped southern region of Calabria. Perhaps unsurprisingly, the impact of his theories extended to the United States, where Southern Italians were quickly deemed undesirables on account of their purported genetic and cultural affinities with African Americans. Lombroso's work circulated in the Anglophone world because Gina translated it into English. Additionally, Lombroso's notions of criminality also deeply influenced the penal systems of both Brazil and Argentina.[9] Cesare Lombroso's shadow, however, not only looms over the interaction the author had with the Italians she met in Brazil, but also over the existing critical scholarship on *Nell'America Meridionale.*

Despite Gina Lombroso Ferrero being an intellectual in her own right—she was among the first women to receive a degree in medicine from the University of Turin—her travel writing has been rarely read on its own. Instead, her work is often read as a source on how her father's ideas shaped the development of the positivist school in Argentina and influenced the establishment of the modern Penitenciaria Nacional of Buenos Aires.[10] Alternatively, anthropologists, such as Livio Sansone, have treated Lombroso Ferrero's *Nell'America Meridionale* as a historical source about her husband's South America trip, specifically to Brazil.[11] But even when read on its own, as political theorist Marcela Varejão shows, scholars cannot divorce Gina Lombroso Ferrero's travel writing from her father's theories. Indeed, literary scholar Tullio Pagano comments that "despite her undoubted talents, she continued to live and work in the shadow of the strong male figures with whom she associated."[12] It certainly makes sense to analyze Lombroso Ferrero's perceptions of South America through the lens of Lombroso's school. It is well known that Gina Lombroso Ferrero collaborated with her father and had been one of his most steadfast interlocutors. Lombroso Ferrero's biographer Delfina Dolza informs us that despite "having a laboratory and an office, [Lombroso] preferred to work from home in order to share his results with his family members and to acclimate them to his activity through various levels of collaboration." In turn, this meant that "Gina and Paola Lombroso precisely because they were the older children, became increasingly associated with their father's work, substituting for their mother who, due to the numerous familial obligations, cannot assist him anymore."[13]

Nevertheless, it is not the goal of this chapter to analyze Lombroso Ferrero's work in relation to her father's. Rather, for my purposes, it will suffice to confine Lombroso's shadow over his daughter's intellectual pursuits to what geographer Carlo A. Gemignani has called a "foreword," by which he means a kind of suggestive paratext. Doing so allows us to privilege *Nell'America Meridionale* as a travelogue rather than as an ersatz "sociological essay."[14] Gemignani's work and the chapter by Pagano on Lombroso Ferrero's travel memoir constitutes the only sustained critical attention that the work has received in the realm of literary studies. Pagano locates the travelogue in a longer tradition of Italian writings about Argentina by offering a panoramic overview and describing it as "insightful."[15] Gemignani identifies gender as one of the narrative threads of Lombroso Ferrero's travel writing and carefully traces Lombroso Ferrero's theories on the role of women in society back to her experiences amid the suffragists' circle in Argentina. However, neither Pagano's poignant description nor Gemignani's gender-centered analysis do justice to the literary scope of a text like *Nell'America Meridionale*. This chapter seeks to fill the gap in the scholarship on Lombroso Ferrero's text by reading it as an exemplary piece of the literary genre known as travel writing. Echoing literary scholar Mary Louise Pratt's observation about the fraught relationship between travel writing and empire making, it aims to show how Lombroso Ferrero's text reveals as much about Italy's colonie in Brazil as it does about Italy itself.

2. *Travel Writing and Empire Making: An Italian Perspective*

In 1889, the Milanese publishing house Fratelli Treves published Edmondo De Amicis's *Sull'Oceano*. In this book, De Amicis described his experience aboard a steamer heading to South America. Within two weeks of the book's first appearance, *Sull'Oceano* had been republished ten times.[16] Its rapid success was surely helped by De Amicis's fame as a journalist. But *Sull'Oceano*'s popularity also shows a growing thirst among the newly created Italian readership for travel writing. Indeed, Italian publishing houses quickly satisfied their audience by including translated works of travel writing from the British and French traditions in their catalogs. They did so because the perception was—and remains to this day—that Italian literature lacks a proper tradition of travel writing. And yet, in reality, it is "the Italian literary canon and . . . its historiography" that "have remained largely impervious to Italy's splendid legacy of travel literature."[17] The case of *Sull'Oceano*, according to literary scholar Loredana Polezzi, is "both exceptional and emblematic." As Polezzi points out, even though De Amicis's previous novel *Cuore* is considered one of the foundational texts of Italian literature—it is included in school anthologies, often as mandatory reading—his once immensely popular travelogue rarely receives any attention. This absence, Polezzi maintains, exemplifies the marginalization of Italian travel writing within Italy's own literary canon. Simply put, the problem lies in the way literary critics have either misplaced or ignored Italian authors who, in other literary contexts, would fall under the category of travel writing.[18]

Italian literary critics tend to deprecate travel writing "due to the uneducated or partially-educated origin of the author, or due to the latter being far from a literary scholar."[19] Looking for a solution to the perceived unliterariness of travel writing within Italian literary circles, Camilla Cattarulla, a scholar of Latin American literature, proposes to expand literary scholar Franca Sinopoli's *scritture letterarie*—a paradigm for the study of migrant writing—to include travel writing.[20] Cattarulla argues that such a material expansion would likewise expand the scope of Italian Studies geographically and epistemologically, since there exists an enormous corpus of "literary or paraliterary texts that have traditionally received very little attention from Italian critics but in fact could be of great interest to those studying the history of emigrations in the Americas (on both sides of the ocean)."[21] Meanwhile, Dante scholar Ted Cachey locates the exclusion of Italian travel writing from the literary canon in the "Italian cultural anxiety about a lack of geographical center, about the territorial absence which is at the heart of its [Italy's] cultural construction."[22] From this perspective, it becomes even clearer why Italian travel writing exists as a "submerged literature."

Few critics have seriously undertaken the study of Italian travel writing.[23] Even fewer have focused on the vast corpus of texts about South America published between 1870 and 1914 that Cattarulla collected in an annotated bibliography. The mere existence of these texts speaks to the interest of the Italian reading public in a place that during those years attracted millions of their compatriots. Cattarulla highlights how these accounts often thematize two inextricably intertwined events: emigration and colonialism. Regarding the former, Cattarulla writes how "travel literature establishes an easy way to attract the general public's attention towards the issue of migration," making central to the broader debate about emigration "the point of view of the travelers, whose direct contact with the emigrants attests to the validity of their statements." At the same time, though, "the politics of colonial expansion seem to be the most general characteristic of these relationships," suggesting an important kinship with the imperialist politics of post-unitary Italy.[24]

In addition to the arguments that Polezzi, Cattarulla, and Cachey have marshaled to explain why the lineaments of a travel writing tradition have remained obscure in the Italian literary canon, I would like to propose another—one that has to do with Italy's "colonial unconscious"—namely, "the discarding, discrediting, and generally repressing of the history of colonial expansion."[25] Perhaps the enduring reluctance to engage with travel writing—a genre that, according to Pratt, played a crucial role in creating "the imperial order for Europeans 'at home' and giving them their place in it"—reflects a latent, self-serving desire to view Italy as the least of the great powers.[26] To foreground travel writing would be to acknowledge not only the breadth of Italian imperialism but also the extent of Italian literature's complicity in that project. After all, it is largely on the strength of postcolonial discourse and what literary scholar Barbara Spackman called the "long-delayed development of the study of Italian colonialism," that we "can now approach texts previously deemed unworthy of our attention as scholars of literary and cultural studies," such as travel writing.[27]

Italian travel writing about South America written at the turn of the twentieth century—which focused heavily on the Italian communities that emerged there—provides a "source for reconstructing the image of Latin America in Italy."[28] Such writing, I contend, also offers invaluable insights into how, through these settlements, Italy (re)imagined itself. Italian travel writing about Brazil reveals a curiously ambivalent relationship with that country, one that, in turn, reflected Italy's own contradictory self-image. On the one hand, the prosperous Italian colonie in Brazil—the prime example of which was the growing city of São Paulo—evoked a spirit of grandeur and prosperity that served, like civilizationist rhetoric more broadly, not only to bolster Italian national pride but also to buttress and legitimize liberal Italy's imperialist ambitions. For nationalists, Italy's cultural and politico-economic sphere of influence could already be said to encompass the settlements and hence explain their phenomenal success. On the other hand, the legacy of slavery that undergirded the mistreatment of Italian workers and threatened to associate them with Brazil's African-descended majority also conjured up biopolitical fears in these selfsame nationalists, revealing their deep-seated anxieties about the ambiguous racial status of Italians in Europe and North America.

3. Colonia, colonos, colonato*: Italian Settlements in Brazil*

The word "colony," in Italian colonia, has at least two meanings: "spontaneous settlements" of Italian emigrants, but also "colonies of direct dominions," such as African possessions under Italian jurisdiction. Historian Mark Choate defined the former as "emigrant colonialism." Already in 1887, with the first legislation on emigration, Choate tells us that Italian Prime Minister Francesco Crispi, "aimed to colonize the emigrant themselves, wherever they traveled. Rather than draining the nation, emigration would expand Italy beyond its boundaries."[29] But, in keeping with the second definition, the prime minister also passionately advocated for the creation of an Italian empire in Africa. He pursued this dream until the anticlimactic Battle of Adwa of 1896, where Emperor Menelik II's troops defeated the ill-prepared and badly organized Italian army. Italy's attempt to assert its imperial prowess on the world stage—the sheer desperation of which stemmed from its rather belated arrival at the imperialists' table—had resulted, as Labanca describes, in the "heaviest white loss in the scramble for Africa."[30]

The year 1896—a decade before Lombroso Ferrero's journey to South America—is a watershed moment for the formulation of Italy's emigrant colonialism, inaugurating what Choate calls "a time of ideological transition crucial for later imperialism" that will last until 1912, with the annexation of Libya as an official Italian (African) colony. After the Italian defeat at Adwa, nationalists increasingly turned their attention toward South America in an effort to satiate their hunger for imperial expansion. In the urban centers of Argentina, Uruguay, and Brazil, Italians had already garnered notable economic success without much support from their motherland. It was mainly the prosperous Italian industries emerging in the Plata region and across the São Paulo state that guided "this geographical and conceptual leap across the Atlantic."[31]

In 1901, the young economist Luigi Einaudi, who would later become president of the Italian Republic, published *Un principe mercante* (A Merchant Prince), which "for a decade was cited by virtually every Italian writer and politician who addressed emigration." *Un principe mercante* proposed capitalizing on the extensive Italian commercial networks already existing in South America, so as to create what Einaudi called "a far greater Italy."[32] The book takes as its case study the industrialist Enrico Dell'Acqua, who made his fortune first selling and, later, manufacturing cotton throughout South America. Such a "self-made man" and "captain of industry," Einaudi argues, embodies the future of the Italian empire. In Einaudi's model, economic supremacy supplants military domination, demonstrating the superiority of Italian colonization to the method employed by Britain:

> We are actually showing the world that Italy is capable of creating a more perfect and evolved type of colonization, in comparison to the Anglo-Saxon variety. Whereas the English were always accompanied by military force during the conquest of the Pacific, Italian colonization has always been free and independent of such force.[33]

But focusing on Enrico Dell'Acqua allows Einaudi and his followers to elide the fact that very few Italian migrants would actually achieve such economic success.[34] The wealth of a few Italian businessmen—"chosen ones," according to Einaudi, "who demonstrate the makings of a new life, one previously unknown, to the masses"—overshadowed the poverty and misery that many Italians found themselves living in once they arrived in Brazil, whether in the coffee fields or in urban centers like São Paulo.[35] Moreover, the myth of the self-made man sought to discourage workers from participation in collective action, which would have threatened the celebrated positions of the few capitani di colonia. In the "far greater Italy" Einaudi envisioned, class struggles evaporated and, as pointed out by historian Claudio Fogu, regional differences between North and South were conveniently obfuscated.[36] In this respect, Einaudi's vision rehearses the suspension of the Southern Question that we discern in the list of products cited by Lombroso Ferrero to demonstrate the overwhelming Italianness of São Paulo.

Although never officially implemented, Einaudi's commercial plan and his vision of creating a "far greater Italy" by exploiting the wealth of Italian colonie in South America recall the relationship between a center and its peripheries. It is not far-fetched, then, to understand Einaudi's model as an imperialist one, particularly in light of what literary scholar Teresa Fiore has described as "Italy's peculiar double colonialism" to illuminate the prismatic relationship between citizens and colonial subjects within the Italian metropole today. For Fiore, Italian postcolonialism must also take into account "the coexistence of multiple colonial legacies," including the "long-lasting and profound inheritance left by its global emigration."[37] The travel writing about Brazil published in the aftermath of Adwa and influenced by the model of *Un principe mercante* lends credence to Fiore's theoretical imbrication of emigration with imperialism.[38] These travelers advised the Italian government on ways to exploit and appropriate the economic success of Italian settlements in Brazil, particularly São Paulo, as a solution to the nation's domestic and foreign affairs. Take, for example, the infamous 1897 account with the unfortunate title *Nel paese dei macachi* (In the country of the monkeys). Here, Italian journalist Ubaldo Moriconi starts his travel writing by directly addressing Italy's ruling class:

> It is now worth giving a general glance at the vast and rich country I study, which is what I will do by rapidly tracing the boundaries of this splendid region of the sun, mentioning the importance of its economic development, *allowing myself the right to show why it should be of interest to our ruling class* and what may be awaiting the Italian workers that, monthly, by the thousands, go there.[39]

Whether focusing on the Italian settlements in Rio Grande do Sul, the southernmost tip of Brazil, or on the coffee plantations across São Paolo, these writings sought to make a case for why the Italian government should throw its support behind these Italian colonos.

And yet these travel writers quickly understood that not all colonie were the same. On the one hand, there were the Italian colonies established in Rio Grande do Sul, where more than 74,000 Italians arrived between 1875–1914.[40] Those who settled there had received a parcel of land from the Brazilian government—either directly from emperor Pedro II, a staunch advocate for European immigration, or, later on, from the state itself.[41] In the colonie of Rio Grande do Sul, Italian colonos hailed mostly from Veneto and Trentino and successfully launched a productive viticulture industry.[42] Such an endeavor could not go unnoticed by the Italian government. In fact,

Italian Congressman Vito De Bellis (1907) dedicated an entire report solely to the viticulture industry in Brazil, and the ways in which the Italian government could and should exploit this network. Other travelers, including the journalists Ubaldo Moriconi (1897) and Alfredo Cusano (1911), looked favorably upon these southern settlements. Such writers touted these settlements as the model for all colonie—what Cusano called an example of "colonizzazione ideale."[43]

By contrast, the State of São Paulo introduced another form of colonia, one that was similar to the settler colonialism of Rio Grande do Sul but with different goals. In the 1880s, Brazilian agents in Italy actively recruited workers for the coffee plantations known as fazendas. Advertising transatlantic journeys to the Americas, the *agente di emigrazione* (emigration agent) mostly operated in and around the Port of Genoa, often for the consular district or on behalf of the target country. The more people that the agente di emigrazione convinced to embark, the bigger his commission.[44] At first, the landowners themselves, the *fazendeiros*, financed the subsidized migration to the State of São Paulo of Italian workers; later, however, it became a government-run affair.[45] Italians comprised the largest group of those who entered Brazil through this program. Colonos, in fact, quickly became identified with Italians, who supplied 73 percent of all arrivals from 1887 through 1900.[46]

The arrival of the Italians coincided with Brazil's transition from slavery to free labor. There can be little doubt that Brazilian landowners and politicians spearheaded the subsidized migration program partly because of the impending abolition of slavery, which occurred in 1888. The sudden lack of captive workers threatened to halt coffee production, which was the number one revenue source of not only the State of São Paulo but Brazil as a whole.[47] Italians thus literally supplanted slaves. And yet despite the abolition of slavery, in the coffee fields one still could encounter "attitudes and customs of the era of slavery."[48] Such lingering attitudes emerge most importantly in how colonos were paid for their work. The form of labor performed by the colono was the *colonato*, which:

> Establishes no salary, but rather a complex form of compensation, usually in three parts: a) fixed annual monetary payment for the cultivation of a given

> number of coffee plants; b) monetary payment proportional to the amount of coffee harvested; c) permission to cultivate a payment in the form of a plot of land dedicated to the growth of basic foods.[49]

The colono needed to borrow tools and other essentials from the landowner in order to be able to cultivate the land. And this meant that the remuneration for his work, which occurred belatedly, or after the colono requested it many times, had to cover his debt with the fazenda first. Not unsurprisingly, Italian travelers frowned upon the exploitation of Italian workers in the fazenda. Moriconi described how the Italian worker in the coffee plantation functioned as a "substitute for the slave, submitted to the arbitrariness and injuries of the fazendeiro," adding that "the faith, the life, and the future of the colono are in the hands of the landowner."[50] Many colonos in the State of São Paulo were simply unable to survive under these conditions. Some decamped for smaller urban centers in the interior of the state, which provided services to the fazenda, while others tried their luck in São Paulo, then one of the fastest growing cities in the Americas.[51]

As Italian travel accounts make clear, the racial politics governing Brazil, where almost half of the population was of African descent, exacerbated what historian Nicola Labanca has called the "Adwa complex"—that is, an intense fear and shame rooted in Italy's military defeat in Ethiopia.[52] If, in the words of the Italian nationalist writer Enrico Corradini, who wrote a popular emigration saga set in Brazil, "under their white skin" Brazilians, showed "the skull structure and the color of the Black man," then who were they to treat Italians as quasi-slaves?[53] I suspect that this Italian racial inferiority complex explains, at least in part, why Argentina, rather than Brazil, became "the darling of Italian emigrant colonialism."[54] It also helps to explain why Italy decided to intervene in Brazil's treatment of Italian migrant colonos when it did.

In 1901, the Italian government created the Commissariato Generale dell'Emigrazione and passed the first law protecting the rights of emigrants. Immediately thereafter, the government sent an emissary, Adolfo Rossi, to investigate the well-being of Italians in the fazendas of the State of São Paulo. But the Italian political class already knew of the exploitative conditions of their compatriots in Brazil. Before the 1896 Battle of Adwa, other travel accounts, such as those penned by Alfonso Lomonaco (1889) and Ferruccio Macola (1894) had revealed that Italians bound for Brazil were replacing enslaved Blacks.[55] In the aftermath of Adwa, however, such a parallelism between colono and slave became both more pronounced and unacceptable. Indeed, the sequence of events suggests that it was not dismay at the colonos' living conditions on the coffee plantations that moved the Italian political class to intervene on behalf of its citizens so much as an increasing sensitivity to the racial optics of the situation now that Italy had been humiliated on the world stage by an African country.[56]

In his 1902 report, *Condizioni dei coloni italiani nello Stato di San Paolo*, Rossi implored the Italian government to protect Italian migrants in Brazil. The situation warranted a forceful diplomatic response, he explained, because "to be better esteemed in Brazil, one must demand respect." Interestingly, his report does not seek to appeal to commercial interests or financial incentives. Instead, turns the treatment of the colonos into a question of national honor:

> Letting the current status quo stand represents a true national embarrassment, since it persuades the Brazilian to believe that, in the eyes of his motherland, Italians abroad don't matter and that the Italian immigrant is coming from a famished country, and thus must be happy with a fistful of corn and beans.

For Rossi, the only solution to end the "exploitation" of colonos at the hand of elite fazendeiros, who "forget too easily that slavery was abolished," is a complete halt to the program of subsidized migration.[57] The political climate made it difficult for the Italian government to remain passive in the wake of Rossi's grim report. Thus, Foreign Minister Giulio Prinetti signed a decree known as the Prinetti Decree, which put an end to all sponsored migration to Brazil.

Lombroso Ferrero's *Nell'America Meridionale* offered one of the first important descriptions of a fazenda since Rossi's 1902 report. Her work clearly seeks to place the part of Brazil "that most interests Italians" in a more favorable light. In fact, she omits the colonie of the Rio Grande do Sul from her account altogether. To forestall any invidious comparisons with slavery, she simply tells us at the outset that the "the modern fazenda . . . has greatly changed." The modification lies in the fact that, unlike the slaves, the colonos were paid for their work, which made the "modern" fazenda more akin to a factory.[58] The distinction is questionable, of course, given what we know of the colonos' numerous complaints about wage theft. Moreover, readers find out soon enough that Santa Veridiana, one of the fazendas she visited, belonged to Antonio Prado, one of the richest fazendeiros of São Paulo, who also happened to be an influential politician. Prado was only one step removed from the subsidized migration initiative, since his brother Martinho had set up camp in Northern Italy to ensnare desperate farmers. Because of the involvement of the Prado family and the fact that Lombroso Ferrero's trip was part of a broader attempt by the Brazilian Foreign Minister to boost Brazil's international image, one must take Lombroso Ferrero's words with a grain of salt. Still, Lombroso Ferrero's description of the fazenda shows the ideological work that travel writing performs and how such writing produces knowledge not just about the peripheries but also the center itself.

First, Lombroso Ferrero makes the fazendas appear akin to Italian villages: "the life that the farmers lead on the fazendas is rather similar to the life led by those in our villages." There, the colono "can continue living his life like he did in Europe" and encounter "a similar organization to the one he left in Italy."[59] Second, in her travel writing, coffee—a quintessential symbol of Brazil—becomes a "shrub *just like our camellias*, with shiny, hard, green leaves, and small scented white flowers *like our jasmine*" and coffee's harvest reminds her of the work in the Italian vineyards since "you [pick] it more or less like we harvest the grapes."[60] By setting up a parallel between Italian and Brazilian agricultural practices, Lombroso Ferrero de-exoticizes the latter, and, more importantly, frees the colonos from the lingering racial stigma imputed to them by other Italian travelers. She does so, additionally, by redomesticating Brazilian agricultural production within a specific Italian economic paradigm. If even the cultivation of coffee—the primary reason Italians were needed in the State of São Paulo in the first place—becomes somehow tantamount to Italian agricultural practices then it is only a short epistemological leap to the conclusion that those Italians working themselves to death in the fields were actually, in some sense, cultivating Italian products. By this logic, even the colonos were actively contributing to the Italian economy. Just as in São Paulo "everything is Italian," so too is everything in the fazenda.[61]

The overwhelming Italianness of São Paulo excites those same Italian travelers who were troubled by the racial implications of the colonato system. Their visits to the city confirmed the transnational Italian wealth exalted in Einaudi's *Un principe mercante*. For example, the journalist Moriconi had staunchly condemned the system of the colonato. But even he did not hesitate to praise the modern comforts of São Paulo, which resulted from the "copious amounts of foreigners living there," pointing out that of "about 200,000 inhabitants, more than 60,000 were Italian." It is these Italians, Moriconi declared, that have lent São Paulo its grandeur. One only needs to observe the rapid urbanization of the Avenida Paulista, then a fledgling symbol of global economic power, "that continues to be populated with many new buildings, all of which [is] thanks to the tireless and efficient Italian industriousness."[62] Indeed, Cusano goes even further in his praise, recounting how in São Paulo "Italian intelligence has shown itself not only in the commercial and industrial realms, but also in medicine, architecture, music and sculpture."[63]

Lombroso Ferrero detects an incongruity in the way the emigrants and the Italian state relate to each other. According to her, the more than a million Italians of São Paulo are "ready to buy Italian goods simply because they're Italian." And yet the Italian state "does [n]othing, nothing . . . for Italians over there, absolutely nothing." This, she avers, is a missed opportunity, for the "love for the homeland" and the "intense thirst for patriotism" that she supposedly witnesses, specifically among the Italians of São Paulo, promise to "be a source of support for Italians in Italy both in the future as well as *in the present*."[64] Echoing Einaudi's model, she locates the basis for Italy's future imperial development in the economic force of Italian São Paulo. At the same time, she insists that the colonos have already performed a great service to their native country. Here Lombroso Ferrero calls upon her readers to acknowledge Brazil as a de facto colonia of Italy, one that is, unbeknownst to them, currently enriching the metropole.

But the economic power of São Paulo was directly related to the power of coffee. After all, many of the Italians in the capital were involved in the growing manufacturing and service industries. As such, the wealth they achieved rested on the shoulders of those maligned colonos in the fazendas. Therefore, without the colonato and the Italian workforce who entered the country through this system, Italians in São Paulo could not have amassed the kind of wealth and influence that so bedazzled these Italian travelers. Lombroso Ferrero, unlike other Italian travelers who quickly condemned the colonato only to then praise São Paulo, understood the relationship that linked the colonos and the Italian commercial elites. But instead of revealing its exploitative nature she camouflages it so that the colonos emerge as the pioneers of the New World. By tracing the change from wilderness to civilization within the Brazilian landscape—a change enacted by the colonos and their cultivation of Brazilian land—she transforms the colonos into settlers. In so doing, she rewrites the history of Brazil, employing a trope that literary scholar Natalie Hester had identified as part of the Medicean epic tradition of suggesting that Italians, rather than the Portuguese, should be regarded as Brazil's true colonizers.[65]

4. Nell'America Meridionale*: Mapping Italy in* and *through Brazil*

Lombroso Ferrero's book opens with a three-page long dedication to the "Italians of America." Choosing to dedicate her book to the Italians whom she encountered on her trip—most of whom she met while in Brazil—betrays her desire to (re)inscribe them into the Italian imperial project as its overseas subjects.[66] As if to lay the foundation for this empire, Lombroso Ferrero traces in her dedication a sketch of the varied contours of Italian geography. Traversing Italy from the north to the south, she reminds the reader of the incredible variety of the Italian landscape: she dwells on the "snow-covered" Piedmont, the "bustling" Liguria, the "smiling" Tuscany, the "sacred" Umbria, the "marshy" Lazio, and the "sweet" Campania.[67] By beginning a travelogue about South America with an overview of Italian geography, she almost seems to want to assure her audience that the term "Italy" names a coherent, knowable object. In this way, she confirms Cachey's suggestion that Italian travel writers suffered from a general insecurity about their country's apparent lack of a discrete geographical referent.

Italy—more specifically, an imaginary Italy entangled in an imperial relationship with Brazil—represents the fourth country (after Brazil, Argentina, and Uruguay) that Lombroso Ferrero discovers during her travels. In fact, she transposes *onto* Brazil that same geographical knowledge with which she opens the book. By using geographical knowledge of Italy to make the Brazilian landscape legible to her audience, Lombroso Ferrero is "remaking space imaginatively as a colonial domain—represented and named within European epistemologies."[68] Yet such an operation implies that Brazil, in turn, reconfigures Italy itself, as well as Italianness. Even Lombroso Ferrero admits that her own Italian landscape appears anew to her after witnessing the "new Italies" of South America.[69]

According to Lombroso Ferrero, one can have "an almost exact idea" of the Guanabara Bay of Rio de Janeiro—the object of travelers' awe and wonder, what De Amicis called the American *Arc de Triomphe*—by standing on the "Capriolo peak, one of the tallest peaks of Monte Rosa." From there one can observe "the summits of the mountain range bathing in the wave of rising sunlight." Lombroso Ferrero cleverly uses language redolent of the sea to strengthen the parallel between these two quite different landscapes. Yet—as if she knew the kind of cogitations required to see the famed beauty of the Guanabara Bay in the Pennine Alps—she quickly clarifies that "the similarity is not limited to appearances." Supplementing her poetic language with some hard scientific facts, she explains how "all over our mountains we find many remnants of shells, which tell us that they were once covered by the sea."[70] Her combination of ecological and literary language renders *Nell'America Meridionale* a text that, much like Alexander von Humboldt's *Views of Nature*, "fuse[s] the specificity of science with the esthetics of the sublime."[71]

Lombroso Ferrero's refraction of Brazil's landscape through Italian geography does not stop at Guanabara Bay. On the contrary, it encompasses each of the spaces she visits, which include the State of Minas Gerais and the State of São Paulo. The latter, which occupies a separate section from the city of São Paulo, resembles "our *langhe* of the Asti region," which, "when viewed from above, look like the waves in a storm."[72] At the time of Lombroso Ferrero's writing, the langhe—a southern area of the Piedmont region—comprised one of the poorest areas of the peninsula, a place plagued by food shortages and mass migration. Making a geographical parallel between the langhe and the State of São Paulo serves a twofold purpose. First, the parallel implies that numerous inhabitants of that Italian region now reside here, which in turn would explain the similarity of these two landscapes. Second, Lombroso Ferrero implies that one may also find that longed-for "America" in Italy because its valleys could easily provide work for these colonos. Hence she not only maps Italy in Brazil but *through* it, indicating to her presumably bourgeois Italian readership the untapped possibilities of their own country. Just as colonie existed outside of Italy, so, too, do they exist in latent form in those areas with similar agroeconomic profiles on the mainland.[73]

Despite neither the langhe nor the interior of São Paulo being near water, Lombroso Ferrero insists on using words evocative of the sea. To be sure, the imagery is highly localized and clearly intended to draw a much more ambitious parallel between the vastness of the Guanabara Bay and the forests she was soon to traverse. Yet in both instances Lombroso Ferrero notices in the variety of these spaces a heterogeneity similar to the Italian one described in the dedication. Both the Guanabara Bay, through its "varying terrains, soils, and waters," and the "untouched forest," which is "never covered by just one species of tree and it never shows, at least in Brazil, a bare soil" recall Italy and its plurality of defining traits.[74] According to Lombroso Ferrero, it is the sense of contained infinitude, of a totalizing variety, which defines Brazil's incommensurable beauty. A similar sense of prodigiousness reappears when she turns her gaze to São Paulo—only, this time, in relation to the city's Italian inhabitants.

The forest prefigures its obverse: first comes the natural heterogeneity, which makes the bay beautiful to the point of ineffability; next, there comes the staggering urbanity of São Paulo, which is defined by its bountiful Italianness. While Lombroso Ferrero's description of the bay reinforces positive feelings, her description of the forest provokes a deep sense of uneasiness and dread. The latter reveals how the natural, unrepresentable Brazil transforms into the modern, civilized Brazil embodied in São Paulo, a fundamentally Italian city:

> But after one, two, three hours, the forest starts to weigh you down . . . when inside such a tight space, life piles into itself, overlapping furiously like in an untouched forest. It is no longer the vast expanse that overwhelms you, but rather loneliness that challenges your strength. . . . There, you no longer struggle with being the loneliest man in the world, but with being the loneliest

> man in a big, animated city, where everyone you meet, everyone you see, lives and stresses about their own needs and desires.[75]

Lombroso Ferrero makes clear that the colonos must burn the forest in order to bring an end to that feeling of alienation described earlier: "after having traveled for hours and hours through the untouched forest, one understands the *revenge* of the men who burned it, not in accordance with any urgent needs, but only for experiencing a feeling of triumph within this untamable nature: only to see it burn."[76] The taming of the "virgin" forest through the practice of burning not only clears the space for a new *cafeeira*—coffee cultivation—to come about; it also brings an end to the solitude and uneasiness that the forest provokes in humans.

The fire, however, also signifies the desire to erase what came before. It reveals the desire to incinerate primitivity and barbarity, to pave the way for the modern metropolis to emerge from the ashes. To convey the devastation brought about by the anthropic fire, Lombroso Ferrero resorts to war imagery: the action itself becomes a "battle"; what is left in the wake of the fire is "a battlefield, still bloody with the dead and wounded."[77] The war unfolds between human and nonhuman (and subhuman) forms, so that modern civilization can come about in the form of the city. Whether done consciously or not, Lombroso Ferrero's rhetoric evokes the brutality of settler colonialism but with an important twist—here colonization begins not with the Portuguese but with the modern programs of subsidized migration.

The tension between the past and the future, which culminates in the image of the fire, becomes visible in yet another rhetorical move: Lombroso Ferrero's usage of a language reminiscent of medieval times. The biggest trees she encounters, the *jequitibás*, become the "*kings* of the forest," which "rise like *towers* from which shredded liana *banners* hang."[78] The invocation of premodern symbols implies that these actions belong to a darker time, yet one that, despite its air of menace, will bring about civilization. Indeed, it is at the end of this Brazilian *medioevo* that Lombroso Ferrero finds São Paulo:

> São Paulo . . . situated on a wide and waving plateau, gives the impression of being located in the outskirts of Florence. It is the pride and joy of all Brazil-

> ians, astonished and proud to have an American city all to themselves, a city with a spirit full of pride, initiative, passion, and constant activity, which was missing from the old urban centers of Brazil.[79]

It is not by chance that, in her peculiar Italian remapping of Brazil, Lombroso Ferrero chooses to situate São Paulo in the outskirts of Florence, rather than, say, Bologna or Rome, both of which are also located amid *un ondulato altipiano*. By likening São Paulo to Florence, she suggests that the former's positive attributes—its pride, resourcefulness, industriousness, and ardor—hearken back to the Italian Renaissance. That is, like the Florence of Leonardo da Vinci and Galileo Galilei that brought light to the dark ages, São Paulo acts as a beacon of civilization at the terminus—literal and figurative—of the primeval forests.

Like other Italian travel writers, Lombroso Ferrero burnishes the aura of exceptionalism surrounding the city of São Paulo at the turn of the twentieth century. Indeed, she goes as far as to suggest that São Paulo is not a Brazilian metropolis precisely because it is *too* modern. Here the term "American" contrasts with the adjective "old" in a surprising way, revealing that for Lombroso Ferrero "an American city" is nonetheless a modern city where "everything is Italian," which is to say, somewhat paradoxically, rooted in the old world.[80] She writes:

> The most pronounced aspect of the city is its Italianness. More Italian is spoken here in São Paulo than in Turin, Milan, or Naples, because, whereas we speak dialect amongst one another in Italy, here all of the dialects blend together under the influence of Venetians and Tuscans who have adopted Italian as their official language.[81]

São Paulo is more Italian than Turin, Milan, and Naples because its residents, Brazilian natives included, speak Italian. However, given that what we understand today as standard Italian had only come about in the second half of the nineteenth century—and, moreover, that most of the people who emigrated to Brazil had low literacy levels and most likely spoke their own regional dialect—such statements seem more like wishful thinking, an effort to imagine the process of "making Italians" championed by elites as a fait accompli.[82] In other words, São Paulo allows Lombroso Ferrero to hypostatize the "imagined community" of Italy.[83] This imagined Italy is, curiously, unburdened by the Southern Question both in terms of consumption—recall the list of "Italian" products cited earlier—and culture. Here Italians have overcome their regional chauvinism and ethnolinguistic parochialism. However implausible this claim may be, it nonetheless reflects a real desire to claim São Paulo as a modern Italian city. While perhaps not equally breathtaking as Rio de Janeiro, São Paulo, where "everything is Italian," epitomizes everything that is modern and civilized in Brazil.

5. *From* colonos *to* colonizzatori*: Erasing and Rewriting Italians in Brazilian History*

If the discourse of geography enables Lombroso Ferrero to remap Italy in *and* through Brazil and narrates a primitive transition from a state of nature to one of urban modernity, it is through history that she negotiates the separation between past and future crystallized in the anthropic fire. Her account of Brazil's history reinscribes Italians into the country's colonial past. That is, through a clever sleight of hand she transforms the Italian colonos (indentured workers) into colonizzatori (colonizers).

Lombroso Ferrero's travelogue includes a sharp critique of Portuguese colonialism, but her critique has less to do with Portugal's exploitation of Brazilian lands, resources, and peoples than it does with the fact that these lands stayed "unpopulated."[84] Although she praises the Portuguese for having brought with them "a cohort of scholars, poets and artists" to Brazil, which ensured that the newly conquered lands would stay "strongly tied to European culture" she insists that the Portuguese never could have risen to the task of conquering a country of Brazil's scale. As she explains, "Portugal . . . was a small strip of land on the Iberian Peninsula . . . it could only give the New World but a few bureaucratic and commercial components and some thousand political and religious exiles." The fact that the Portuguese "were always scarce" left room for other colonizers, namely the French and the Dutch, to arrive in Brazil and set up their own colonies.[85]

Italians, too, were among those colonizers, she reminds us: "Venetians and Florentines went all around Bahia, amongst whom a member of the Cavalcanti family, a family once referenced by Dante, who left a great number of descendants and had an important role in Brazilian history."[86] According to Lombroso Ferrero, the presence of Italians in Brazil, far from being only a contemporary phenomenon resulting from specific socioeconomic conditions, can be traced back to the seventeenth century. Lombroso Ferrero was almost certainly familiar with the epic poem *L'America* (1650) by Girolamo Bartolomei, in which the author narrates Amerigo Vespucci's navigation to the Americas, Africa, and Europe. In the last canto, Bartolomei depicts a glorious Vespucci founding the Brazilian city of Salvador in Bahia. Literary scholar Natalie Hester explains how in Bartolomei's epic "the Portuguese colonization of Brazil is written over, as a Medici subject provides the remedy to the ills of European expansion. Vespucci is the expression of a Florentine invention of the New World, the symbolic naming—and therefore possessing—of a territory to be known as America." Much like Bartolomei, Lombroso Ferrero overwrites the Portuguese colonization of Brazil. But instead of casting navigators such as Vespucci as the founders of an Italian colony in Brazil, she inserts the figures of the Italian colonos. What the juxtaposition makes clear is that in both the Medicean epic tradition analyzed by Hester and the fin-de-siècle travel writing about South America discussed in this chapter, "a tale of Italian travel allows for the development of a substitute narrative of Italian might."[87] Lombroso Ferrero wants to insinuate Italians into the colonial history of Brazil to justify her imaginary colonial map. She seeks to legitimate the emigration of the colonos and further mystify their miserable working conditions by making their presence part of a longer, noble legacy of Italian colonization of Brazil, a process that reaches its apex with the rise of São Paulo.

In addition to linking Brazil's colonial past to Cavalcanti and to the *italianissimo* Dante, Lombroso Ferrero suggests that the current wave of Italian immigrants might serve as better colonizers than the Portuguese, not least because "as a Portuguese colony, Brazil was never subordinate to its dominant country, like Peru, Chile, Argentina and Mexico were to Spain, or the U.S. to England."[88] For Lombroso Ferrero, the Portuguese are only nominal colonizers of Brazil. And this, consequently, makes room for the industrious and populous Italy to lay claim to it. Yet the Portuguese *did* populate Brazil, through the forced displacement of millions of African slaves. Lombroso Ferrero's desperate attempts to establish the desolateness of

Brazil speaks to the nature of settler colonial projects more broadly, which depend on the violent erasure and subjugation of vulnerable peoples. Like her account of the colonos, her description of slavery sanitizes that brutal system. "The agricultural exploitation of Brazil," she explains "would have never been possible without the *help* of enslaved Africans."[89] The use of the word *aiuto* (help) trivializes forced labor, implying that the master/slave relationship was akin to the one between employer and employee, albeit one characterized by an uncommon degree of intimacy.

In this respect, she anticipates the work of sociologist Gilberto Freyre whose 1933 influential text *Casa-grande e senzala* (translated as *The Masters and the Slaves*) constitutes a fundamental turning point in Brazilian racial politics. Cultural historian Lamonte Aidoo writes that, according to Freyre, who was a student of famed anthropologist Franz Boas, "what made Brazilian society so exceptional was precisely its miscegenation." For Freyre, "the absence of racism in Brazil was due to the nation's history of peaceful miscegenation between European, indigenous, and African peoples." Additionally, Freyre argued that "slavery was more benign and humane as a result of these intimate relations among the races."[90] Sex and intimacy became the regulating processes through which Afro-Brazilians became included in Brazilian society. The problem however, as highlighted in Aidoo's book, lays in the fact that the intimacy Freyre talks about was not consensual, and more often than not came about in the form of rape. Anthropologist Livio Sansone highlights how Lombroso Ferrero's observations about race in Brazil "are proof that ideas similar to those later developed by Freyre were already circulating among certain elites well before their popularization."[91] Anticipating Freyre by several decades, Lombroso Ferrero finds the seeds of Brazilian racial harmony within the family: "familial bonds accustomed whites not only to love Blacks but also to appreciate them." The love allegedly shared by masters and slaves made it so that "Brazil never had such disdain for Blacks as did North America still today."[92]

The idyllic race relations depicted by Lombroso Ferrero are dubious, to say the least. Even so, they foreshadow the myth of Brazilian racial democracy popularized in the 1930s by thinkers like Freyre.[93] Despite the fact that Freyre's *Casa-grande e senzala* often gets cited as the most exemplary theorization of Brazilian racial democracy, Freyre himself did not employ the expression until much later in the 1960s within the context of Portuguese colonialism in Africa. In any case, his theorizations of Brazilian miscegenation and ethnic amalgamation allowed for the belief that everybody, no matter their race, enjoyed social mobility in Brazil.[94]

To frame larger conversations about race occurring in Italy, Lombroso Ferrero goes as far as to use her proto-Freyrian understanding of Brazilian race relations:

> Miscegenation saved Brazil from the racial issues that plague North America. In fact, it formed a new race that held no lesser status to its Black and white counterparts that were its roots, contrary to the theoretical assertions of modern anthropologists who want to invalidate the potential for perfection in our mixture with Hamitic races.[95]

Miscegenation is conceived of here as a salve to the race problem both in Italy and in Brazil. Brazilian society furnishes evidence to dispute the claim that the Italian race, on account of its admixture with Hamitic blood, must occupy a subordinate position within the racial hierarchy of Europe. Here it should be noted that the foremost proponent of the Eurafrican hypothesis was anthropologist Giuseppe Sergi, who aggressively responded to theories of Aryan superiority by proposing in his 1898 *Arii e italici* "that the racial roots of all European whites were in Africa, and that Aryans had brought nothing to Mediterranean Europe." Employing Lombroso's methodology of cranial morphology, Sergi concluded that "racial mixing was . . . the condition for racial evolution, not its demise." But for all his research proving the superiority of the Mediterranean race, Sergi nonetheless succumbs to racist thinking when it comes to Southern Italians who he, like many of his contemporaries, regarded as inferior to their Northern counterparts. Miscegenation likewise reappears here as a solution. Like Lombroso Ferrero, Sergi proposes to resolve the Southern Question through means similar to the ones championed by Brazilian elites: "the organized 'immigration' of Northern Italians to the South and sexual intermixing with southerners."[96]

In the case of Brazil, the fact that the country "continues to visibly become whiter" reassures Italians that their eventual mixing with the local populace will lead to the creation of a "new race." This is because, according to Lombroso Ferrero's positivist outlook, "the condition of the mulatto is temporary." Since the mulatto "will never marry a Black woman," Lombroso Ferrero reasons, "the children will, after a few generations, be more or less white or, at the very least, be considered as such."[97] With this disquisition on race, Lombroso Ferrero seeks to dispel fears about the racial stigmatization of the colonos that may have troubled Italian travelers and politicians before her. Whatever new race emerges from the Brazilian experiment will be, she assures us, one in which the Italian element, imported specifically to mix with the local populace, remains superior.[98]

Lombroso Ferrero's stance toward miscegenation, however, becomes of even greater interest when we consider how she avoids discussing Italians and Black Brazilians in the same context. As we have seen, the notion that Italians have come to Brazil to substitute enslaved peoples haunts other Italian travel accounts about Brazil. Disturbing parallels between Italian laborers and Black captives abound, especially when it comes to the coffee fields. But for her part, Lombroso Ferrero studiously skirts them. The simplest explanation for this would be that she could not criticize the fazendas she visited lest she offend her patrons. But another likely explanation lies in Lombroso Ferrero's deeper understanding of the biopolitical role Italians stood to play in the Brazilian racial system. After all, as Sansone points out, Lombroso's travelogue shows more than a passing familiarity with current racial debates in Brazil and the finer points of Brazilian literature. For example, Lombroso Ferrero calls Brazilian writer Graça Aranha, who also happened to be their guide, "foremost . . . among the poets and writers of the younger Brazilian generation" and defines his controversial masterwork *Canaã* (1902) as the "national poem of Brazil," going so far as to compare it to the American *Uncle Tom's Cabin* in terms of its local impact.[99] In closing, I would like to suggest that the extensive references to *Canaã* found in Lombroso Ferrero's text offer a clue to understanding her silence on Black-Italian relations in Brazil.

Literary scholar May E. Bletz describes *Canaã* as "one of the first works that overtly engages [the] search for a perfect race through the process of *mestiçagem*." Lilia Moritz Schwarcz also highlights *Canaã* as emblematic of a series of works of fiction published in these years which project the future emergence of a progressively white Brazilian ethnic type thanks to miscegenation.[100] The novel takes place in the southern region of Espírito Santo; its protagonist Milkau is a German immigrant who "is optimistic and dreams about a new tropical race, a fusion of all people." Yet Milkau's dream founders on account of his fellow countrymen, who do not share his enthusiasm for assimilation and even refuse to so much as learn Portuguese. In this respect, the novel is an accurate depiction of German settlements, which hindered the process of miscegenation that Graça Aranha and others "proposed as the inevitable and ultimate solution of Brazil's lack of national unity."[101] Lombroso Ferrero's mentioning of the novel hardly seems like a coincidence. It suggests that the distinction between the German story and the Italian one was not lost on her and that she intuited—rightly—that Italians' success in Brazil depended principally on their ability to avoid the fate of their German precursors. In other words, what mattered was neither that Italians had to contend with Brazil's African presence nor that their mistreatment occasionally brought to mind the legacy of enslavement. Rather, what mattered was whether Italians would have the good sense to capitalize on their status as uniquely privileged vectors of whiteness in this new world. One look at the teeming streets of São Paulo, where Italians seemed to have taken over, was perhaps enough to quiet the old racial fears. But if, as the century progressed, Italians became more associated with the urbanity of São Paulo than the provincialism and backwardness of the countryside, it was not, as Lombroso Ferrero might have hoped, by dint of their pride and industriousness alone. In this they had help from, among other things, the Brazilian modernist movement, which, as we shall see in Chapter Two, extended and revised the tradition of Italo-Brazilian representation that Lombroso Ferrero pioneered.

TWO

Cidadão italiano residente em São Paulo

Modernism, Cannibalism, and the Italians of São Paulo

In the preface of *Brás, Bexiga e Barra Funda*—whose title refers to the São Paulo neighborhoods famously inhabited by Italians—Antônio de Alcântara Machado informs his readers that a new breed of Brazilians was born from the mixing of the Italian "jovial race" with the local Brazilian people (originally made up of "three sad races": the Indigenous, the Portuguese, and the African).[1] From this new mixing, the author muses, "The *italianinhos* were born. Gaetaninho. Carmela. Brazilians and Paulistas. Even *bandeirantes* [the early settlers of São Paulo]." Italians, for Alcântara Machado, became not just mere native city dwellers but the progenitors of a new urban landscape, what literary scholar May Bletz has called "urban *bandeirantes*."[2] Just as São Paulo incorporated the *italianinhos* and transformed them into Paulistanos, so, too, did Italians leave a visible mark on the urban, cultural, economic, and political landscape of São Paulo.[3]

And yet this was neither as simple nor straightforward a process as perhaps the above quote from Alcântara Machado makes it seem. Rather, it was a dialectical one that involved a complex negotiation between a tendency toward assimilation or incorporation on the one hand and a tendency toward ethnocentrism on the other. To a certain extent, the cultural assimilation of Italians into a Paulista society conceived of as generically "white" has tended to obscure the crucial role that they played in establishing an image of São Paulo as the crowning achievement of what historian Barbara Weinstein calls "the region's exceptional capacity for progress and modernity" vis-à-vis the rest of Brazil, especially the highly Africanized northeast. In fact, if Italians were embraced for their industriousness and their assimilability, they nonetheless held fast to their distinctive speech patterns, their religious *festas*, and their culinary traditions, not least because these eventually became markers of Paulista prestige. In this chapter, I turn to the modernist and proto-modernist Brazilian writers who not only captured this process but, in so doing, helped to ensure that certain aspects of *italianità* would morph into a specific São Paulo identity—called "paulistinidade" by Weinstein—associated with modernity and progress.[4] To reconstruct this process, I adapt one of their most famous and controversial literary tropes: the figure of the cannibal. I propose that this trope offers a useful theoretical framework for understanding the cultural encounter between Italians and São Paulo or, more specifically, how Italians became Paulistanos and, conversely, how São Paulo became Italian in the Brazilian popular imagination.

Cannibalism, understood as a literary trope for thinking about the interlinking of two or more cultures, animates some of the most canonical artistic productions of Brazilian modernism. Modernist writer Oswald de Andrade famously asked, in his 1928 *Manifesto antropófago* (Cannibalist Manifesto), "Tupi or not Tupi, that is the question." The Tupi people were the largest group of Indigenous people in Brazil before its colonization. For him, 1556—the year when the Aimoré Indians killed and devoured bishop Pedro Sardinha—marked the beginning of Brazilian history. He saw cannibalism, or *antropofagia* in Portuguese, as the quintessential Brazilian sign and practice. No longer simply relegated outside of history, the Indigenous cannibalistic act subverted European values of time and space and truly revolutionized "traditional" (i.e., colonial) institutions.

Literary critics have largely interpreted Andrade's notion of cannibalism as the act of devouring and ingesting the foreign—particularly the

European—as a means of producing an authentically Brazilian national culture that mitigates and resolves differences.[5] Others, namely literary scholar Sara Castro-Klarén, have instead highlighted how Andrade's epistemological dilemma of whether to be Tupi or not, and the subsequent cannibalistic act, rejects dialectical synthesis as a Western and patriarchal mode of being in the world.[6] For Castro-Klarén, cannibalism constitutes "an operation of turning into, of becoming another" that does not end. Likewise, literary scholar Isabel Gómez locates the source of this infinitude in the reciprocity of the cannibal act, which she interprets as a practice of cultural exchange founded on nonassimilation. Literary scholar Zita Nunes also notes the impossibility of a completed process of synthesis since the cannibal act requires "a remainder" or a "left over" that cannot be ingested. In her analysis, the problem with thinking about cannibalism as a metaphor for national synthesis is that the remainder—that is, the Black Brazilian body—"prevents a sense of completion and haunts the discourse on/of national unity, undermining the ideology of racial democracy, even as it makes it visible."[7] Thinking about the cannibal act along the lines proposed by Castro-Klarén, Nunes, and Gómez—that is, understanding it as reciprocal and continuous—allows us to better understand how Italians in São Paulo have become Brazilians even while retaining identifiably Italian contours. At the same time, it is precisely through the cannibal trope that Brazilian modernists successfully cement, in the literary realm, the association between Italianness, São Paulo, and modernity.

An underappreciated corollary of the rhetorical work carried out by the modernists is that, in São Paulo, this association between Italians and modernity occurred decades before it did in Europe or the United States. In some circles, it was perhaps not until after World War II and the "Made in Italy" boom that it became possible to speak of Italy and modernity in the same breath without eliciting the utmost skepticism. Indeed, the Italian identity that Mussolini sought to project on the world stage—to disastrous effect—stemmed largely from his country's subaltern position in Europe, which, as historian Ruth Ben-Ghiat has observed, "led many Italians to associate modernity with the achievements of more dominant nations." Anthropologist Mia Fuller points out that "whether during the Liberal or Fascist era, efforts to modernize Italy were driven by the state's growing confrontation with nationwide poverty, cholera epidemics, sanitation problems, illiteracy, and social instability."[8] By contrast, across the Atlantic, Italians had supposedly spearheaded an unprecedented economic boom in the most powerful capitalist city in South America and hence become the apotheosis of modernization. Recuperating the discourse that constructed this alternative Italian identity in São Paulo—what I have chosen to call throughout this work the New World Italian discourse—compels us to reexamine the totalizing narratives of Italian backwardness and underdevelopment, which inspired much of Italy's foreign and domestic politics during the first half of the twentieth century.

1. An Italian language for São Paulo? Juó Bananére and the Italo-Paulistanos

The figure of Juó Bananére, the Italo-Paulistano journalist-barber invented by Brazilian civil engineer and writer Alexandre Machado Ribeiro Marcondes, first appeared on São Paulo's journalistic scene in a 1911 edition of *O pirralho*, a magazine founded by Andrade. When Andrade left for his sojourn in Paris—from whence the prominent modernist famously returned with a copy of Filippo Tommaso Marinetti's *Futurist Manifesto*—Bananére took over his satirical column "As cartas d'abaixo piques."[9] The column already had an Italian flavor, since Andrade wrote it under the Italianate pseudonym of Annibale Scipione. Marcondes, the pen behind Juó Bananére, had no connection to Italy; however, he had attended school in the immigrant neighborhood of Bom Retiro, where he picked up on the changing soundscape of urban São Paulo. His subsequent work as an engineer afforded him the income and leisure time to pursue a literary career writing in the voice of Bananére until his premature death in 1933. Although Marcondes was familiar with the Italian social milieu in São Paulo, critics have tended to see his linguistic innovations—which incorporated the street argot he had likely heard in places like Bom Retiro—as idiosyncratic literary invention rather than a faithful reproduction of the speech of Italian immigrants living in the city at the time.[10]

Nevertheless, it is indisputable that he effectively Italianized Portuguese, often by rendering some Portuguese sounds through Italian phonemes. For example, the Portuguese word *minha* (mine) becomes *migna* in the language used by Bananére in an obvious play on the similarity of the sound *nh* in Portuguese and *gn* in Italian. But *migna* does not exist in standard Italian; rather, the first-person possessive pronoun is *mia*. He also sprinkles in Italian words to give his diction a more authentic feel. For example, the word *robba* from the Italian *roba* (things, stuff) often appears in his writing. Bananére does not engage with the diurnal realities of immigrant life, nor does he seek to demonize the immigrant per se. Instead, his works satirize the São Paulo political scene using a fictive immigrant outsider's voice. Marcondes became so adept at this faux ventriloquism that local politicians of all persuasions dreaded any mention of their names in Bananére's columns. But what does it mean to write political satire in an Italian-inflected Portuguese?

Marcondes's linguistic choices mark an important moment in Brazilian literary production because they transcribe—loosely, to be sure—a popular, urban voice that brought a breath of fresh air to the rarefied cultural milieu of the Paulistano belle epoque. São Paulo's established bourgeoisie, a highly educated and cultured group who read *O pirralho*, laughed with *and* at Juó Bananére. These were the same people who would overwhelmingly support São Paulo's 1922 *Semana de Arte Moderna* (Week of Modern Art), a series of talks and exhibits crowning the city as the capital of Brazilian modernism. This bourgeois audience gravitated toward modernist art partly on the belief that to maintain one's class status in a changing São Paulo—where the intense process of industrialization led to a reconfiguration of power relations among the city's elites—one needed to be au courant. In fact, as literary scholar Randal Johnson points out, the fluctuating valences of high and low styles mirrored the undulations of class mobility caused by modernization.[11] In his extensive analysis of Bananére, literary scholar Maurício Martins do Carmo convincingly argues that Marcondes uses the Italian language to convey an aesthetics of everydayness. He points out that Marcondes's wordplay often involves changing the diction of existing poems to undermine their "erudite presumption." Indeed, not long after joining the staff of *O pirralho*, Marcondes shifted his focus from urban chronicle to poetic parody.[12]

In 1915, Bananére published a collection of poems, *La divina increnca* (The Divine Mischief), an obvious play on Dante's *Divine Comedy*. It became a bestseller and was subsequently adapted into a play in 1918 and performed thirty-six times. While the original 1915 edition comprised forty-four pages, by 1925, with the publication of an expanded ninth edition, the count stood at 134 pages. The cover of the first edition clearly shows Bananére, in a scene taken from the *Inferno*, dressed like Dante and standing alongside Virgil and other characters who resemble various politicos of the time. Marcondes possessed a vast literary knowledge and cleverly drew on the *Divine Comedy* to create incendiary political subtexts. Marcondes's erudition surfaces also in the poems he chose to Italianize, which included those by Machado de Assis, La Fontaine, Edgar Allan Poe, Luis de Camões, and Gonçalves Dias. Thus, Bananére's allegedly "democratic message" contrasts starkly with the relatively elite literary education that his reader must have to grasp much of his text's satire. He certainly "had a wide, admiring readership in a society significantly composed of Italian immigrants and Italian Brazilians."[13] Even so, such readers of Bananére, even any Italians among them, likely belonged to the upper echelons of society. And, in any case, Italian immigrants most likely did not read Bananére because they had their own newspapers and magazines, as we shall see later in this chapter.

In Bananére, the sound of Italian, despite its association with the demotic, nonetheless modernizes and innovates a static and pompous literary tradition. That Italian could exercise such a modernizing force in Brazil comes as a surprise, given the linguistic situation unfolding on the Italian peninsula at the time. Even in the early twentieth century, most Italians did not speak the artificial language of "Italian," which for many represented nothing more than the imposition of the Tuscan dialect. The value attributed to these Italian dialects, however, changed as they crossed the Atlantic. Far from the peninsula, where dialects would quickly be understood as such, these languages acquired the esteem attributed to their speakers and became, ipso facto, standardized. After all, to a listener accustomed to Brazilian Portuguese, all the Italian dialects shared a similar sound, one referred to as "Italian" and, consequently, associated with São Paulo's ongoing industrialization and modernization.

At the same time, Marcondes's use of Dante as a starting point for his parodic poetry collection reveals that even as the Italian language belonged to the streets and to the popular domain, it had also produced one of the most lauded works of world literature, the *Divine Comedy*. The mythologization of Italians as agents of modernization on the basis of their association with a specific moment of peak industrialization and urbanization in São Paulo goes hand in hand with the status enjoyed by Italian literature in that city. Italians in São Paulo became the ideal modern subjects because, while their presence challenged the preexisting order by bringing about streetwise ways of expressing oneself and creating a new urban soundscape, they did not necessarily threaten to upend the status quo. The highbrow artistic production associated with the peninsula functioned both as a shield from discrimination for Italians and as a source of pride for Brazilians, who could now claim to have internalized parts of it themselves.

In other words, Paulistano society accepted and consumed Bananére, despite his humble origins, because of his *alegria* (joviality) and his Italian heritage. Even so, Marcondes understood that it was precisely his accented Portuguese, combined with his vast literary and political knowledge of Brazil, which allowed him and his nom de plume to penetrate Paulistano society. Each part interpenetrated and consumed the other. Perhaps more than any other figure, Juó Bananére epitomizes the reciprocity of the cannibal act, or what Castro-Klarén and Gómez have interpreted as a constant process of becoming, a cultural exchange rooted in nonassimilation. At the same time, the centrality of laughter and the parodic in Bananére's production directly recalls the element of the discursive joke, which literary scholar Lucia Helena rightly identifies as a key component in Oswald de Andrade's conception of literary cannibalism.[14] Bananére, the Italo-Paulista barber-cum-journalist, with his elitism masked by a vernacular flair, heralded the emergence of a new Paulistano identity, one both cosmopolitan and modern.

Among the Paulistano modernists, it was Alcântara Machado who most clearly understood the importance of Bananére. While literary scholars such as Mario Carelli recognize Marcondes as "the most radically anthropophagist creator of his generation," a kind of proto-modernist, Marcondes was never attached, properly speaking, to the Brazilian modernist movement. In fact, Carelli informs us that Andrade, Brazil's foremost modernist poet, was decidedly ambivalent toward him, at first downplaying his success and, only later in the 1940s, calling him the "master of Brazilian satire."[15] By contrast, Alcântara Machado, Andrade's protégé, writing in *Cavaquinho e Saxofone*

(Cavaquinho and Saxophone), promptly recognized him as "the most popular journalist of the city," adding that "Juó Bananére, citizen of São Paulo, always remained deeply Italian."[16] But what does it mean for an invented character—in this case, a native-born Brazilian's alter ego—"to remain deeply Italian"? For that matter, what does it mean for such a figure to be a citizen of São Paulo? These questions are central to Alcântara Machado's work and suggest that he developed the Italian characters in *Brás, Bexiga and Barra Funda* with the model of Bananére in mind.

2. *Alcântara Machado among the Modernists: The 1922 Week of Modern Art and Its Legacies*

The "unparalleled pages" of *Brás, Bexiga e Barra Funda* mark the first time an Italian immigrant appears as "the exclusive subject of a literary work" and form an "ample canvas of the Italian presence in early twentieth century São Paulo."[17] At the same time, literary scholars regard Alcântara Machado's work as "a unique account of a frantic and evanescent São Paulo" and lionize its prose as the quintessential example of Paulistano modernism.[18] Hence the first and most exemplary literary representation of Italians in Brazilian literature doubles as the ultimate manifestation of the country's modernist movement. Simply put, it was Brazilian literary modernism that crystallized the conflation of São Paulo, modernity, and Italians for decades to come.

It was with the 1922 Week of Modern Art, so the conventional story goes, that Brazil declared its artistic independence, subsequently launching its modernist movement.[19] Held at the São Paulo Municipal Theater from February 11 to February 18, the Week of Modern Art showcased lectures, exhibits, and performances that exhorted artists to break free from obsolete artistic traditions incapable of representing Brazilian reality. Initially, rather than participating in the Week of Modern Art, Alcântara Machado—then only nineteen years old—protested it outside the Municipal Theater. Yet he, too, was soon caught up in the modernist fever. Just two years later, in 1924, he wrote an article for the *Jornal do Comércio* titled "O que eu disse a um comediógrafo nacional" (What I Said to a National Playwright), in which he called on writers not only to Brazilianize (*abrasileirar*) the country's theater but to Saopaulistanize it (*apualistanizêmo-lo*).[20]

In Alcântara Machado's preface to *Brás, Bexiga e Barra Funda*, he outlines the *italianinhos*' arrival on the Brazilian scene, the result of a symbolic process of reciprocal cannibalism in which the Brazilian body politic figuratively devours Italians and incorporates Italianness. This depiction sums up nicely the prevailing beliefs of some of São Paulo's modernist intellectuals. Take the organizing committee of the 1922 Week of Modern Art: its members were Oswald de Andrade, Tarsilia do Amaral, Anita Malfatti, Menotti del Picchia, and Mário de Andrade. Although these artists and writers followed quite divergent ideological paths, they nonetheless all imagined the Italian immigrant as a crucial player in Brazil's modernization process, a process that, of course, had São Paulo as its cynosure.[21]

In 1928, Alcântara Machado was at the editorial helm of the famous *Revista de Antropofagia* (Journal of Cannibalism), which published Oswald de Andrade's *Manifesto Antropófago*, his second manifesto.[22] There, Andrade—whom literary critic Alfredo Bosi described as the "tip of the spear of the spirit of '22"—proposed a much more violent understanding of Brazilian history, one than refutes the amicable mixing of races believed to be the basis of Brazilian national formation. In the identification with the Tupi Indian—"Tupi or not Tupi, that is the question," his well-known quote famously puns in English—Andrade found the final rejection of Europe and, in cannibalism, "the most extreme concept of opposition to the morality of Western civilization."[23] According to Johnson, the cannibal act "expresses, in allegorical terms, the revolt of the colonized against the colonizer . . . it represents an attempt to devour the advantages of the former without being culturally decharacterized or destroyed." Far from resulting in a synthesis, Andrade's cannibalism becomes synonymous with perpetual transformation, what Castro-Klarén calls "an endless voyage toward an infinite and indetermined alterity."[24]

Antropofagia, the movement Andrade founded based on his ideas about cannibalism, constitutes the first and most visible splinter of the 1922 Week of Modern Art organizing committee and of the Brazilian modernist movement writ large. The circle of intellectuals around Antropofagia—other than Andrade and his wife, painter Tarsilia do Amaral—included Alcântara

Machado, who, in fact, had become Andrade's protégé. A full-blooded member of São Paulo's Portuguese aristocracy, Alcântara Machado counted among his forebearers some illustrious academic and political figures. He had, moreover, no direct knowledge of Italy or Italian, apart from a trip to Europe he undertook between March and November 1925. To this day, it still bewilders literary critics that he was the one to write the definitive literary account of Italians in São Paulo, instead of, say, his contemporary Menotti del Picchia. Such confusion is exacerbated when we consider that Picchia, a writer who was famously proud of his Italian heritage, was also one of the co-organizers of the seminal Week of Modern Art. But although Picchia's Italian identity informed his work during this period—most notably his self-published poem "Juca Mulato," which critics consider the first expression of Brazilian modernism—he did not write explicitly about his own ethnic community until much later.[25]

In 1926, Picchia, Plínio Salgado, and Cassiano Ricardo launched the *Movimento Verde-amarelo* (The Green and Yellow Movement), which embraced and foregrounded the inherent cultural nationalism of Brazilian modernism. Literary scholar Antonio Arnoni Prado calls the Verde-amarelo a "false vanguard" and links it to the development in the 1930s of Brazil's homegrown fascist movement known as integralism led by none other than Salgado (discussed later in Chapter Four). As a participant in the Verde-amarelo, Picchia begins to reflect more forcefully than in "Juca Mulato" on the integration of different ethnicities under the Brazilian flag, whose colors are green (verde) and yellow (amarelo). Picchia also bestowed upon Italians the same kind of virility attributed to bandeirantes, São Paulo's early settlers, to the point that, for him, the arrival of "emigrant bodies" had "viscerally" changed Brazil's "ethnic environment." Salgado's participation in the Verde-amarelo and the publication of his 1926 novel *O estrangeiro* (The Foreigner) are likewise central to the movement's rhetoric. In his novel, Salgado portrayed Italian Humberto Mondolfi as a model migrant compared with the protagonist, a Russian named Ivã. At one point, Ivã contrasts his own inability to overcome his status as a foreigner with Mondolfi's ability to assimilate. The difference lies in the fact that "Italians bring here a strength of intimate cohesion, which grounds them and makes them allies of the land."[26] In this view, Italians emerged from the crucible of migration better suited to become one with Brazilian land—a view not unlike the one espoused by Lombroso Ferrero in her travel writing. Moreover, according to Picchia and Salgado, Italians engender the allegedly peaceful synthesis, or integration, that the authors of Movimento Verde-amarelo championed.

The Verde-amarelo's vision of Brazil's racial origins differs significantly from the one that emerges from the *Manifesto Antropófago*. While Antropofagia exalted the aggressive, violent native warrior who practiced cannibalism, the Verde-amarelo idolized the docile, collaborative native Brazilian whose legacy in Brazil ensured the absence of racial prejudice within Brazilian society.[27] However, both movements share a similar understanding of the immigrant, especially the Italian one. Whether in the urban space of São Paulo or in the coffee fields of the Paulista interior, this immigrant remains a fixture in both groups' imaginative and essayistic productions. For their part, Salgado and Picchia saw in the Italian immigrant a like-minded Brazilian: someone whose cordiality and joviality fit well in the harmonious racial fusion that they envisioned as quintessentially Brazilian. As for Andrade and Alcântara Machado, their enthusiasm for the Italian element of São Paulo emerges as early as 1911 in the satirical columns the former wrote under the pseudonym of Annibale Scipione in *O pirralho* and culminates in the latter's collection of short stories *Brás, Bexiga e Barra Funda*.

And yet, to be sure, not all the modernists saw Italians in a positive light. Consider, for instance, Mário de Andrade, another member of the organizing committee of the 1922 Week of Modern Art and the most outstanding figure of the modernist movement. Literary historiography places Mário and Oswald de Andrade (no relation) at the center of Brazilian modernism and often imagines them as complementary: whereas Oswald, belonging to a rich, landowning family, possessed the charisma and the resources, Mário, the timid son of mixed-race, middle-class parents, had the creative genius. Oswald is often credited with discovering Mário after reading the latter's collection of poems *Paulicéia Desvariada* (Hallucinated São Paulo). São Paulo takes center stage in these poems, which, in turn, means that various Italian characters also appear in Mário's verses. Hardly a flattering portrayal of Italians, *Paulicéia Desvariada* marks the first in a series of attacks against Italians in Mário's poetics, what Carelli calls "the queasiness of Mário de Andrade vis-à-vis the Italians of São Paulo."[28]

In 1928—the same year Oswald published his *Manifesto Antrópofago*—Mário de Andrade debuted an experimental novel, the literary masterpiece *Macunaíma: O herói sem nenhum caráter* (Macunaíma: The Hero without Character). With *Macunaíma*, Mário delineates the third splinter of Brazilian modernism. As the protagonist of the novel, Macunaíma allegorizes, in his own person, the "three sad races" that make up Brazil: his mother is Indigenous; he himself is Black; and he eventually becomes white after bathing in a magical pond. His search for the *muiraquitã*, a talisman that symbolizes his cultural ties to a specific Amerindian legacy, lands him in the yard of "a giant eater of people" in São Paulo. The ogre who stole the precious amulet is Venceslau Pietro-Pietra, or Piamã, an Italo-Peruvian Brazilian industrialist. The novel's primary villain, then, just happens to be Italian *and* a "giant eater of people," that is, a cannibal. Thus, in the most studied Brazilian modernist novel, the Italian community of São Paulo is defined by cannibalism—indeed, far more so than the folkloric group that Macunaíma himself claims as part of his heritage.[29] The trope of the cannibal helps Mário condemn the economic ambition and self-interest of Italians like Piamã, whose factories eat up the italianinhos. Thus, Mário casts a negative light on the economic ambitions of the Italians of São Paulo, who willingly devour their own kind, so to speak, to achieve social status. Yet the same cannot be said for Alcântara Machado, who instead, while also depicting an Italian class of small business owners eager to thrive, celebrates them as true Italo-Paulistanos. Following the line of thinking elaborated by his mentor, Oswald de Andrade, Alcântara Machado uses antropofagia to explore the relationship between Italians and São Paulo, elaborating in his prose a unique Italo-Paulistano identity in which the Italian immigrants retain some cultural specificity while at the same time assimilating to and modernizing the city of São Paulo.

3. Consumption and the Italo-Paulistanos *of Alcântara Machado*

The eleven stories contained in *Brás, Bexiga e Barra Funda* show "the varying degrees and methods of integration into paulista society achieved by Italian immigrants." The book's opening story, "Gaetaninho," revolves around an Italian child who dreams of riding in an automobile only to die after getting hit by a tram; the concluding story, "Nacionalidade" (Nationality), depicts an Italian business owner whose Brazilian-born children refuse to speak Italian. But in all Alcântara Machado's stories, "Italo-Paulista types" seek only wealth.[30] The italianinhos not only became the principal engine of the transformation of São Paulo, but they also represent the most privileged consumers of the products brought about by these transformations.

Take, for example, the story "Carmela." The eponymous heroine is a young Italian girl who works in a textile factory and finds herself daydreaming of romance when a young wealthy man driving a Buick begins stalking her on the street. The man, who has glasses and whom Alcântara Machado calls "four-eyes," invites Carmela to meet him in the evening behind the neighborhood church; he tells her that "the *barbeirinho* can stay at home," referring to Carmela's Italian boyfriend, Angelo Cuoco. The nickname is literally translated as "the little barber." The flashy, bespectacled suitor clearly holds the Italian man in contempt. Carmela, an avid reader of the romance saga *Joana a desgraçada ou A odisseia de uma Virgem* (Joana the Disgraced One or An Odyssey of a Virgin), cannot resist the temptation and meets the wealthy man in his Buick.[31]

Alcântara Machado depicts Carmela as a gleaming piece of ripe fruit, ready to be devoured: "Carmela's dress, tightly fitted to the body is of green organdy. Naked arms, naked neck, knees out. Green shoes. A grape of ripe Marengo for the lovers' lips." Her beauty and sexualization, which suggest nourishment, provide a counterpoint to the Black women, who "dirty" the streets of São Paulo while Carmela wanders off to meet her mystery man. But she is not so unlike her Black counterparts in her lasciviousness. "Grape of ripe Marengo" that she is, Carmela allows herself to be tasted, if it means that she herself can savor, if only temporarily, the fruits of wealth. After all, Angelo Cuoco does not have a car. When a friend asks her, "What about Angelo?" Carmela responds that Angelo "is something else. He is for marriage." Understanding the imperative toward social reproduction that bedevils these italianinhos, Alcântara Machado implies that Carmela will eventually wed her beau. Such a marriage, however, can transpire only after Carmela has broken with the more traditional societal norms that we imagine an immigrant Italian family would impose on its young daughter—that is, after Carmela has allowed herself to be consumed by a Brazilian man in exchange for a joyride and thereby has become a modern, liberated citizen of São Paulo.[32]

Marriage and cars reappear again in one of the most written-about stories of this collection, "A Sociedade" (The Society), in which the son of a wealthy Italian man marries the daughter of a decadent aristocratic family with roots in Brazil. Alcântara Machado has the young man, Adriano Melli, drive a Lancia around the woman's house as she watches him longingly from a balcony, a modernist take on Romeo and Juliet:

> The long-awaited howl of the car horn closed the book by Henri Axel and brought Teresa Rita from the office to the terrace . . . The Lancia passed by reluctantly. Almost stopping. The gloved hand matched the Borsalino hat. Uiiiiia-uiiia! . . . Lancia Lambda, red, shiny, strutting around the road. A Camilo dress, green, attached to the skin, slithering on the balcony.[33]

Alcântara Machado pays extreme, almost obsessive attention to the clothes worn by these italianinhos. Melli, the Brazilian-born son of an Italian entrepreneur, simply exudes coolness: he drives a sporty new car while donning a Borsalino hat. Ângelo Cuoco, despite being belittled as a barbeirinho, also has a touch of the dandy about him: "Ângelo Cuoco in red pointy shoes, white socks, tiny ties, hat *à la* Rodolfo Valentino, coat with only one button." The garish outfits and the obsession with brands go hand in hand with the sense of newness, or modernity, that emanates from these characters. Their clothes become status symbols and reinforce the idea that Italians, even when mere barbers, know how to consume goods in a proper modern fashion—with style.[34]

In "A Sociedade," the marriage between Adriano Melli and Teresa Rita—which occurs despite the mother of the bride's insistence that her "daughter will not marry the son of the *carcamano*!"—turns out to be good business for both families. In fact, in a key moment of the story, Adriano's father, Cavaliere Ufficiale Salvatore Melli, proposes a partnership with Teresa's father, who just so happens to own the plot of land next to Melli's factory. Melli wants the land so that he can build apartments for his workers to either rent or buy—a callous plan, considering that he could simply allow them to remain there for free.[35] Melli assures him that it is going to generate "assured profit, more than assured, super assured."[36] When the Brazilian aristocrat responds that he, too, had had a similar idea, but he does not have the necessary capital, Melli responds:

> *Per Bacco*, doutor! Mas *io* tenho capital. O capital *sono io*. O doutor entra com o terreno, mais nada. E o lucro se divide no meio.
>
> Oh gosh, doctor! But I have capital. The capital is me. The doctor enters with the land, nothing else. And we split the profit in half.[37]

The parvenu Salvatore, who made his fortune by starting out as a fruit seller, has become the fuel of São Paulo's modernization. That is, capital is anthropomorphized here in the form of the Italian entrepreneur, who, in turn, literalizes the cannibalistic qualities of capital production, with its relentless consumption of human labor power, machinery, and surplus value. But what is perhaps most surprising in this story is that Teresa's mother—who twice calls Salvatore a carcamano, a pejorative term for Italians that refers to the practice among Italian grocers of placing a hand on the scale to exact higher prices for goods (literally *cargar a mano*)—might *also* be Italian. Her name, Isotta Franchini, certainly has an Italian ring to it. And Salvatore reminds her during the wedding toast that "he used to sell her onions and potatoes, Lucca's oil and salted cod, always on credit and without writing it down."[38] Thus, Isotta Franchini most likely married into Brazilian wealth and relinquished her national allegiances—to the point that she is the only character in the stories who uses an ethnic slur for Italians. Alcântara Machado's far-from-flattering portrayal of the Italians of São Paulo reveals the effect that modernization has on an ethnic community whose unity is undermined by the promise of social mobility. As I discuss later, the form of the short story collection allows us to view the city's Italians as a collective protagonist, but the stories nonetheless call into question the coherence of such a collective subject, especially along class lines.

If Isotta Franchini treats one of her own, so to speak, with such hostility, one can only imagine how Italians treated other immigrants, who, likewise took part in the industrialization of São Paulo. The story "Armazém Progresso de São Paulo" (Emporium Progresso of São Paulo) engages in exactly that exercise. The story details how Natale, owner of the emporium Progresso (literally "progress," a name already pregnant with meaning) plots to take over his Portuguese neighbors' struggling store next door. The story implies that the neighbors' business is failing because the Portuguese man, Paiva Couceiro, lacks the industriousness of Natale, who "always stood at the counter from dawn to sunset, working like a madman." Natale's hard work has clearly paid off: "The emporium Progresso started with one door on the right side of Rua da Abolição. Now it had four on the left side," a description that accentuates the Italian's progress over his struggling neighbors. Natale checks on the Portuguese couple daily because he knows they will not be able to stay afloat. He imagines that, once they declare bankruptcy, he will buy all the merchandise they have. He seems especially interested in their onions, which were "rotting in the store." Natale has heard from a customer, João Espiridão, "the mulatto, the one from the Provisions Committee," that there will soon be a hike in the price of onions due to the scarcity of the latest harvest. Natale knows exactly where he can get some, and so does João Espiridão, who tells him: "Look here, my friend Natale: you've got to grab all you can. Do not be silly. Those higher-ups that today spit on the head of the people got rich in this way."[39] The goal is to make as much profit as possible. Italians become Paulistanos in the stories of Alcântara Machado by hustling, showing good business savvy, and voraciously gobbling up their competitors. At the same time, São Paulo takes on *a jeitinho italiano*—literally, "a way of being Italian"—in its sounds, colors, foods, names, and religious fairs.

Eventually, Natale makes a profitable deal with the clueless Portuguese couple. It is so profitable that Natale's wife, Bianca, who also "sweated every day in the kitchen and worked the *bocce* courts," falls asleep shortly afterward while daydreaming about living "in the most expensive building on the Avenida Paulista."[40] Bianca's dream holds some truth: not long after the publication of *Brás, Bexiga e Barra Funda,* Italians began moving to other more expensive and fashionable neighborhoods, such as Higienopolis. As if anticipating this wave of internal migration, Alcântara Machado sets one story there.

In "Notas Biográficas do Novo Deputado" (Biographical Notes of a New Congressman), the orphan Gennarinho is given a new name after adoption and becomes Januário. After his father, João Intaliano, who took care of the *fazenda* owned by Colonel Juca Peixoto de Faria, dies, Gennarinho is shipped off to live in São Paulo with the colonel and his wife. The childless, aging couple live in the chic neighborhood of Higienopolis, a world quite different from Brás, the neighborhood where Gennarinho was born. Eventually, the family adopts him as their own, but of course a name change must occur:

> This business of Gennarinho is not right. Gennarinho is not a name of our people. Now your name will be Janúario, which is the translation. I already investigated it. Did you hear me? . . . your name will be Janúario. Did you hear me?[41]

In the previous story, the Italian man becomes capital; in this second story, the Brazilian-born Italian child becomes the new lifeblood of Brazilian society. Not by chance does Alcântara Machado make the couple infertile. The italianinho supplants the child they wanted but could not have, to the point that, after Colonel Peixoto de Faria leaves Gennarinho at a boarding school, he rushes off to amend his will. All their fortune, mostly made up of lands and titles, will go to Gennarinho, in a symbolic transfer of wealth from the old Brazilian aristocracy to the new Italian bourgeoisie. There is a caveat, though. Only once Gennarinho assumes the name Januário—which he proudly does when arriving at the boarding school—can such a process take place. The name change, a direct translation of his former name, symbolizes the invention of a new Brazilian identity, emerging from the presence of these Italians in São Paulo. Some have read his transformation into Januário as indicating a progressive abandonment of Italian heritage.[42] But I propose that we pay attention to the title of the story. If the story is indeed supposed to detail the biographical notes of a new Brazilian congressman—supposedly Januário—then his Italian roots are not so forgotten after all. Instead, they are remembered as a crucial part of his biography.

Such retentions are further illustrated in the concluding short story of *Brás, Bexiga e Barra Funda*, "A Nacionalidade." Tranquillo Zampinetti is the proud owner of a barbershop who entertains his customers by reading out loud reports of the Italian conquests in Libya from *Fanfulla*. When a patron named Ferruccio asks Zampinetti to vote for him in the upcoming judicial elections, the barber responds in Italian: "I am not a voter . . . because I am Italian, my dear." Ferruccio quickly explains that one's nationality does not matter; after all, Ferruccio himself is Italian and will become a judge. Ultimately, Zampinetti chooses to vote—but for someone else. This decision opens a series of possibilities for him and his children, who, to Zampinetti's disappointment, refuse to speak Italian. By the time World War I unfolds in Europe, we learn that Zampinetti has become:

> The owner of four buildings in Rua do Gasômetro, two in Rua Piratininga, an influential leader of the Partido Republicano Paulista, and the beloved compadre of Brás's first deputy; [his son] Lorenzo, partner of the company Vanziello & Cia. And engaged to the older daughter of Major Antônio Del Piccolo, member of the governing administration of Bom Retiro; [his other son] Bruno, vice president of the Athletic Association of Ping-Pong and a freshman in the public lycée.[43]

Zampinetti realizes that, by participating in the political life of Brazil, he can achieve more wealth than when he did not vote.

During World War I, committees to raise money for the Italian troops mushroomed across the Americas. Historian Vittorio Cappelli has explained how "the general discovery of the patria among the Italian communities across the world came about in the new century with the Great War."[44] Zampinetti had intended to give money to his friend Carlino in charge of organizing these funds. However, upon discovering this scheme, his wife, Dona Émilia, vehemently objects. She thinks it is a rather naïve way to spend their money, which they amassed not by virtue of their attachment to Italian patriotic values but precisely because Zampinetti became involved in Brazilian political life.[45] In the Zampinettis' household, no one cares about Italy or its wars: not the wife, and certainly not the children who make fun of Italian General Cadorna's inability to take possession of Trieste. The story ends with Bruno, Zampinetti's son, now a lawyer, applying for the naturalization of his father, "Tranquillo Zampinetti, Italian citizen resident in São Paulo." In the end, though, Zampinetti, much like Juó Bananére, remains deeply Italian.[46]

Alcântara Machado seems to have written "A Nacionalidade," the closing story of his collection, specifically so that literary critics could point toward it as an example of how Italians and their children became assimilated into Brazilian society. Zampinetti uses the fact that he has become a voter as an excuse to avoid giving money to support the Italian campaigns during World War I. The acknowledgment of the Zampinettis that their wealth depends on forsaking their loyalty to Italy is central to the story of Italians' assimilation in Brazil. At the same time, Alcântara Machado specifies, in the last sentence of his book, that Tranquillo Zampinetti is a *cidadão italiano residente em São Paulo*, an Italian citizen resident in São Paulo. Tranquillo Zampinetti remains Italian—despite the naturalization process his son has begun on his behalf.

Alcântara Machado's Italian characters become the face of the modern São Paulo, by literally taking the place of the dying, landowning aristocracy or by becoming the capital that fuels its modernization, while holding on to key remnants of their Italianness, either by ultimately marrying one another or by carrying on cultural mores and traditions that they brought with them across the Atlantic. It is as if they symbolically stage a cannibal act between São Paulo and Italians. In other words, Alcântara Machado's characters re-signify Italianness in *and* through São Paulo, so that instead of holding meaning within a specific geopolitical national reality, Italianness becomes a marker of ethnicity informed by the very same subjects who act in its name and within a transnational space. However, if these stories stage or thematize a cannibal act, so, too, does the literary form whereby readers encounter them. That is, the very form of these stories instantiates the tension between assimilating and othering that marks the encounter between Italians and São Paulo and points toward the reciprocity of the cannibal act.

4. Brás, Bexiga e Barra Funda*: The Newspaper of the Italo-Brazilians of São Paulo*

The preface of Antônio Alcântara Machado's *Brás, Bexiga e Barra Funda* poses a formal provocation. Cleverly called "artigo de fundo"—"editorial" in English—it warns us against reading this collection as if it were a book:

> This book was not born a book: it was born a newspaper. These short stories were not born short stories: they were born news. And so this preface also was not born a preface: it was born an editorial. *Brás, Bexiga e Barra Funda* is the organ of the Italo-Brazilians of São Paulo.[47]

Three of the eleven stories that form the collection first appeared as standalone stories in *Jornal do Comércio*, the newspaper where Alcântara Machado had originally published his piece on the need to Brazilianize (*abrasileirar*) Brazilian theater. "Gaetaninho," "Carmela," and "Lisetta"—all dedicated to Italian children or young adults—were understood to be intended for a book project tentatively titled *Italo-Paulistas*. However, on the suggestion of Oswald de Andrade, Alcântara Machado ultimately chose the more "suggestive" title *Brás, Bexiga e Barra Funda*—the Italian neighborhoods of São Paulo—to create "a rhythmic effect."[48]

Yet Alcântara Machado's choice of the newspaper form goes beyond the simple fact that these three short stories had previously appeared in an actual newspaper. The newspaper form asks us to focus on the totality of the stories rather than their fragmentary nature. It also echoes the fundamental role that the Italian press played in São Paulo. And, in general, the newspaper seeks to make collective experience legible by containing and repackaging it, while simultaneously trying to give the impression of novelty and happenstance in the events it recounts. Thus, on the one hand, Alcântara Machado wants to incorporate these Italo-Paulistanos into a coherent whole, all the while keeping them fragmented. On the other hand, he absorbs and embellishes the ethnic newspaper, so as to align it more fully with an overarching Paulistano discourse. Both in its contents and its form, *Brás, Bexiga e Barra Funda* materializes the tension of simultaneously assimilating and othering that lies at the heart of the encounter between Italians and São Paulo. The literary medium performs a cannibalistic act, whose reciprocity results in a fragmented narrative product.

When read in its totality, Alcântara Machado's short story collection mirrors other modernist formal experiments—such as James Joyce's *Dubliners* (1914) and John Dos Passos's *Manhattan Transfer* (1925)—that have become categorized as composite novels. According to literary scholars Maggie Dunn and Anne Morris, a composite novel "is a literary work composed of shorter texts that—though individually complete and autonomous—are interrelated in a coherent whole according to one or more organizing principles." They identify five sometimes overlapping "principles of composite-novel organization": "setting," "single protagonist," "collective protagonist," "pattern," and "storytelling." *Brás, Bexiga e Barra Funda* shows evidence of being governed by all of these.[49]

Most notable perhaps is how the Italian community of São Paulo in Alcântara Machado's work forms a *collective protagonist*. As Dunn and Morris explain, collective protagonists are common when the contents of the composite novel touch upon questions whose nature is multicultural or multigenerational (as is the case with *Brás, Bexiga e Barra Funda*). The composite novel allows Alcântara Machado to create the semblance of a "patchwork," while applying to each story essentially "the same identical story pattern or . . . motif patterns."[50] In other words, the newspaper format of *Brás, Bexiga e Barra Funda* affords Alcântara Machado the ability to create unity through ostensible fragmentation. Its seemingly miscellaneous parts add up to a rather tendentious operation—namely, that of homogenizing the different experiences of Italians into one grand tale of social mobility and capital accumulation.

At the same time, calling *Brás, Bexiga e Barra Funda* a composite novel also creates certain problems. After all, Alcântara Machado explicitly instructs us in the preface *not* to read this as a book. His insistence on treating his work of literary fiction as if it were printed news reflects the modernists' anxieties about changes in technology, mass media, and the urban landscapes that nurtured their artistic practices. As Barbara Foley has shown, turning to the documentary novel became one way for modernists to cope with such anxieties. Foley explains that the documentary novel "locates itself near the border between factual discourse and fictive discourse, but it does not propose an eradication of that border." In other words, the documentary novel, "aspires to tell the truth, and it associates this truth with claims of empirical validation."[51]

Brás, Bexiga e Barra Funda does not fit neatly, however, in the subcategories of this genre delineated by Foley either. Even so, its formal experimentation speaks directly to the tradition of the documentary novel and its aspiration, for better or worse, to truth-telling. In fact, part of the tendency to read *Brás, Bexiga e Barra Funda* as a document of 1920s São Paulo has precisely to do with the way Alcântara Machado has set up the "editorial." Besides telling us that "this is not a book," he ends the editorial by insisting that his composite novel "is a newspaper. Nothing more. News. Only. It does not have a political party nor an ideal. It does not comment. It does not discuss. It does not expand." By emphasizing the supposedly objective qualities of his prose, Alcântara Machado invites readers to adopt a specific perception of his characters, one that does not apprehend them altogether as fictional but that sees them as historical, that is, as part of a specific material and social reality. As Foley argues, following psychologist E. H. Gombrich, "There are no innocent perceptions: if perception is to produce cognition, it must invoke a framework of prior assumptions about what is being seen." It is no surprise that literary critics have followed Alcântara Machado's lead, then, when reading *Brás, Bexiga e Barra Funda* and at times overlooked the very fact that the form itself aspires to the tell the truth but nonetheless remains a work of fiction, even if a documentary one at that.[52]

For my purposes, the question of whether such stories tell the truth matters little. However, the form in which Alcântara Machado presents them poses an interesting dilemma. In fact, as I mentioned earlier, the composite novel allows Alcântara Machado to weave a set of stories, somewhat different yet similar when looking at their plot pattern and motifs, which make one whole text. As Dunn and Morris recognize, "The composite novel is a single text composed of shorter texts: its aesthetic is one that insists on a coherently developed whole text, even though that whole text must, for the most part, be composed of individually autonomous pieces."[53] Insofar as the composite novel incorporates fragmented narratives into a whole, the literary form of *Brás, Bexiga e Barra Funda* already lends itself to being understood through the cannibal trope. This becomes even more compelling when we consider the fact that Alcântara Machado chose the newspaper form, thus directly interpellating the Italian ethnic press, which constituted one of the largest news apparatuses in the city, to speak of and for Brazilian modernism.

The *Fanfulla*, the most widely circulated Italian-language newspaper of São Paulo, reached a circulation of 15,000 copies in 1909—second to only the *Estado de São Paulo*. It would have probably circulated even more copies if it had not had to split its audience with four other important Italian newspapers, *Tribuna italiana*, *Corriere d'Italia*, *l'Avanti!*, and *Il Secolo*. Historian Pantaleone Sergi explains that the "pedagogical and political functions" of the ethnic press "appear more forcefully" with *l'Avanti!*, which he defined as "the most important initiative among the socialist press," and with the anarchist paper *La Battaglia*, which I discuss at length in Chapter Five.[54] These publications supported literacy campaigns and, most importantly, raised class consciousness across the Italian community by pointing to the deplorable working conditions in the factories, which were typically owned by Italians. They expressed no interest in promoting Italian nationalism, and they instead advocated for solidarity based on social class. Literary scholar Joseph Pecorelli convincingly shows how these socialist newspapers promoted community development and collective identity along class lines rather than those of ethnicity. However, *Fanfulla*, despite the competition, remained the preferred ethnic newspaper for both the industrial bourgeois and lower-class migrants for five decades, from 1893 to 1942. Its appeal and longevity, then, raise the question of whether class trumped ethnicity as the driving interest of the Italian community in São Paulo. In fact, in contrast to the socialist papers, the *Fanfulla* "argued for parallel loyalties" to Brazil and Italy.[55] This type of loyalty is precisely the one we see reflected in the character of Tranquillo Zampinetti, who Alcântara Machado tells us also reads the *Fanfulla*.

The *Fanfulla*'s politics, as historian Samuel Bailey explains, "wanted and sought . . . a chance for the Italian workers to become sufficiently adapted to the host society to be able to survive and prosper." Its pages supported the naturalization of Italian immigrants as Brazilian citizens so that they could participate in the political life of their new homeland; yet they remained firmly loyal to Italy, nonetheless. In other words, the *Fanfulla*, a "vital communication link" for the Italian community of São Paulo, promoted the social assimilation of Italians while advocating for the preservation of their ethnic qualities. Such ambitions were mediated by the paper's continued use of the Italian language, its celebration of Italian national holidays and festivities, and its defense of Italy whenever the country became embroiled in geopolitical conflict. The *Fanfulla* and its readership, which by the late 1930s numbered 40,000, acknowledged that, in order to economically succeed in São Paulo, Italians had to, so to speak, become Brazilian, even while retaining identifiably Italian characteristics.[56]

On a subtler level, Alcântara Machado's style lends credence to his claims about his literary work being a newspaper. Indeed, his short, verb-laden, staccato-style sentences convey the author's documentarist intention. As literary scholar Roch Duval has posited, Alcântara Machado's stories perform an actual translation of "the haecceity of São Paulo in the 1920s."[57] The book clearly aspires to transcribe the action and the vernacular of the streets with uncommon immediacy. Consider Alcântara Machado's description of a soccer game between Palestra Italia (today's Palmeiras) and Corinthians (these are two of the most important teams of São Paulo to this day), which epitomizes the author's style's immediacy along with its dynamism.

> Biagio alcançou a bola. Aí Biagio! Foi levando, foi levando. Assim, Biagio! Driblou um. Isso! Fugiu de outro. Isso! Avançava para a vitória. Salame nele, Biagio! Arremeteu. Chute agora! Parou. Disaparou. Parou. Aí! Reparou. Hesitou. Biagio Biagio! Calculou. Agora! Preparou-se. Olha o Rocco! É agora. Aí! Olha Rocco! Caiu.
>
> Biagio got the ball. Go Biagio! He went on to carry it, carry it [up to the goalie]. That's the way, Biagio! He dribbled pastone [player]. That's it! He avoided another [player]. That's it! He was advancing toward victory. Make a "salame" of him, Biagio! He attacked. Shoot now! He stopped. He shot. He stopped. There! He adjusted [himself]. He hesitated. Biagio Biagio! He calculated [the shot]. Now! He prepared himself. Look Rocco! It is [happening] now. There! Look Rocco! He fell.[58]

The Portuguese language lends itself more easily to such a verb-centered prose because, as this short passage makes clear, one can generally elide subjects and objects. The verbs do most of the work, much like the Italians, whose actions they recount, supposedly do most of the work behind the transformations taking place in São Paulo. The sounds of this game also seep through these pages. Alcântara Machado carefully uses two separate verbs for "shoot," *chutar* and *disparar*, to create the alliteration *parou-disaparou-parou*. Perhaps such a choice also has to do with the likely fact that such a live, play-by-play chronicle of the soccer match would be heard through the stadium speakers—a possibility that further reinforces Alcântara Machado's intention of capturing and fixing in time the changing reality surrounding him. At the same time, this description includes Italian expressions that would end up becoming loan words in Brazilian Portuguese, like *salame*, meaning, in this case, to make a fool out of someone.

Along with the flurry of verbs and the action-centered prose, Alcântara Machado reinforces his documentarist style by imitating the work of a camera.[59] In a manner akin to the way a director frames a scene, Alcântara Machado masterfully moves his "camera" from the action in the foreground to the scenes unfolding in the background. In the same short story quoted above, "CORINTHIANS (2) vs PALESTRA (1)," he offers us a shot of what happens outside the field:

> Girls eating toasted peanuts sitting on cars' hoods. The shadow advanced on the poorly attended lawn. *Mulata* women in blue dresses earn pinches. And they laugh. Fans argue with gestures.[60]

The stage-setting techniques of Alcântara Machado's stories show us how prose can evoke live action, making us feel that we are watching events unfolding in real time. One should note that when the camera, as it were, offers us a wider angle, other groups begin to appear side by side with the Italians, specifically, the Brazilians of African descent who had also recently taken up residence in São Paulo. These characters are often women of mixed-race heritage, and we find them indulging in what bourgeois society considers immoral behaviors, such as prostitution, sexual promiscuity, and public drunkenness. Here Alcântara Machado reproduces images of Black Brazilians found throughout the mainstream media of the time, depicting them as primitive, uncivilized, and a threat to bourgeois order.

His reification of racist tropes notwithstanding, Alcântara Machado acknowledges a somewhat puzzling truth: that these two ethnic groups, who often symbolized divergent social mores in the popular imagination, shared the same spaces. This is illustrated in the short story "O Monstro de Rodas" (The Wheels Monster), which is about a child who dies in a hit-and-run, and its description of a lively discussion about the burial that occurs in the parents' home:

> In the living room they were discussing the hour of the burial. Aída thought that in the afternoon was better. . . . With the son sleeping on her lap, Dona Mariângela thought the same. The smoke from the husband's smoking pipe danced all the way above the coffin. . . . Sitting on the floor, the *mulata* woman was offering a glass of orange flower water. . . . The Black woman with sandals without socks began [reciting] the chaplet a second time.[61]

Two Black women appear in this scene: one, most likely a domestic worker for the family, is serving water; the second one, clearly darker in complexion and poorer—hence her bare feet—keeps the chanting of the rosary going.[62] Here, Italians and Black Brazilians share not only public but also domestic space. Through such panoramic shots, Alcântara Machado shows us that the Italians of Brás, Bexiga, and Barra Funda lived on intimate terms with Black Brazilians. I will have more to say about Black-Italian relations in São Paulo in Chapter Three. But, for now, it is worth pausing to consider why the presence of Afro-Brazilians in Alcântara Machado's collection has received so little attention.

To be fair, the book does not exactly prime us to read it as a story of cross-racial intimacy. *Brás, Bexiga e Barra Funda* is dedicated to "the triumph of the new *mamelucos*"—that is, the Italians and Italo-Brazilians who took São Paulo by storm. In his dedication, Alcântara Machado lists eighteen names, including António Augusto Covello, Menotti del Picchia, Victor Brecheret, Anita Malfatti, Conte Francisco Matarazzo Junior, and Teresa di Marzo. Alcântara Machado practically announces at the outset that the collective protagonist of his composite novel is the Italo-Brazilian community and enjoins us to read it accordingly.

But to paraphrase the British modernist D. H. Lawrence: trust the tale, not the teller. The stories speak for themselves. And the fact is that Black Brazilians often show up in them as marginal characters (in five of the eleven short stories) or as important secondary ones (in "Armazém Progresso de São Paulo"). The lack of critical analysis about these characters in the numerous works written about *Brás, Bexiga e Barra Funda*, in addition to the uncritical acceptance of Alcântara Machado's dedication, which has helped it to become the urtext for both documentary evidence of Italo-Brazilian experience and Brazilian modernism, poses particular dangers, given the complicity of the New World Italian discourse in upholding white supremacy in Brazil. The trope of the cannibal act I have employed in this chapter for understanding the relationship between Italians and São Paulo becomes all the more useful when we consider the relationship between Italians and those Afro-Brazilians who were clearly not celebrated as constitutive elements of the modern São Paulo imagined by Paulistano modernists. The fact that, in all these modernist accounts, Italian residents of São Paulo remain "deeply Italian," that is, they held on to their Italianness while becoming Paulistanos, reveals yet another dimension of their status as vectors of whiteness in Brazil.

As this chapter has argued, the privileged position afforded to Italians and *italianità* in Brazil's racial hierarchy—a status that endures to this day—was underwritten largely by the Italophilia of Brazilian modernists, who conflated Italians in São Paulo not only with modernization but modernism as such. If this holds true, then demystifying the mythical narrative constructed by Brazilian modernists about Italians is one necessary rhetorical step toward dismantling that racial hierarchy. By focusing on São Paulo's flourishing Black press during the modernist period and one of its chief exponents, José Correia Leite, Chapter Three explores how those figures relegated to the background in Alcântara Machado's work sought to place themselves in the foreground and contest the efforts of Italo-Brazilians and their advocates to monopolize the discourse of modernity in São Paulo.

THREE

I perchè nu so naziunale?

José Correia Leite, Blackness, and New World Italians

The first independent and longest-running Black newspaper of São Paulo, *O Clarim*, debuted on January 6, 1924. That inaugural issue also saw the first column written by someone calling himself "Prof. Dott. Juó P. Carretta."[1] Along with its byline, the style of Carretta's column, titled "Naziunale," strikes one as peculiar for its obvious solecisms, malapropisms, and oscillations between Portuguese and Italian. Stranger still is the column's content, which revolves around what the author perceives as a great personal injustice: the fact that despite working his way up from several menial jobs, marrying a Brazilian woman, and sending his son to an elite professional school—in short, having done all of the things associated with the New World Italian narrative of upward mobility discussed in Chapter Two—he still did not feel fully recognized and accepted as a Brazilian national.

Why does this column, which would later be accompanied by an illustrated portrait of the author that depicted him as a stereotypical Italian dandy, appear in what was to become one of the most important Black newspapers of São Paulo? The simplest explanation is that José Correia Leite, who cofounded and edited the journal and was one of the most prominent intellectuals of the Black Brazilian Movement, saw fit to put it there.[2] Indeed, the columnist was entirely his invention. Writing under the pseudonym Carretta, Leite—himself the product of a union between a Black woman and a white man—cleverly emulated the idiom of a certain segment of Italo-Brazilians in São Paulo and captured their anxieties vis-à-vis native-born citizens. In so doing, he ironized the conventions, affectations, and assumptions of the New World Italian discourse. At the same time, this racial ventriloquism allowed Leite to explore the possibility that Italians and Black Brazilians might not be so different after all. Leite would reprise his role as Carretta in the pages of *O Clarim* five more times, and each time he would find a new way to satirize the Italians of São Paulo. These columns clearly progress toward an unexpected idea: that of a cross-racial coalition between these two groups, sanctioned by the shared banner of Brazilianness. Where the previous chapters have traced how the New World Italian discourse took shape and became institutionalized, this chapter focuses on its significance for Black Brazilians in São Paulo. Using Leite as a case study, it argues that the Black Brazilian intelligentsia found unique ways to interpellate the New World Italians in their midst.

That Leite was among the first to do so should not come as a surprise. Orphaned at a very young age, he had spent his formative years working and living with an Italian family in Bexiga, at the time a mixed Italian and Black low-income neighborhood of São Paulo. In his autobiography, satirical columns, and political essays, Leite displays such an intimate knowledge of Italian cultural mores that one is tempted to describe him, somewhat paradoxically, as a Black New World Italian. Indeed, one can imagine that, given his status as a fair-skinned mulatto and his familiarity with the city's dominant white ethnic group, he could have easily spent his life taking advantage of the special privileges that Brazil's famously flexible color line afforded him and denied more phenotypically "African" subjects. And yet he refused to do so. Instead, he became one of the first intellectuals to publicly embrace the term *negro* (Black), identifying himself unequivocally with the bottom rung of the country's racial hierarchy, and urged others to do the same.

This chapter posits that Leite's upbringing among Italians and his exposure to their language and culture played crucial roles in the development of his racial consciousness. I argue that Leite's privileged position, what literary theorist Homi Bhabha would define as "in-between," allows him not only to interrogate the New World Italian discourse but also subvert it. Drawing on literary scholar Graziella Parati, I propose that we understand Leite's writings as "acts of talking back." Parati uses this expression in reference to "the fragmented voices that question . . . the hegemonic construction of an imagined Italian community" within the geopolitical confines of the contemporary Italian nation.[3]

At first glance, it might seem odd to include Leite among such "fragmented voices." But Leite encounters a discourse of Italianness no less hegemonic and exclusionary than the one Parati has in mind. Indeed, this discourse had the effect of turning Leite into something of a migrant in his own country: first, it made him "feel Italian," to borrow an expression from literary critic Thomas Ferraro; second, this feeling failed to confer on him the same privileges available to white Italians; finally, this feeling led his fellow Black Brazilians to regard him as a foreigner.[4] Leite's story shows us that non-whites were driven to scrutinize and contest homogenous notions of Italian identity long before such acts of talking back became commonplace in the metropole. In fact, if the *questione*—literally, the question mark—is, as literary scholar Vetri Nathan puts it, "a central image that constantly . . . haunts the essentialist discourse of the Italian nation as a complete whole," then this is all the more reason to suspect that informal colonies like São Paulo, which fundamentally destabilize notions of Italian identity, are spaces where such questions become acutely legible. Indeed, the heteroglossia of Leite's columns, although clearly exaggerated for comic effect, provide an invaluable record of Luso-Italian speech patterns and constitute an important intervention in the debate over the relationship between the Italian language and national belonging—otherwise known as *questione della lingua*.[5]

Just as prevailing conceptions of the Mediterranean have tended to mystify and downplay Italy's long-standing history with Africa, the New World Italian discourse has often obfuscated the complex exchanges between Italians and Blacks in Brazil. One of the basic premises of the discourse is that these groups essentially belonged to two disparate Brazilian worlds: one modern, the other premodern. To be sure, there were important differences between them. Because of their European provenance and access to various forms of cultural and financial capital, Italians enjoyed greater opportunities for social mobility than Black Brazilians. As this book's final chapter will show, the benefits of white racial privilege even extended to the substantial population of Italian socialists and anarcho-syndicalists, who often faced less repression than Black radicals.

But if the very presence of Black Brazilians in São Paulo shaped how Italians understood their position of superiority in this transatlantic space, it did so partly because the two groups often lived side by side. Indeed, Afro-Brazilians and Italians lived on much more intimate terms in urban spaces like São Paulo than they did in North American settings, a fact which the discourse of racial, economic, and cultural superiority accompanying the assimilation of Italians has helped to elide. As the historian Kim Butler has explained, just as there were no wholly Black neighborhoods in São Paulo, there were likewise no fully Italian enclaves. Thus, although contemporary Paulistanos recognize Bexiga as their version of Little Italy, a space akin to New York's Mulberry Street, it is important to acknowledge that Black Brazilians have as much of a historical claim to the neighborhood as do their counterparts of Italian descent.[6] Moreover, it is no coincidence that Bexiga, with its dense mixture of Black and Italian residents, was one of the main incubators of the New World Italian discourse that I anatomize throughout this book.

And yet the reverse is also true. At the turn of the twentieth century, the massive influx of Italian immigrants into São Paulo also determined how Black Brazilians, many of them having recently migrated to the city from the interior and the northeast as freed captives or their descendants, came to define themselves. Hence, it is likewise no coincidence that Leite, one of the intellectual architects of the Black Brazilian Movement, also emerged from Bexiga. For all their concerns with Italo-Brazilian identity, Leite's columns nonetheless reveal an incipient Black Brazilian consciousness and, as this chapter shows, prefigure both his and other expressions of Black ethnonationalism in São Paulo. This is because Leite understood that the discourse of Italian supremacy could be reformulated to articulate a new agenda, one that Butler has defined as "alternative integrationist."[7] Italians had been celebrated as settlers and modernizers, but who was to say that this rhetoric could not be turned around, that this story could not be rewritten from a Black perspective? After all, as Black intellectuals in the 1920s and 1930s never tired of pointing out, *they* were the true nationals, the ones who truly belonged to Brazil because of their long connection to its land and distinctive cultural traditions.

In Chapter Two I showed how the discursive link between Italians, modernization, and whiteness crystallized in the Brazilian literary imaginary following the 1922 Week of Modern Art, which heralded the arrival of the modernist movement in São Paulo. But that event and the mythologization of Italo-Brazilian whiteness unfolded against the backdrop of Black-Italian interracial intimacies and a flourishing Black press. In this chapter I explore instead how the New World Italian discourse developed in dialectical tension with Black literary activism in São Paulo and partly inspired the counternarratives of the Black Brazilian Movement.

1. Everything Was Italian? Black Brazilians in São Paulo

As I explained in Chapter One, Gina Lombroso Ferrero and other Italian travel writers in Brazil, to say nothing of Brazilian state officials, adduced a body of knowledge that comprised statistics, anecdotes, and theories of race to calibrate the whitening of São Paulo and hence its progress toward civilization. Lombroso Ferrero went so far as to claim that everything in the city, from its population to its commodities, was overwhelmingly Italian. In so doing, she helped cultivate the image of São Paulo as a modern, Europeanized city.

More recent histories tell a more complicated story. Most notably, Carlos José Ferreira dos Santos's *Nem tudo era italiano* (Not everything was Italian), whose title directly invokes Lombroso Ferrero's claim, questions such claims, and casts considerable doubt on the evidence marshaled to support them. According to Santos, neither eyewitness accounts like Lombroso Ferrero's nor official reports recorded reality. Instead, as Santos rightly points out, these accounts often reflect a "willingness" on the part of São Paulo's elites to believe "that the population of the city were of

European and white origins." Because of this "latent desire," "national" Brazilians from groups deemed undesirable and inimical to progress—namely, the poor, Afro-Brazilian, and Indigenous people—were simply erased from the record.[8]

The active erasure and omission of poor nationals dwelling in the city further sustains historian Barbara Weinstein's trenchant critique of São Paulo's "racialized images of modernity and progress." Weinstein argues that "the economic success of São Paulo has cemented the widely assumed association between whiteness and civilization, between whiteness and modernization, between whiteness and productivity." Perhaps even more concerning, Weinstein explains, the rest of Brazil—but especially the Northeast, São Paulo's impoverished, heavily Africanized obverse—became associated with racialized ideas of backwardness and decadence, fomenting a relationship similar to the one cultivated in Italy between North and South, what anthropologist Jane Schneider called "orientalism in one country."[9] Much like the Italian *meridionale*, which became the racialized, inferior other, the Brazilian *nordestino* embodied the backward other, against which Paulistas could define their own progress and racial integrity.

This discourse about São Paulo's racialized modernity deeply informs the New World Italian discourse. That is, Italian immigrants to Brazil, regardless of the province whence they hailed in Italy, benefited tremendously from the celebratory and xenophilic discourses that facilitated their arrival in the city. "There is not one noble and generous idea, denoting the progress and the advance of this province," opined the *Correio Paulistano* emphatically in 1883, "that has not met immediate and efficient support among the Italians (the bigger colony of immigrants) living among us." This discourse became so entrenched that, almost thirty years later, an official government document, under the heading "Progress, Civilization, Immigration," could breathlessly proclaim: "This [progress] has always been reproduced in São Paulo [ever] since its colonization by the intensified Italian element, bringing to this city force and new energy, elevating [São Paulo's] progress and contributing to its degree of civilization."[10] These pronouncements overlook the fact that, as Santos points out, São Paulo's "foreign element," to borrow a term frequently used for immigrants in official documents and newspapers, existed cheek by jowl with "nationals": those poor Brazilians who were largely racialized as Black, Indigenous, or mixed.[11]

Although Black Brazilians in São Paulo accounted for about 2.7 percent of the population in the city in 1890, by 1940 that percentage had jumped to 12.6 percent, alongside São Paulo's overall population increase. Italians made up the most numerous groups of migrants in the city, constituting somewhere between 41 and 63 percent of the "foreigners" arriving in São Paulo between 1890 and 1940. But the fact that the population of Brazilians of African descent grew during São Paulo's demographic explosion indicates that the city also became an important destination for internal migrants. Molly Ball indicates that as early as 1900 the Hospedaria de Imigrantes—a dedicated welcome center for immigrants located in the Brás neighborhood—began accepting internal migrants as well as city residents who were looking for employment. Hence, insofar as it epitomizes what Butler called a "tale of immigrants and dreams," the story of Black Brazilians in the city of São Paulo mirrors that of Italians. "Afro-Brazilians flocked to the capital," Butler writes, "with much the same motivations as the European immigrants." These nationals also exhibited patterns of behavior and expectations similar to those of foreigners: they often moved their entire families; they tended to settle near other families from their same village; and they imagined the city offered unique opportunities for upward mobility.[12] In other words, Black Brazilians moving to São Paulo also saw the city as a beacon of progress and modernization.

But although Black Brazilians migrated to São Paulo with the same hopes and dreams as other immigrant groups and often lived alongside them, their experiences could not have been more different. First, Butler tells us that "Afro-Paulistas lacked the seed capital necessary to establish a foothold in the private business."[13] Second, Black Brazilians faced extreme racial discrimination in the job market since factories owned by immigrants tended to hire immigrant workers hailing from the same country of origin. For example, 81 percent of the workers employed by the factories *Fábrica Mariangela*, owned by Francesco Matarazzo, and 82 percent of the ones working for Rodolfo Crespi in his *Cotonifício*, were foreign-born. Of these percentages,

94 percent and 89 percent, respectively, were Italian.[14] Historian George Reid Andrews has shown how a preference for foreign (white) workers had nothing to do with them being better acquainted with skilled labor, as some sociologists had hinted at before. On the contrary, these immigrant Italian workers often came from rural backgrounds and were unfamiliar with the machinery used in these factories. Thus, they effectively leapfrogged over recently emancipated slaves who were equally qualified. Under these similar circumstances, then, Black Brazilians' hopes for a better future came to an abrupt halt in São Paulo. They quickly understood that, despite their status as native-born Brazilians, they existed as second-class citizens. They became, as historian Paulina Alberto aptly put it, "foreigners" in their own country.[15]

The neighborhoods in which Black Brazilians settled, although today marketed by the city as exclusively Italian, harbor forgotten stories of cross-racial and cross-ethnic intimacy. Today the streets of "the oldest black enclave in São Paulo," Bela Vista's Bexiga, are lavishly adorned with Italian flags; such ostentatious displays of ethnic pride belie the fact that, during the first half of the twentieth century, "Italian immigrants . . . rented their basements to black families" and "employ[ed] black women as domestics."[16] In areas like Bexiga, Italians did not only have Black neighbors, they actually interpenetrated each other's households. Yet even this reveals the extent to which Italians could feel secure in their social status. In contrast to the United States, for instance, Italians in Brazil did not feel threatened by their physical proximity to Black Brazilians, since their circumstances did not readily translate into or augur a deeper imbrication with Blackness as such. On the contrary, the presence of these nationals made Italians' socioeconomic superiority more salient. Ironically, although Brazil's color line was more porous than the one that governed social life in North America, the power of the New World Italian discourse all but ensured that Italians in Brazil, unlike their US counterparts, *couldn't* become unmoored from their purported whiteness. This is why it is unsurprising that Leite grew up in the streets of Bexiga. Here, the proximity with Italians made him become conscious of his racial status. Thus, this is also where he staged his political activism, starting with the foundation of the Black newspaper *O Clarim.*

2. *José Correia Leite Among Italians: Not Black Enough or Too Black?*

In 1992, the Black Brazilian writer and activist Cuti curated and published the posthumous memoirs of José Correia Leite (1900–1989), which were the result of numerous hours of recorded conversations between the two men. Aptly titled . . . *E disse o velho militante José Correia Leite* (. . . And so said the old activist José Correia Leite), this work offers a glimpse into the life of the man who, for decades, embodied "the single source consulted by all researchers" on all things related to the Black Brazilian Movement.[17] In the first chapter, Leite mentions one of the most important theoretical shifts that his newspaper inaugurated: "we, the people behind *O Clarim*, treated the mulatto as if he were Black." Leite is perhaps too modest here. In fact, in the pages of his newspaper *O Clarim*, he became the first major *mulato* (mulatto) public figure to proudly embrace the Brazilian term negro. In so doing, Leite and his paper directly challenged Brazilian racial ideology.[18]

In the United States, where the one-drop rule of hypodescent prevailed, Leite's distinctions would have seemed trivial or moot, but in the Brazilian context such a declaration was provocative indeed. The Brazilian word negro—which I will translate, for lack of a better word, as "Black"—"had pejorative connotations," especially during slavery. Even in post-emancipation Brazil, the word remained all but synonymous with the word "slave." Thus, since "light skin color" conferred, according to Butler, a "socially sanctioned form of access," if a mulatto chose to self-identify as Black, it would likely hinder their social mobility. Certainly, those white Brazilians that might have accepted a mulatto would have found it off-putting to hear him identify as Black. The breakdown of what Butler has called the "traditional distinction between blacks and mulattos" precipitated by Leite and the consequent "redefinition of blackness to include mulattoes" became "an important tenet of Afro-Brazilian political philosophy." Leite's 1992 memoir chronicles such a conversion, so to speak, from mulatto to Black. Importantly, as Alberto notes, it was Leite's "closeness with white Italians," which is chronicled in his memoir, that "eventually led to this self-definition as a *negro*."[19] In many ways, *E disse* is a conversion narrative about Leite's transition from mixed-race to Black.

At the same time, *E disse* also offers a unique perspective on how the Italian community of São Paulo interacted with Black Brazilians. His reflections occupy an exceptional place within the documented experiences of Italians in São Paulo because they were produced by someone who "was witness to the racial insults Italians frequently hurled at Brazilians of color."[20] Such insults included, somewhat paradoxically, the appellation *Menelik*. To this point, historian Valter Zanin writes how the Italian vicissitudes in Ethiopia—known as the First Italo-Ethiopian War—left a deep mark in the memory of Black Brazilians. He mentions specifically how Italians themselves are partially to blame for this and explains how despite the contradiction—Menelik did after all defeat the Italians—the use of this term underscores the Brazilian social hierarchy, in which Italians occupied a higher social status than former captives.[21]

These instances of racism became immediately labeled as *foreign* to the nation, because they were, supposedly, very *un-Brazilian*. A "real" Brazilian, so the logic went, would neither resort to hurling racial slurs nor discriminate on the basis of race. This fact alone is enough to make Leite's memoirs of interest to scholars of race and Italian history. But what's more, Leite's narrative reveals how this discourse weakened Brazilian colorism and prefigured negotiations of the color line in late twentieth-century Italy.

Leite's childhood dream, as he tells it, was to become literate. However, since he had to work in order to help his mother—"a Black woman, a housekeeper, a true fighter"—provide for the household, he could not attend school.[22] His white father abandoned them early on and "did not acknowledge his paternity."[23] However, after the death of his mother and numerous failed attempts to enroll in makeshift neighborhood schools and other charitable programs, Leite was forced to temporarily abandon his dreams of an education.

This desire for schooling, a wish not fulfilled until his early twenties, explains much of the "alternative integrationist" agenda to which Leite would later subscribe. According to this alternative integrationist model, "individuals could improve their conditions based on merit" using an interest group model. Struggling to find a literacy program that would accept him—a poor, orphaned child—Leite became acutely aware of the lack of Black mutual associations. Conversely, he realized just how plentiful such associations were for Italians. As early as 1905, the Italian newspaper *Fanfulla* noted that 135 such organizations had sprung up in São Paulo alone.[24]

Although Leite could not take advantage of the benefits provided by Italian mutual aid associations, he nonetheless became immersed in the Italo-Brazilian community when he subsequently found employment with an Italian family in Bexiga. He started out assisting them in the acquisition and distribution of wood for residential buildings. The job came with room and board, on top of a small monthly salary. Moreover, given the family dynamics, Leite also ended up taking care of the children and running errands for the family when he was not working with the "old Italian" patriarch. Thus, Leite not only worked for an Italian family, but, as he tells it, he also spent most of his time "in the middle of Italians."[25]

Unlike most other exponents of *italianità* discussed in this book, Leite had neither Italian parentage nor a formal background in Italian letters. Even so, his immersion in the everyday, quotidian life of the Italian community of São Paulo made him Italian *culturally*—certainly more so than the Brazilian modernists discussed in Chapter Two.[26] As a consequence of this, Leite spoke the same dialect as Italians in Bexiga and enjoyed the same music, theater, and athletic activities as the Italians with whom he lived. And, years later, after having discovered the limits of racial tolerance among New World Italians, he would draw extensively on his knowledge of italianità—not only to exact revenge on those who had failed to accept him as truly one of their own, but to articulate a Black Brazilian identity.

In the São Paulo of Leite's time, his lighter complexion made him, on the one hand, "too black to be considered a member of the family," but, on the other hand, "not too black" to socialize with the Italians of Bexiga.[27] For example, Leite recounts how, although Italians encouraged him to play soccer with them—even going so far as to invite him to join a club named after Italy's "Heroes of the Piave"—they nevertheless forbade him from participating in the neighborhood's dances lest he dance with an Italian girl. Thus, while Italians welcomed Leite's racialized body in a fraternal, homosocial context, they deliberately excluded that same body from those formal spaces where it might participate in youthful heterosexual intimacies. That is, the Italians of São Paulo countenanced Leite's Blackness in their world insofar as it fulfilled their white masculinist fantasies and their need for labor power.

But the presence of his Blackness in the realm of mating rituals—at least, to the extent that it suggested the possibility of sexual relations between Black Brazilian men and white Italian women—was simply a bridge too far.

This was in spite of the fact that, as discussed in Chapter One, Italians were literally imported to Brazil with the explicit purpose to whiten the nation by mixing with the local populace. Surely, then, acts of sexual intimacy (if not outright violence) did indeed happen, but behind closed doors, and certainly not during the colony's dances and *festas*. One finds important parallels here with the exploitative, paternalistic relationships between Italians and subjects racialized as Black in the Italian African colonies. The practice of *madamato*—socially sanctioned concubinage between Italian men and local women, openly practiced until its ban in 1936—allowed for interracial relationships to occur, albeit on the margins of legality and with no protections for the women involved. Children born from these unions faced extreme difficulties in accessing Italian citizenship, which recalls, to an extent, the resistance that Leite confronted as a similarly hybrid figure among the Italians of Bexiga. Likewise, the Italian practice of recruiting Eritrean soldiers, known as *ascari*, to fight for the Italian army in their colonial wars reflects, albeit in far more pernicious form, the same tendency to accept interracial homosociality that Leite encounters on the soccer field in São Paulo.[28]

Leite's treatment within the Italian community he grew up in reflects the dialectics of what French philosopher Étienne Balibar has called a "fictive ethnicity"—that is, a collectivity united under one common national ideal. According to Balibar, it is the inextricable link between language and race that makes "fictive ethnicity" possible. Thus, while Leite carried himself like the Italians he grew up with and was conversant in the New World Italian discourse, he failed to conform to the national ideal on the axis of race. If, as Angelica Pesarini notes in the context of fascist East Africa, the "racial body . . . is performatively constituted by discourse," then the New World Italian discourse, which drew inspiration from both Italian and Brazilian conceptions of Blackness, ascribed to Leite a racial identity that was axiomatically incompatible with italianità.[29] In other words, Leite's story helps to make clear that this discourse represents a tradition of both cultural and racial nationalism. Indeed, it is perhaps more indicative of the latter since, historically, those who appear racially white but have only the most tenuous connection to Italian culture can nonetheless lay claim to an Italo-Brazilian identity more credibly than those who, like Leite, are steeped in Italian culture but racialized as Black. In this respect, the New World Italian discourse anticipated developments in contemporary Italy where the *jus sanguinis* law allows the great-grandchildren of emigrants from Italy in the Americas and elsewhere—the majority of whom have never set foot in Italy and cannot speak Italian—to obtain Italian citizenship. Yet the same law makes it extraordinarily difficult, if not impossible, for such citizenship to be achieved by the mostly non-white children of immigrants that have resided in Italy their entire lives.

To be sure, in Leite's São Paulo, and more specifically within the city's Italian community, the color line, although present, was far from strict. This was because, as Leite himself explains, no such strictness existed within Brazilian society, which by those years had, as historian Micol Seigel notes, largely "relinquished biological determinism in favor of environmentalist and culturalist paradigms" under the banner of racial democracy.[30] Nonetheless, Leite found that Italians "had their own restrictions toward Black people, in their ways." He continues by confirming that "the Italians adapted to perfection the Brazilian model of treating us. They knew up to which point they could go." Whether or not a Black person was well-liked by the community determined how far that point might be. In the case of Leite, his adoptive family, as it were, grew rather fond of him, and he thus spent much of his time sitting at the same table with them, eating their food, and enjoying their conviviality. But his Blackness prevented him from actually "being considered a member of the family."[31] The constant feeling of being only "halfway" integrated into the community ultimately induced Leite to abandon the Italo-Brazilian world altogether.

At age twenty-two, after realizing that he had been "wasting time with these Italians," he began to seek out connections with Black Brazilians, whom he affectionately refers to as "my people." Around the same time that he severed ties with the Italian community, he also resumed his efforts to secure an education. He found a tutor in Jayme de Aguiar, who would later cofound and coedit *O Clarim* alongside Leite. Aguiar taught Leite arithmetic and helped him learn to read and write proficiently. At first, Leite's

Portuguese was so poor that within his newfound Black community "everybody was shocked by [his] Italian way of speaking. [He] would talk as if [he] was singing and this was made fun of."[32] It is no wonder that, writing as Prof. Dott. Carretta, Leite was so adept at reproducing Italo-Brazilian speech patterns, particularly to comic effect. Leite had not only once expressed himself in just such an awkward polyglot mixture of Italian and Portuguese, but, also like Carretta, had been made the butt of jokes for doing so. This fact goes as far toward explaining Leite's later insistence on the need for literacy programs among Brazilians of African descent as it does his use of dramatic irony in his Carretta columns. For Leite understood, perhaps better than anyone, that the New World Italian discourse's portrayal of Italo-Brazilians as an enlightened cultural elite was fundamentally at odds with how they appeared to many everyday Brazilians. Indeed, if his own process of self-discovery was any indication, to many Black Paulistas, Italo-Brazilians sounded like bumpkins.

Hence, we should not underestimate the role of language in Leite's intellectual development and his contributions to the Black Brazilian Movement more broadly. It was only after Leite learned to express himself competently and eloquently in Portuguese that he became a celebrated Brazilian intellectual. It was the mechanism that mediated his discovery of his own fictive identity. Not only was this inconceivable with the Italian—or "italianado," as he preferred to call it—he grew up with; it was also downright inimical to such a process. For Leite, italianità would always evoke, on the one hand, a powerful interest group to which he would never belong and, on the other hand, a benighted cultural and intellectual existence vis-à-vis Brazilianness. He would equate speaking Portuguese, the Brazilian national language, with being a true national, someone who belongs in and to Brazil. By this logic, Blackness would articulate more closely with Brazilianness than Italianness. If New World Italians wanted to be true nationals, Leite suggests in his columns, then they would have to learn proper Portuguese, adapt to Black cultural norms, and invent a place for themselves in Brazil's premodern past alongside African slaves. In a city dominated by Italians and organized around ethnic patronage, Black Brazilians such as Leite promptly concluded that their survival depended partly on their ability to create their own public sphere. Perhaps unsurprisingly, they turned to newspapers to create a hitherto unprecedented version of what Benedict Anderson has termed an "imagined community" in Brazil.[33]

3. Italians in the Black Press: The Case of Prof. Dott. Juó Carretta

If demography is destiny, as the saying goes, then surely the more Africanized cities of Rio de Janeiro or Salvador de Bahia should have been the birthplace of the Black Brazilian press. And yet this was not the case. Rather, it was São Paulo that engendered the most prolific and storied Black publishing scene in Brazil. Indeed, it was the minority status of Black Brazilians in this seemingly Italian city that spurred the desire to articulate a Black "racial ethnicity" in the public sphere. Alberto observes that Black Brazilian "writers' *negro* identity . . . came not from a cultural identification with an African heritage, but from the sense of being small, denigrated minority in an immigrant city." Another way of putting this is to say that the Black press in São Paulo developed largely in response to the New World Italian discourse elaborated by native-born Brazilian elites and second-generation Italian immigrants.[34]

A defining feature of São Paulo's Black press was its strong nationalist polemics. Even when the Black writers, who embodied an "opinion elite" and an "an ideological vanguard," took issue with Brazilian racism, they nonetheless professed a vehement attachment to the Brazilian nation.[35] At the same time, however, Black opinion makers expressed their sense of belonging by invoking the concepts of progress and modernization, which had become synonymous with São Paulo. To be sure, much of this was performative, insofar as this "ideological vanguard" was aware of the discrimination enacted against them but nonetheless understood the need to stress their national belonging over and against the foreignness of the immigrants populating the city.

Black Brazilians seized on the language used by policymakers and elite opinion makers to describe the country's whitening process, exploiting its negative valences. Terms like "foreignness" and "nationality" reverberated throughout the Black press of São Paulo, with Black writers seeing this distinction—one drawn by white Brazilian power brokers themselves—as a crucial ground on which to formulate a form of nativism that cast Brazilians of African descent as more authentically "Brazilian" than foreigners, namely, Italians.[36] As Alberto explains, they "would seek to define the categories 'native' and 'foreign' to their own advantage by addressing two major concerns: their relationships with European immigrants and their relationship with Africa."[37] We can see evidence of this motive in Leite's tendency to deploy the term "national" in his satirical columns targeting Italians. Despite being welcomed with open arms, Leite insists, these New World Italians seem to possess an ineradicable taint of "the foreign element," which prevents them from fully assimilating into Brazilian society. The evidence he leans on to demonstrate their status as unassimilable is, quite frequently, their inability to speak proper Portuguese. From this perspective, the Italian language and, more broadly, Italianness, becomes not a mark of prestige but of shame.

As mentioned above, the persona of "professor" and "doctor" Juó P. Carretta appears in the very first issue of *O Clarim*, just two years after Leite had turned his back on the Italo-Brazilian community and embarked on a journey to rediscover his Black roots. Newly literate and thus keenly aware of his erstwhile ignorance, Leite somewhat unsurprisingly trains his satiric impulse on what he knows best: New World Italians and the unlettered. As it turns out, the two are mutually imbricated. The potshots begin with the byline itself. The double honorific suggests the presumptuousness and pretension of the classically insecure parvenu, for whom such titles convey power and importance. That the titles are mere puffery is made clear by the fact that Carretta never bothers to tell us what he is a "doctor" or "professor" of. Dramatic irony is established by the prose itself, which betrays little in the way of professional excellence. Obviously, the good "doctor" is simply putting on airs.

The caricature that accompanies the second installment of the column reinforces the irony. It depicts Carretta as gangling man with a long beard, sideburns, and an aquiline nose, who gestures matter-of-factly toward the text with his left hand. On his right arm hangs what appears to be a walking stick and his right hand is hidden in his pocket. His feet are evenly spread, and his abdomen—or, perhaps more accurately, his crotch—juts out almost lewdly in the direction of the headline, which reads "U Clarino." His posture befits the kind of bumptious mountebank who would sign his name with a double honorific. The figure's body language is striking, but his clothes stand out even more. The top hat, the checkered trousers, the cut-away frock coat draw the eye, but they are not stylish. Rather, his clothes seem rather passé, evoking the nineteenth-century flaneur more than a twentieth-century cosmopolitan elite. By depicting the quintessential New World Italian as a dandy of a bygone era, Leite exposes him as a fraud. There is nothing modern about him.

The irony doesn't only inhere in these paratexts, though. It's also riven through the text of the columns themselves. The text of Carretta's first column, "Naziunale," makes further mockery of the glorification of Italians as modern and white subjects in Brazil. In this short but stinging paragraph, Leite shows how Carretta—despite following the supposed path toward assimilation sanctioned by the Brazilian reformulation of italianità—fails to count as a national in the eyes of Brazilian society.

> *Naziunale*
>
> Io gosto molto du Brasile e dos brasileiro. Ma io fico cheio de indignacò quando sento aparlare que io nun só naziunale. I perché si a moglie mia é una bella mulatinha que parla o portoghese corretamente. Io só inleito du Nicolau ingoppa a Bella Vista, só nicociante di banane lá abbaixo o Bò Ritiro, tengo danaro a bèssa, os minho figlio so studante nu commercio giunto co Matarazzo. I perchè nu so naziunale? Và dottore dé un gieto nisso, e bona notte
>
> *National*
>
> I like Brazil and Brazilians very much. But I am filled with indignation when I hear people saying that I am not a national. And why not, if my wife is a beautiful mulatta who speaks Portuguese correctly? I am under the protection of Nicola up in Bella Vista, I am a seller of bananas down there in Bom Retiro, I have a lot of money, my son is a student at the commercial institute together with Matarazzo ['s children]. And why am I not a national? There, doctor, fix this, and goodnight.[38]

Leite recapitulates the Italian upward mobility narrative that lies at the heart of the New World Italian discourse. All the key tropes are there: Leite has done his part to whiten the population by marrying a mulatta; the reference to "Nicola up in Bella Vista" underscores the Italo-Brazilian patronage system; Carretta's status as a fruit vendor and his claim to "have a lot of money" point to Brazilians' tendency to conflate Italianness with industriousness and wealth accumulation; and, lastly, his boasting of sending his children to the same "commercial institute" as Francesco Matarazzo's recalls how Italians sought to reproduce their class privileges through schools like the Istituto Medio Italo-Brasiliano Dante Alighieri. The litany of accomplishments conjures the cliché that Italians were agents of modernization and hence model immigrants.

Nevertheless, Italians were not nationals. This much is conveyed through the text's thematization and exemplification of language politics. Carretta complains of not being a "*naziunale*," combining the Italian *nazionale* and Portuguese *nacional*, making the "o" vowel appear as "u" to reflect Portuguese phonetics. This despite his having married "una bella mulatinha" who "parla o portoghese corretamente." Here Carretta betrays not only the stereotypical predilection for light-skinned women of color among Italian men—a stereotype that persists to this day—but also a deep insecurity about his own language skills. That his insecurity is warranted is made abundantly clear by his Bexiga brogue, which Leite satirizes through transcription. Leite recreates the sound of the language heard in the streets of Bexiga by using Italian words but with a spelling that signals to Portuguese speakers and readers how it would sound in Italian. Thus, in addition to "naziunale," the word "indignation," which in Portuguese is *indignacão* and in Italian *indignazione*, becomes a truncated *indignacò* with the grave accent commonly used in Italian as opposed to the acute one, which is more of a hallmark of Portuguese. Similarly, *arrivederci* becomes *arrivederche*. Later, Leite would add to the realism of the columns signed by Carretta by punctuating them with Italo-Brazilian colloquialisms such as "*pa maronna*" ("for the love of Mary"), an expression that remains in use among contemporary Paulistanos. Leite's knowledge of the "italianado" spoken by Italian immigrants allowed him to mimic in writing the sounds he had been hearing his entire life. His exceptional ability to capture the oral quality of this language in a written format might stem from his becoming literate in his twenties. Thus, in addition to talking back to the New World Italian discourse, Leite—through Carretta—also challenges traditional and normative understandings of what makes a "good" writer.[39]

More important for my purposes, however, is how the column indicates that Black Brazilians, who would have comprised most of the audience of *O Clarim*, clearly grasped the New World Italian discourse and Leite's mockery of it. As Alberto explains, "the column demonstrated . . . black writers' and readers' proficiency in the culture and language of their city, state, and nation."[40] In other words, it demonstrates that the Italians, Brazilian elites, and Italo-Brazilians were not the only ones preoccupied with the making of that discourse. Nor was the figure of this new migrant class always someone to be revered or celebrated. On the contrary, in Leite's hands, this figure became the plaything of Black Brazilians, who understood it as a backhanded affront to their history and dignity. Behind Leite's wordplay one detects a certain bitterness that, in turn, becomes the basis for national consciousness. By mocking Italo-Brazilian dialect and suggesting that Black Brazilians who speak correct Portuguese are more authentically Brazilian than favored Italian immigrants like Carretta, he draws a connection between language and nation that recalls both Benedict Anderson's imagined community and Balibar's fictive ethnicity. To speak good Brazilian Portuguese means to belong to Brazil in ways that Italian immigrants could only imagine—or hope to attain through marriage to a Black Brazilian. Perhaps unsurprisingly, literacy would become one of the most pressing issues in Leite's ethnonationalist political activism.

Ironically, Leite's literary nationalism also reminds us of an important fact about the Italians of his time: they did not necessarily speak what we understand today as standardized Italian. Consider that around the time of the proclamation of the Kingdom of Italy in 1861—a moment that also marked the unification of the peninsula, joining together two regions, North and South, that experienced drastically different historical development—"only between 2.5% and 12% of the newly established nation's entire population knew Italian."[41] In fact, it was only in the second half of the twentieth century that Italian "became an actual mother tongue (that is, spoken at home since the speaker's birth)."[42] Italians immigrating to the Americas did not speak a unified Italian language so much as, to borrow a formulation from historian Nancy Carnevale, a multiplicity of "Italian languages." They spoke dialects they brought with them from their respective regions, dialects visible also in the creole Leite reproduces in his Carretta columns.

These dialects did not amount to simply "regional variations of standard Italian, but 'sister' languages that evolved from Latin."[43]

Carretta's *italianado*, what today we might refer to as an act of translanguaging, adds together expressions coming from Northern and Southern Italy, as well as phonetic sounds that mix the closed, nasal vowels of Portuguese with the more dental, staccato Italian. Contrast Carretta's language with what Carnevale calls Italo-American, a creole that combined elements of English, dialect (primarily Neapolitan), and standard Italian.[44] Here, Carretta's italianado includes fewer words from Portuguese but more of its sounds, and fewer affinities with Neapolitan in favor of closer alignment with Northern Italy's *dialetto settentrionale* and Italian. Some of these differences are purely linguistic and phonological, the product of closer similarities between Portuguese and Italian than exist between Italian and English. But that should not occlude the material difference of divergent migration patterns—more Northern Italians, especially those from Veneto and Lombardia, migrated to Brazil than they did to the English-speaking Americas. Taking a closer look at Italian immigration to Brazil, then, also shows how Italian emigration was not only a phenomenon that had to do with the so-called Southern Question, but one affecting the entirety of the peninsula.

Meanwhile, as these Italians abroad created their own "insider's language, that reflected immigrant life and shaped it," the Italian government went to great lengths to ensure that its citizens at home and abroad became or remained fluent in Italian.[45] After all, as linguist Mariella Totaro-Genevois notes, language planning "is not an idealistic and exclusively linguistic activity, but a political and administrative activity." State officials in Italy and in densely populated informal colonies, such as São Paulo, saw language retention as a way to preserve strong ties between these emigrants and the motherland. Brazil's Dante Alighieri Society and, later, Italy's fascist regime both encouraged linguistic chauvinism among Italians abroad to promote an image of national unity and strength. Efforts to promote linguistic homogeneity undertaken by the Italian institutions abroad functioned as a means to elevate a specific notion of Italian culture and, hence, to "make Italians."[46] Such efforts reflected a belief in the "genius of language," which literary scholar Paola Gambarota characterizes as "the ideological nucleus of linguistic nationalism."[47]

Nevertheless, these initiatives did not always produce the desired outcomes. Brazil is a case in point. There, Italians did resist learning proper Portuguese. One indication of this is that Leite wrote his satires of São Paulo's Italians in 1924, almost three decades after the mass migration from Italy took place. At the same time, however, much to the frustration of the Italian government, these Italian migrants did not, by and large, commit to becoming fluent in standardized Italian. In fact, it would be unfair to describe the language that Leite heard in Bexiga in such terms. When we read Gina Lombroso Ferrero's enthusiastic accounts of hearing more Italian in São Paulo than in any other city in Italy, for instance, we should be skeptical. The sound of italianado might very well have tricked her or—and this is the more likely scenario—her interactions in São Paulo occurred principally among the more affluent Paulistanos of Italian origins. As Carnevale has observed, both in Italy and abroad "language took on marked class overtones as it became increasingly clear that the majority of Italians who were struggling for mere survival could not afford the luxury of sending their children to school to learn Italian."[48] Given her own class status and predilections, Lombroso Ferrero, so enthralled by the Italian spoken in São Paulo, might very well have avoided encounters with the Italo-Brazilian arrivistes whose native language was closer to italianado.

Leite, by contrast, scrupulously transcribed it and, in so doing, disclosed the contradictions of the New World Italian discourse, which tended to ignore the discrepancies between the way Italians in Brazil actually spoke and the standardized Italian promulgated by the protean Italian government with which elites on both sides of the Atlantic aligned themselves. His columns allow us to see how the *questione della lingua*—one of the founding and unresolved tensions at the basis of Italian unification—operates from a transnational standpoint. Far from resolving it, Leite revels in it, showing that the homogeneity of standardized Italian is but an artificial construct. In the streets of Bexiga, one communicated through hybrid forms of Italian regional dialects and Portuguese. This polyglot environment enabled the people of São Paulo to develop conceptions of Italian culture and national identity at once redolent of the so-called homeland but irreducible to it. In other words, Leite's italianado proposes an alternative language to standardized Italian, one that more faithfully reflected the language spoken within the Italian diaspora in São Paulo. That said, he nonetheless reiterates the union between nation and language (the "genius of language"), invoked by Italian nationalists at home and abroad when he suggests that Carretta's inability to speak standard Portuguese undermines the latter's claim to Brazilian citizenship. That is, Leite deconstructs the Italian language undergirding the New World Italian discourse, while simultaneously reappropriating its linguistic nationalism to benefit the cause of Black Paulistanos.

And yet what is perhaps Leite's most profound attack on the fictive identity of the New World Italian discourse falls more squarely on the axis of race than that of language. Carretta, for instance, belongs to the large group of small Italian peddlers who take up odd jobs alongside some of the Black Brazilians who read Leite's paper. One of the activities Carretta lists that makes him a "naziunale" is that of "nicociante di banane lá abbaixo o Bò Ritiro." Selling bananas was a common activity among jobbers, laborers hired on the spot, who often received produce in exchange for their labor. Not coincidentally, most of them were Black. It was so common to find them selling fruit in front of the Barra Funda train station that the station area became known as Largo da Banana.[49] Thus, in addition to being married to a Brazilian woman of African descent, Carretta works a job normally associated with the Black urban community. Such details would seem to suggest that Carretta, his inability to speak Portuguese notwithstanding, is—just as he insists—as much a national as any Black Brazilian.

But, in keeping with the tone of the caricature that would accompany Carretta's second column, here Leite is satirizing the New World Italian discourse, particularly its assertion of white racial exceptionalism. The fact that Carretta performs the same racialized labor as Black Brazilians shows that, in fact, there is nothing particularly special about him and the Italo-Brazilian community he represents. The same message is communicated by Carretta's claim that he is "inleito du Nicola ingoppa a Bella Vista" or "under the protection of Nicola from the Bella Vista" neighborhood. To be sure, as Donna Gabaccia reminds us, "patronage was an integral dimension of Italian life at every level of society," but this was no less true among Brazilians generally and Black Brazilians in particular.[50] Indeed, ethnic patronage was according to Butler "the underlying principle of social relationships" in Brazil.[51] Unlike Black Brazilians, however, Carretta can also claim—using the

Italianate expression "a bèssa," which roughly translates to the Northern Italian idiom "a bestia" to signify a large quantity of something—to have made a fortune. With such money he can afford to send his son to study commerce alongside the children of Matarazzo. This perhaps refers, if obliquely, to the Istituto Medio Italo-Brasiliano Dante Alighieri I discuss in Chapter Four and thereby draws another important distinction between himself and Black Brazilians.

By invoking Matarazzo, who historian Warren Dean describes as "the most successful and loquacious of the immigrant industrialists, but also as its doyen, shrewdest and oldest in experience," Leite mocks the aspirations of the many Italian peddlers who dreamed of turning themselves into "capitani di colonia" à la Matarazzo, while also acknowledging that their dreams were at least founded in reality. As Angelo Trento reminds us, such success stories were few and far between, but they were certainly more common among Italo-Brazilians than Brazilians of African descent. Leite understands that not all patronage was created equally: Carretta could go from fruit peddler to parvenu like Matarazzo because of a system that favored white Italian immigrants over native-born Black Brazilian citizens. Anticipating his later political essays, Leite here strives to inform readers of the extent to which race informs their everyday lived experience in the city.[52]

Leite further subverts the New World Italian discourse by questioning Italians' racial status, in ways that echo North American rhetoric about immigrants from Southern Italy. In the column published after the Carnival of 1924, for instance, Leite attributes Carretta's love for the rather sensual and morally dubious festivities directly to the latter's blood.

U Clarino . . .

U pissuálo da ridação ficarao chein de indignaçó porque io virei surbeto nu carnevale. Ma qui curpa io tengo di sere farrista? Isto djà e di familia, perche istá dentro do mingo sango. Caros Leitores! . . . Io quando iscutei bem in sima da città quello bruto baruglio du carneval juguei pru aris o piato di macarré e disgambei como maluco p'ro Braiz p'ra Avenida e p'ra tudus cantus ondi si deixava impirá o bello e formso ré Momo. Ainda isto isculiambadu di tantas baguncias qui ovi im goupa das sucietá. Per Dio! No proximo numero io vô faze moltas coisas p'ra o minho Clarino. Arrivederche! Prof. Dott. João P. Carretta

The Clarino . . .

> The editorial staff were indignant because I went missing during Carnival. But who can blame me for being a *farrista*? This is a family trait, because it is in my blood. Dear Readers! . . . When I listened good from the very top of the city to that ugly noise of Carnival I threw the plate of macaroni in the air and I ran like a madman toward Braz and the Avenida and to all the corners where the beautiful and handsome king Momo was allowed to reign. I am still dazed because of all the pandemonium that took place. By God! In the next number I will do many things for my Clarino. See you! Prof. Dott. João P. Carretta[53]

Being a "farrista"—that is, someone who enjoys partying—"is a family trait, because it is in *my blood*," Carretta explains. Thus, the reason for his absence from the issue published during Carnival—an absence to which the otherwise hardworking editorial staff apparently took umbrage—lies in Carretta's genealogy. Such a confession only serves to further undermine the supposed differences between Italian and Black Paulistanos. After all, the celebration of Carnival, to say nothing of the extensive organization behind it, was a distinctly Black affair. As Butler writes, "Neighborhood-based social groups organized around events such as . . . Carnival were a new form of black collective in post-abolition São Paulo"—so much so that "organized samba became a fixture of black Paulistano culture with the emergence of *cordões carnavalescos*" or organized neighborhood Carnival groups. The stigmatization and criminalization of Blacks, especially males, in the Brazilian imagination dates back to these "less formal cultural manifestations [of the Carnival] taking shape in the poorer black communities, where bars . . . became a meeting point for music, billiards, dancing, and drinking."[54]

Carretta places himself squarely in this seedy world when he confesses to having visited "tudus cantus." Although sociologists like Florestan Fernandes would later depict social disorder as a "Black" issue, Leite insinuates, through Carretta, that whites and Blacks alike contributed to it. This account is confirmed by Andrews, whose extensive investigation into race relations in São Paulo highlights how "crime, poverty, and anomie" were widespread among "poor whites and immigrants" as well.[55] Leite's depiction of Carretta discarding his plate of pasta and heeding the primordial call of the samba drums in an almost Pavlovian fashion adds another layer of irony.[56]

It suggests that the people touted by Brazilian elites as the avatars of whiteness and modernity have an atavistic connection to the very cultures of Africa which supposedly threaten to keep the country mired in its premodern past. Italians like Carretta might not be nationals, Leite implies, but they nonetheless bear traces of racial Blackness.[57]

The structural similarity hardly seems like an accident. Leite's rhetoric betrays an awareness of the discourse surrounding Italians in North America, where the influx of Southern Italians in the late nineteenth century was conflated with the "mongrelization" of the United States. As the historian Gary Gerstle notes, "in the eyes of native-born Americans, Southern Italians were seen as a group that, of all the European immigrants, most closely resembled blacks."[58] The Italian American festas—Carnival-esque street parades honoring minor saints—that took place in cities like New York, Boston, and Chicago were, much like their Brazilian counterparts, regarded as primitive and degenerate. Given the well-documented exchanges between the Black press in the United States and Brazil, it is not unlikely that Leite and his audience encountered stories of such racial attitudes—which ultimately led to the passage of laws that placed strict limits on Italian immigration to the United States—in pieces reprinted from Black American newspapers. And the ironies would not have been lost on them. At the same time, though, by revealing how Carretta enjoys Black popular culture one might also infer that Leite's purpose is precisely that of showing that these two groups, Italians and Black Brazilians, are the same. In other words, Leite is redefining the meaning of Blackness by going beyond the binary of Black and white and proposing a cross-racial discourse which, under the banner of Brazilianness, defies the segregation based on color embraced by the New World Italian discourse. After all, proving his Blackness meant that Leite had to impersonate an Italian.

In his final Carretta column, Leite, having thus challenged Italians' status as both agents of modernization and paragons of whiteness, targets the New World Italian discourse's revisionist accounts of Brazilian history. As we have seen, writers like Lombroso Ferrero have asserted that Italians not only ushered Brazil into the world of modern industrial capitalism but also played a central role in the alleged discovery of the New World and the subsequent founding of Brazilian civilization. Leite turns this narrative on its head by taking aim at Giuseppe Garibaldi, the so-called hero of the two worlds that, along with Christopher Columbus and Amerigo Vespucci, served to legitimize the presence of Italians in contemporary Brazil. In the 1830s and 1840s, Garibaldi fought across South America with his voluntary legions of Italian political exiles. Historian Lucy Riall recounts how, upon his return to Italy—where, despite his Republican beliefs, he fought for the Crown of Savoy in its pursuit of a "unified" Italian Kingdom—"Garibaldi's life and actions were recast as a heroic narrative . . . in which he personified a lost national tradition of selfless physical bravery and the promise of Italian regeneration." Garibaldi, more so than any other historical figure, exemplifies the link between the political realities of nineteenth-century South America and Italy. And this was a fact that fascist propagandists in Brazil and Argentina exploited.[59]

Leite's farewell column reads:

> **Sempri avanti!**
>
> Sempri avanti dizia u grandi Garibaldo na bataglia a do Itororó p'ro suo valoroso exercito. Assim també eu digo p'ros pissuaio du CLARINO, nada di disanimo perché a primiera itapa istá vencida, bilhantemente. Isto numero vou fichare u primiero simestro di dificultá i di lucta insana mais apisare di tuto isto a direçó ista firme a mantenere u grandi programa di açó desta foglia, u anno passa i as conquistas ficam sigundo aparló u minho barbiero nu Bó Ritiro e io cumo num so troxa sumento disejo qui u pissualo du Clarino cu a penna na mó conquiste as gloria qui ellis mirece, assim sendo inte u proximo numero.
>
> **Always Forward!**
>
> Ever onward said the great Garibaldi in the battle of Itororó to his valiant army. The same thing I say to the people of *Clarino*, there is nothing to worry about because the first match has been won, brilliantly. This number is going to close the first period of difficulty and struggle but despite all of this the editorial board is committed to maintaining the great plan of action of this paper, time goes by and victories remain, according to what my barber in Bom Retiro said, and since I did not get a raise I hope that the people of the Clarino with pens in hand win the glory that they deserve, may it be like that till the next number.[60]

It is easy to interpret this as merely a parody of the New World Italians' efforts to insert themselves into Brazil's national mythology. No doubt Carretta's comparing himself to Garibaldi is but another of his delusions of grandeur. In his desperate attempt to affiliate himself with one of the most important figures in italianità, however, he seems to commit two comic gaffes. First, he belittles the war hero by equating his efforts on the battlefield with managing a newspaper. Second, he gets the facts about Garibaldi wrong. Garibaldi famously fought in the Revolução Farropilha (1835–1845), during which Brazil's southernmost province, Rio Grande do Sul, declared its independence from the Brazilian Empire. According to historian James Sanders, Garibaldi's interest in joining the struggle grew from the Italian mercenary's broader anti-imperialist views and his attitudes toward other imperial powers, particularly the Hapsburgs and their dominion over Italy.[61] But despite Carretta's assertion above, there is no evidence that Garibaldi took part in the 1868 Battle of Itororó (or Ytororó), which marked the first in a series of victories in the war that the Triple Alliance (Brazil, Argentina, and Uruguay) waged against Paraguay from 1864 to 1870. The victory of the Brazilian imperial army on the Itororó River consecrated the figure of another *condottiero* named Marshal Marquês de Caixas, a Brazilian, who allegedly incited his soldiers with the battle cry: "Follow me, those of you who are Brazilians." By misattributing this episode to the biography of Garibaldi, Carretta further reveals his anxiety about failing to qualify as a Brazilian national.

But it is also true that Leite's parody of the New World Italian discourse is double-voiced: it is an attack on the white supremacist ideology and ethnonationalism undergirding life in São Paulo, but also an ode to Black creativity. Leite's audience would have known, at this point, that a Black writer was impersonating an Italo-Brazilian parvenu. This makes the invocation of Garibaldi all the more provocative, for Leite, in the guise of Carretta, appropriates the hero to rally the editorial staff of a Black newspaper. Leite-cum-Carretta recasts himself as Garibaldi, anticipating, as we shall see in Chapter Four, the Italo-Brazilian fascist Miguel Reale, who envisioned himself as the reincarnation of Dante. But these speech acts differ sharply in their intent. Where Reale invokes Dante to reify Italianness and white racial superiority in Brazil, Leite channels Garibaldi to inspire Black ethnic consciousness and expose Brazil's racial democracy as a sham. He correctly identifies the public sphere as a battlefield, comparing the pen of the editorial staff to a weapon that brings glory to the people of *O Clarim* and, by extension, the Black Brazilian community. In this discursive arena, the Black community can exploit the symbols of Italians—to say nothing of their labor power, since Carretta fails to "get a raise"—for their own purposes. And yet, through Carretta, Leite also hypothesizes a possible collaborationism between these two groups. The progression of the columns, from Carretta's pompous and insecure posing, to being somewhat flummoxed at his own attraction to Carnival, to now cheering on the progress of *O Clarim*, hints at a complete subversion of the New World Italian discourse: one in which Italians are portrayed as not only wanting acceptance as Brazilians, but even almost wanting to be Black, although without quite knowing it. Thus, Leite flips the script on the discourse of racial, economic, and cultural superiority accompanying the assimilation of Italians by turning it into a mechanism that redefines Blackness at large. His final column as Carretta foreshadows how he will become a figure that fosters unity and militancy in the Black Brazilian Movement.

4. *The Italian Immigrant: A Model or an Enemy?*

At a certain point during the 1920s, *O Clarim* was forced to become *O Clarim da Alvorada*, because another newspaper under its former name already existed. The newspaper promptly fell under the sole direction of José Correia Leite after Jayme de Aguiar left his editorial position to dedicate time to his family. The name change and staff shake-up heralded a shift in tone and content. No longer oriented toward satire, Leite retired his character Dott. Prof. Juó P. Carretta. Under his leadership the newspaper became the premiere platform for spreading a political message of solidarity and strength among the Black Brazilians of São Paulo.[62] Leite's experience within the Italian community convinced him that the creation of a mutual aid association represented the first step toward full emancipation of the Black masses.

In his new signed columns, Leite sounds graver, more confrontational and accusatory. In the one that appears in the 1925 issue honoring his own birthday, he lamented the fact that, despite his various calls to action, there had yet to materialize a "center for Black men in this State or in the entirety of Brazil for asserting the full power of [their] representation, much like . . . the foreigners do who reside here have." The creation of such a central organization, he writes:

> Depends only on our willingness, we live in our land in worse conditions than the foreigners who have recently arrived here, these [people] after some months of labor and unity, accomplish what they planned, this in virtue of unity and labor, while we do not value anything and we are hostile when they do not treat us as if we also contributed to the great advancements of our land.[63]

Here Leite measures the progress of Black Brazilians according to the social mobility narrative promulgated by the New World Italian discourse. If hard work and solidarity enabled groups like Italians to climb the socioeconomic ladder, then these should suffice for Black Brazilians. The problem is that, unlike the Italians, Black Brazilians failed to valorize their labor and fight for their collective interests. It might seem that Afro-Brazilians lack the capacity to climb the social ladder in the manner of their "white brothers"; that they have failed to move beyond an antiquated mode of production; that they do not have the numbers to form a united front and demand better wages—yet none of this is case. Where Brazilian elites seek to frame Brazilians of African descent as backward and anachronistic, Leite insists that they have played no less of a role in the nation's progress than recent immigrants from Europe and continue to do so.

Where previously Leite ridiculed the figure of the Italian parvenu for his ethnonationalism, he now espouses, unironically, an ethnonationalism of his own. His complaints about the low regard for Black Brazilians mirror Carretta's own calls for recognition. Thus, while Carretta may have disappeared from the *O Clarim*, the figure of the foreigner—who, for Leite and other Black Brazilians in São Paulo, was epitomized by the Italian immigrant—continues to haunt its pages and shape the rhetoric of the Black press. As historian Regina Pahim Pinto has shown in her exhaustive work on the Black Brazilian Movement, the figure of the immigrant provoked feelings of both repulsion and admiration among Black Brazilians. They denounced the favoritism shown toward what they continued to call foreigners, even though these people, by the 1920s, had Brazilian-born children. But, at the same time, they admired the foreigners' qualities or at least the model minority narrative that accompanied their reception in Brazil. For Pinto, the mix of grudging admiration and resentment toward immigrants is crucial to understanding the Black Brazilian Movement.[64] Such a tension is visible in Leite's writings who, at first, mocked and subverted the New World Italian discourse through the figure of Carretta, but also increasingly chose to use that same discourse to promote the betterment of Black Brazilians in São Paulo.

By the mid-1920s, Black dissatisfaction over working conditions and preferential treatment toward foreigners in the labor market of São Paulo had reached a fever pitch. At this point, "the conditions were ripe," according to Butler, for the birth of the "first Afro-Brazilian activist organization of São Paulo." Thanks in no small part to the advocacy of Leite, that year the Centro Cívico Palmares—a mutual aid association for Black Brazilians—finally came to life. The name Palmares was drawn from "an independent African republic founded in Brazil by fugitive slaves that lasted from approximately 1604 to 1696," and was "the quintessential symbol of Afro-Brazilians resistance."[65] The nomenclature signaled the extent to which Black intellectuals in São Paulo had begun to see themselves as not only nationals but specifically *Black* nationals. In other words, the Centro Cívico Palmares reflected the same ethnocentric paradigm espoused by the Italian mutual aid associations that Leite had admired for so long from afar.

The Palmares started off as a mostly cultural and educational space for the Black urban community. By the 1930s, however, it had become a key force in articulating and advocating Black political interests. In its transition from a cultural center to a political advocacy organization, it grew increasingly oriented toward an extreme form of ethnonationalism. Indeed, the Centro Cívico Palmares constituted the "embryo" of the political party Frente Negra Brasileira (FNB), the Black Brazilian Front, which was the first formally instituted Black political party in the Americas. This proved too much even for Leite. Despite campaigning for the center and advocating for Black self-determination, he drew the line at the FNB.

And not without good reason. Under the aegis of Black politician Arlindo Veiga dos Santos, the FNB promoted a series of ideas that bore a disturbing resemblance to those embraced by both integralists in Brazil and fascists back in Italy. Historian Jessica Lynn Graham calls the FNB's ideology a "conservative illiberalism," and highlights the ties between Santos and Brazilian Integralist Action (AIB) leader Plínio Salgado. The FNB's internal structure partially mirrored AIB's, which, in turn, resembled that of the Italian National Fascist Party (PNF).[66] According to Graham, the popularity of fascism in Brazil, especially São Paulo, did not simply result from the large influx of Italian immigrants. On the contrary, fascism found fertile ground because of the limits of Brazilian liberal democracy when it came to racial justice.[67] That is, Brazilian fascism, although clearly derived from fascism in Italy, was multiracial and homegrown.

Fascism is one of the main nodes of Black-Italian relations in the history of São Paulo—one for which Leite served as an unwitting conduit. The question of interracial and intercultural intimacy with which I started this chapter reappears here, in the concrete history of Brazilian fascism. Not coincidentally, it was the neighborhood of Bexiga—whose Black history both predates and overlaps its reinvention as São Paulo's "Little Italy"—that housed the headquarters of the FNB and its literary organ *A Voz da Raça*.[68] Even less coincidentally, the FNB's propaganda was very much suffused with the anti-immigrant rhetoric that newspapers like *O Clarim* had trafficked in for years. As Graham states, "the FNB . . . was uninterested in foreign blood on Brazilian soil."[69] But one must be careful not to exaggerate Black hostility to immigrants at this time. As mentioned earlier, Black Brazilians' expressions of xenophobia often went hand in hand with a strong sense of admiration for all that these—mostly Italians—immigrants had accomplished. As I illustrate in Chapter Four, the key to understanding the connections between the integralists and members of the Black Brazilian Front lies precisely in their shared investment in the discourse promoting the racial, economic, and cultural superiority of Italians. After all, the members of both the AIB and the FNB wanted to be Brazilians. In the eyes of both groups that meant actively contributing to the modernization process of São Paulo, a process that, in the popular imagination, Italian immigrants had monopolized. Thus, both parties took the New World Italian discourse as a point of departure from which to articulate their ultimately divergent visions of Brazilian racial nationalism.

FOUR

Sob o signo da Dante

Miguel Reale, Italianness, and Fascism

In 1903 São Paulo's Consul General Pio Gherardo di Savoia wrote an inflammatory memo to the headquarters of the Dante Alighieri Society in Rome, in which he claimed to not be "interested in redeeming the transoceanic Italian proletariat from its dejection."[1] Instead, Gherardo di Savoia expressed a desire to assist the Italian bourgeoisie who "have no idea where to send their children to get educated conveniently and *italianamente* (in an Italian manner)." An Italian secondary school for this class of Italians, he reasoned, would surely prove to be *un ottimo affare*, "a great deal."[2] Gherardo di Savoia's intuition proved to be true: ten years later the Istituto Medio Italo-Brasiliano Dante Alighieri opened its doors on Alameda Jaú. It soon became one of the most prestigious schools in the city. And, more than a century later, it still continues to be an important institution in the educational lives of São Paulo's elite class.

Amongst its most illustrious students, one in particular stands out: Miguel Reale. Political scientist Michael Mitchell has written that Reale has "[u]nquestionably . . . exerted a pervasive influence over Brazilian intellectual life."[3] Born to an Italian family that immigrated to the State of São Paulo, Reale was a Brazilian politician who cofounded the Brazilian fascist party Ação Integralista Brasileira (Brazilian Integralist Action, AIB) in 1932 and openly supported and collaborated with the twenty-one-year-long military dictatorship that started in 1964. But before his pivotal role in Brazil's fascist movement and military dictatorship, Reale attended the exclusive secondary school Istituto Medio Italo-Brasiliano Dante Alighieri of São Paulo. Funded by a consortium of local Italian elites, the Italian government, and the Dante Alighieri Society, the Institute was, according to historian Patrizia Salvetti, "the first and only [institution] of this kind."[4] While those who attended the Institute did not necessarily have to be of Italian descent, they did have to belong to the local upper class. It was this prerequisite that, as Reale demonstrates, helped to further cement Brazil's long-standing social hierarchy, which was predicated on the intertwining of wealth and racial superiority. Brazilian elites made sure to exclude Indigenous and Afro-Brazilians from the national project of modernization initiated in the late nineteenth century, often by appealing to theories of scientific racism that regard the Black race as an impediment to modernization.[5] Due to their exclusion from the more coveted positions in the labor market, few, if any, Black and Brown people would have had the means to send their children to a place like the Institute, which was—and remains to this day—a school designed to produce a professional managerial class in São Paulo that maintains a deep cultural and economic attachment to Italy. Indeed, there is no doubt that the Institute's unique amalgamation of Italian cultural nationalism and de facto racial exclusivity contributed to Reale's developing a commitment to fascism and other strains of political conservatism.

By taking as its central objects the political essays and autobiography of Reale, this chapter explores the affinities between the New World Italian discourse and the competing versions of *italianità* championed by liberal and fascist Italy. I show how Reale's autobiography, written decades after the period of Italian mass migration, illustrates the success of the practice identified by historian Mark Choate as "emigrant nationalism," that is, the state promotion of "*italianità*, a subsidized and somewhat artificial Italianism, as a portable, enduring ethnic identity for transnational emigrants." At the same time, through Reale's political essays, I trace what historian Federico Finchelstein has described as the "global connections that were essential for fascist ideology to travel (or replicate itself, so to speak) from one side of the ocean to the other."[6]

By the time Reale had embarked on his literary and political career in the 1930s, the processes of miscegenation and upward mobility had already brought about a second generation of Italians who—like Reale—identified as Brazilians. Their sense of Brazilianness, however, had been mediated by what Mitchell calls "the conservative intellectual tradition on modernization and race." Hence for Reale, "Brazil exists as a racial democracy"—so much so that Brazilian race relations "represent something of an achievement of national pride."[7] This belief lays the basis for *integralismo* (integralism), the Brazilian strain of fascism that he pioneered.

Yet that celebration of multiracialism obfuscates the true intention behind miscegenation: the elimination of a racial population in Brazil considered to be a drag on the modernizing process itself. Reale fully espoused the project of national modernization pursued by the Brazilian elite, which promoted removing the racial barrier to progress through a gradual whitening (*branqueamento*) of the Brazilian population. By the same token, Reale understood that the Italian contribution to Brazil's fledgling racial democracy should be protected and elevated. Therein lies the contradiction: on the one hand, one should integrate; on the other hand, one should preserve a privileged space for Italo-Brazilians in relation to those races considered an impediment to modernization. How could one embrace the whitening project, while, at the same time, insist on the importance of maintaining the ethnic and racial integrity of one's group? Reale almost answers this question directly in one of his earliest works, *O Estado moderno*, first published in 1935:

> One of the characteristics of integralism's organic unity is precisely that of integrating while discriminating [*integrar discriminando*]. The whole should not absorb all the parts, as in the case of totalitarianism, but integrate common values while respecting specific and exclusive values.[8]

Thus, while Reale emphasizes the importance of highlighting the heterogeneity of the Brazilian people—thus satisfying his desire for a nationalism that truly reflected Brazilian society—he also posits that not all components that make up Brazilian society are equal. On the contrary, the Italian blood that runs through the new, modern Brazilian race must remain "specific and exclusive."

As I illustrate in this chapter, the Italian cultural nationalism that has shaped Reale's emotional, social, and intellectual formation greatly informs his version of Brazilian nationalism. Such a dual sense of national loyalty emerges as a result of the New World Italian discourse, which, as we have seen, established the association of Italians with whiteness and modernity upon their arrival in Brazil. I argue that Reale weaponized the New World Italian discourse by articulating it with authoritarian political projects, namely fascism and militarism. Reale's autobiography reveals not only how laying claim to an Italian heritage in Brazil became closely associated with racialized notions of social belonging; it also discloses the results of this association—how Italianness became increasingly conflated with racial superiority. By foregrounding the Institute's role in Reale's formation and his political and literary writings, this chapter sheds light on the most conservative and racist aspects of the New World Italian discourse, demonstrating how these aspects have informed mainstream understandings of what epitomizes an Italian subject in both Brazil and Italy.

1. Forged in Italianness: The Istituto Medio Italo-Brasiliano Dante Alighieri in São Paulo

Miguel Reale was born in 1910 in São Bento de Sapucaí in the province of São Paulo to a family with Italian roots. His mother, Felicidade Chiaradia, was the daughter of Italian immigrant Miguel Chiaradia, who came to Brazil to work in the orchards in the interior of São Paulo. His father, Brás Reale, was a doctor from Naples who had served in the Italian army. Like many bourgeois status-conscious Brazilians of Italian descent, Reale's parents sent their son to study at the prestigious Istituto Medio Italo-Brasiliano Dante Alighieri in São Paulo.

The Institute opened its doors in 1913 on Alameda Jaú, about two blocks from the posh Avenida Paulista, in a building designed by the prominent Italian architect Giulio Micheli. Founded by a group of eleven Italian entrepreneurs, the school received funding from the Italian government, the privately managed Dante Alighieri Society, and the Italian elite *in loco*. It was initially managed directly by Italy's Dante Alighieri Society, which had been founded in Rome in 1889. The society's mission was to promote Italian language, literature, and culture among Italians abroad, in the hope that doing so would strengthen their links with the motherland.[9] In fact, the Dante Alighieri Society was founded the same year Italian Prime Minister Francesco Crispi passed a law safeguarding the operations of Italian schools abroad. Crispi saw these institutions as a means of "cultural and political influence and of commercial penetration."[10]

The Institute comprises part of a broader cultural imperialist project whose goal was to promulgate a specific idea of Italy as one of the great modern European nations. One should not underestimate the extent to which the existence of a school like the Institute testifies to "the [Italian nation's] desire for more political prestige as a new nation among the major European states."[11] After all, historian Mark Choate notes how "cultural expansion had always been a cornerstone for Italy's foreign policy."[12] Although Italian foreign policy in those years looked more favorably upon Argentina, "the darling of Italian emigrant colonialism," it is in Brazil that the Dante Alighieri Society managed to establish its most prodigious and longest-running school. If no such school exists in Argentina, it is not for lack of effort or interest: a similar project was undertaken in Rosario but ultimately failed.[13] The singular achievement of Italians in Brazil has to do not only with the amount of financial and social capital they had amassed locally—itself a reflection of the comparatively different class composition of Italians in São Paulo—but also with a confluence of interests among Italo-Brazilians, the native-born Brazilian upper class more broadly, and the Italian government. Chief among these was a shared desire to ensure that Italianness would become synonymous with racial, technological, and cultural amelioration.

What the Brazilian elite behind the push for subsidized migration had not foreseen was that with Italian labor came Italian ideas *about* labor. São Paulo's labor movement was, in fact, very much a transnational Italian product, one animated largely by anarchism and other radical traditions. As historian George Reid Andrews points out, the mainstream media in Brazil tended to associate subversive ideas with racialized laboring populations.[14] Thus, Italians who had been hailed as purveyors of progress could, in the same breath, be relegated to the category of the lumpenproletariat alongside Black Brazilians and other racial undesirables. Because it had poured considerable sums into the Italian immigration fund, São Paulo's ruling class had a material interest in counteracting this turn of events it. Hence, it makes sense that Brazilian elites joined forces with the Italian government to establish the Institute. For their part, upwardly mobile Italo-Brazilians, in addition to cementing further their privileged place in the city's cultural and economic establishment, could, by way of investing in the school, imagine themselves as key participants in the transnational creation of a great state power.

The origins of the school can be traced back to 1903, when São Paulo's Consul General Gherardo Pio di Savoia wrote in a memo the need for a school to educate the children of the Italian entrepreneurial class. An Italian secondary school for this class of Italians, he reasoned, would surely prove to be *un ottimo affare*, "a great deal."[15] Despite initial objections from members of the Dante Alighieri Society and Italians in São Paulo, who argued that such a school would not serve the entirety of the Italo-Brazilian community, Pio di Savoia's idea gradually began to take root. The most pressing issue concerned money. It would take three years of back-and-forth between the various stakeholders before the budgeted £500,000 was attained.

The first major contribution came in 1906, when the Dante Alighieri Society committed £20,000 to the creation of an institution of secondary learning, which would train teachers of Italian and permit students to access a Brazilian baccalaureate. Later, with this commitment in hand, Rodolfo Crespi, an Italian immigrant who made his fortune in São Paulo's textile industry, began collecting money from a group of noteworthy Italians in Brazil. By 1908, thanks to his large and wealthy circle of friends, Crespi had collected £200,000.[16] Finally, Bonaldo Stringher, then-president of the Banca Generale d'Italia and vice president of the Dante Alighieri Society, persuaded Italy's Minister of Foreign Affairs Tommaso Tittoni to approve the allocation of £300,000 for the creation of a private institute of secondary education in São Paulo. This investment was to be disbursed in three installments directly from the treasury of the Commissariato Generale dell'Emigrazione, which had been established in 1901 to support Italy's impoverished emigrants.[17] Ironically, the Commissariato ended up using money earmarked for citizens languishing under adverse conditions abroad to fund one of São Paulo's most elite schools.

Not long after its inauguration, the Institute earned a reputation as one of the most esteemed schools in the city. Consequently, it became responsible for educating generations of children belonging to middle- and upper-class families, such as the sons of industrial magnates, entrepreneurs, lawyers, doctors, and landowners from all over the State of São Paulo.[18] As it turned out, an Italian education provided practical benefits for both Italians and non-Italians alike. Since Italian was the only official language spoken in the school, and since the subjects closely resembled those found in Italian educational institutions, a diploma from the Institute allowed students, including those not descended from Italian nationals, to study in Italian universities, giving them access to what was, at the time, an extremely coveted European education.[19] Indeed, the fact that Brazilians of all stripes aspired to send their children to a school where, for decades, Portuguese counted as a foreign language is a profound testament to the success of Italian cultural imperialism in São Paulo and the extent to which Italians have functioned as the principal vectors of whiteness in Brazil.

Between 1913 and 1937—the year that marks the prohibition of obligatory schooling in a language other than Portuguese—an entire generation of children born to a rising upper middle class had received what was, for all intents and purposes, an Italian education. This generation would go on to reshape the political and cultural elite of the State of São Paulo. The elite saw, in the Institute's mission of preserving and bestowing Italianness through education, a possibility to redeem and solidify their own professed racial superiority. By gaining exclusive access to what they understood as a modern European institution of upper-class social reproduction, they would succeed in distancing themselves even further from the stigma of Africanness commonly associated with Southern Italians in Italy, as well as the Brazilian masses.

After 1923, the Istituto Medio Dante Alighieri became increasingly fascist despite the fact that some faculty members held views that were distinctly opposed to the regime.[20] But that mattered little since the school's tendency to identify italianità with fascism reflected the interests of its leadership, as well as broader trends in Italian public discourse. For example, President Rodolfo Crespi, who, as noted earlier, was also a primary donor and cofounder, welcomed the introduction of fascist ideas and their proponents at the Institute. Under his stewardship, several distinguished guests visited the school, including Italian dramatist, novelist, and poet Luigi Pirandello and Italian Minister Italo Balbo. In fact, Crespi was such a staunch supporter of Mussolini that he listed the leader as a beneficiary in his will. Other major industrialists of São Paulo, such as magnate Francesco Matarazzo, as well as the Italo-Brazilian petite bourgeoisie also openly supported fascism. Historians disagree, however, on whether they chose to do so primarily out of sincere ideological commitment or political expediency. On the one hand, historian Angelo Trento insists that the adherence to fascism among these classes was motivated by "deep conviction, which pushed everybody to embrace the cause with enthusiasm . . . as the continuous and generous donations in favor of the regime's organizations suggested." On the other hand, historian João Bertonha implies that the relationship between the well-to-do and fascism was primarily a marriage of convenience, rooted in the material interests of the Italian upper class.[21]

The situation at the school reveals how easily a preexisting Italian cultural nationalism was adapted to fit the needs of Mussolini's burgeoning fascist regime. To be sure, as historian Phillip Cannistraro writes of this period, "Italians were to be made to feel that they were a vigorous, industrious people, filled with pride in being Italians—not in being fascists."[22] But where did such cultural nationalism end and fascism begin? Insofar as both tended to celebrate narrowly circumscribed identities and hierarchies of political belonging, the discourses of Italian cultural nationalism and fascism dovetailed quite nicely. Historian Tamara van Kessel confirms as much when she writes: "there appears to have been a gradual process of ideological convergence between the Italian fascist ideals and those of the Dante Alighieri Society, both of which were infused with nationalist sentiment." Given its fundamentally conservative remit, it comes as no surprise that "the Dante Alighieri Society decided to support Mussolini's government in its imperial ambitions and to emphasize the broader mission of spreading Italian culture across the world."[23]

It is in this academic atmosphere, steeped in Italian fascist politics, that Miguel Reale—who later cofounded with Brazilian politician and writer Plínio Salgado the fascist-inspired party Ação Integralista Brasileira, or Brazilian Integralist Action (AIB), at only twenty-two years of age—began his intellectual apprenticeship. Reale's intellectual formation at the exclusive Istituto Medio Italo-Brasiliano Dante Alighieri would shape his political views in profound and consequential ways.

2. *Transatlantic Exchanges: From Fascism to Integralism*

In 1931, Serafino Mazzolini, while serving as Italy's consul in São Paulo, had already communicated with Rome about the emergence of a new local fascist movement, the AIB. Historian Gianni Rossi highlights how "Mazzolini had an original idea and was able to make it win and win with it: give to the particularistic Paulista current the total support of the Italian masses." In fact, in 1932, the Paulista elites, infuriated at the loss of political and economic power after the military coup of 1930, which put an end to the Old Republic and installed *gaúcho* Getúlio Vargas as president of Brazil, attempted to secede from the Federal Republic of Brazil (known as Constitutionalist Revolution). Historian Barbara Weinstein argues that, during these uprisings, Italians became part of the Paulista imaginary through a careful renegotiation of their role in the political life of the city and the state. And, indeed, it should come as no surprise that the Italian Ministry of Foreign Affairs entertained the idea of supporting the São Paulo separatists on the grounds that the majority of them were of Italian descent. Fascist support for the Constitutional Revolution raised some concerns among foreign governments, particularly the United Kingdom, because they feared the possibility of a fascist military alliance between Italy and the State of São Paulo.[24]

Around the same time, Italy launched an intense fascist propaganda campaign in the Brazilian press. This was not the first effort on the part of Rome to reach the numerous Italian communities of São Paulo. One of the major channels through which this had taken place prior to 1931 was the *fasci italiani all'estero* (Italian Fascist Abroad), political and cultural associations that operated as the proxy for the Partito Nazionale Fascista, or Italian National Fascist Party (PNF), overseas. While, during the first years of the regime, the fasci all'estero carried out violent actions like the ones employed by fascist militias, in the 1930s they focused their energies primarily on conquering the cultural and social worlds of Italians living abroad. According to historian Emilio Gentile, the fasci all'estero aimed to: "claim a monopoly abroad for the fascist organization as the sole representative of *italianità*; encourage, with massive propaganda, the sense of Italian identity among Italian citizens and descendants abroad; [and] create public opinion favorable to fascism by encouraging the celebration of Italy's past and forwarding fascist ideology and the regime as expressions of a renewed Italian glory." Foreign countries tolerated their existence because the fasci all'estero were supposedly prohibited from interfering with the politics of their host countries.[25]

Although the fasci all'estero were more numerous in Brazil than in other Latin American countries—seventy-five fasci existed in Brazil, thirty-two of which were concentrated in the state of São Paulo—the total membership was "derisory" if compared to the hundreds of thousands of people of Italian descent living in Brazil.[26] In fact, Bertonha observes that a larger number of Italians participated in activities that were not restricted to members of particular fasci. This shows, then, the success of these fasci in becoming repositories of italianità. It was precisely through their cultural activities that they penetrated the Italian community, where many, their qualms with fascism as a political philosophy notwithstanding, proved willing to enjoy events organized or sponsored by the PNF.

To reinforce the cultural apparatus of the fasci all'estero, the fascist regime implemented abroad the *Opera Nazionale Dopolavoro* (the National Afterwork Club), a social policy that, largely inspired by Fordist rationalization of the workforce, aimed to colonize the free time of Italians. The dopolavoro social club was extremely successful, especially in São Paulo, where, in 1935, it counted more than 7,000 members, far exceeding the numbers officially affiliated with the fasci. Bertonha explains that in Brazil, the dopolavoro "had a deep impact, indoctrinating thousands of people, attracting several tens of thousands to their cultural, recreational and welfare activities, assuming a clear political function, in the sense that . . . [they] influenced in a pro-Italian and pro-fascist way the masses of immigrants."[27] The broader success of the dopolavoro's subtler propaganda further reinforces the idea that the fascist regime was able to penetrate the lives of the Italian communities abroad and in São Paulo specifically by cornering the market in leisure activities.

The increased interest of the fascist government in extending its influence to Brazil also reflects the growing imperialistic tendencies of the Duce, who viewed the creation of "a great bloc of Latin and fascist nations attached to Rome" as the way to dismantle US hegemony in the region.[28] The Italian invasion of Ethiopia in 1935 provided yet another incentive to circulate pro-Italy articles and photos. In Brazil, the PNF directly controlled the União Journalística Brasileira (Journalistic Brazilian Union), through whose channels the party spread pro-Italian articles in numerous Brazilian newspapers. At the helm of the fascist-controlled Journalistic Brazilian Union was none other than Italo-Brazilian modernist Menotti del Picchia. As Angelo Trento writes, "the African campaign marks the apex of the consensus amongst the Italian community [in Brazil] which mobilized itself with large demonstrations, gold collection, [and] the boycott of goods coming from the country who sanctioned Italy's invasion, shipping of goods, and volunteers."[29] Bertonha remarks that although "the Abyssinian War seemed to have changed the good image of fascism in countries . . . like France, the UK, and the USA . . . in Brazil . . . [the war] did not have a negative impact on the fascist image."[30] On the contrary, the massive presence of fascist propaganda in Brazil led not only to the normalization of extreme right-wing political discourse but also widespread support for fascist criminality and violence.

Indeed, the fascist party encountered few obstacles when it came to spreading its ideology in Brazil not least because it enjoyed the sympathies of the newly elected President Getúlio Vargas, whom the PNF saw as "a great player." Additionally, the fascists had monitored closely the emergence of the integralist movement and quickly discerned that its actions "were inspired by distinct sympathy for fascism." Ironically, as if to demonstrate its fealty to power over ideological purity, the fascist party expressed a preference for Getúlio Vargas over his opponent Plínio Salgado, head of the AIB, because the latter supposedly lacked "combat spirit."[31] Tellingly, in 1937, when Vargas instituted a state of emergency based on false documents about a possible Communist coup (manufactured by the integralists themselves) and banned all political parties, Rome promptly sided with Vargas.[32] Salgado and Reale first attempted to overthrow Vargas but after they failed, they both had to go in into temporary exile, the former to Portugal and the latter to Italy. From the standpoint of fascist Italy, Vargas's Brazil was the key to upending the entire South American democratic system.

While the AIB lasted a mere five years, the party's existence changed the face of right-wing politics. One might even go so far as to say that the AIB fundamentally altered the way of doing politics more broadly in Brazil. After all, it was Brazil's first mass political party with a national base. Hélgio Trindade, in his study *Integralismo: O Fascismo brasileiro na década de 30* (Integralism: Brazilian Fascism in the 1930s), provides a clear picture of the origin, formation, and ideology of the AIB:

> Integralism is a fascist movement because of the social composition of its adherents; the motivations of its militants; the type of organization of the movement; the explicit content of [its] ideological discourse; the ideological attitudes of its adherents; [and] finally, the movement's expression of solidarity with the fascist international.[33]

Trindade's findings show that, while integralism as such cannot be explained without the rise of Italian fascism, its popularity did not depend on the fact that it appealed to Italian migrants. Rather, most Italian-born residents of Brazil did not align themselves with the AIB but remained faithful to the vision of italianità promoted by the fascist spokesmen in their respective cities.

To be sure, a third fascist-inspired movement also animated the political life of São Paulo in the 1930s. The rise of the AIB is coterminous with the emergence of the *Frente Negra Brasileira* or Black Brazilian Front (FNB). The FNB was founded in São Paulo in 1931 by Arlindo Veiga dos Santos, a lawyer from Bahia with a Jesuit education who espoused reactionary political theories and was one of the leaders of *Patria Nova*, a party that advocated for a return to monarchical order.[34] The FNB was a nationalistic and xenophobic party that promised to uplift the Black working class. Its promises to its members mirrored those of the AIB, so much so that, as historian Jessica Lynn Graham has shown, the two movements openly supported each other.[35] In fact, Andrews finds that both movements "shared a contemptuous disdain for liberal democracy [and] despite their rejection of foreign political philosophies, an open admiration for European Fascism." The FNB even adopted the integralist motto "for family, for country, and for God," adding "for race." Such mutual admiration stemmed not only from what historian Sandra Deutsch calls AIB's "racial tolerance" but also from their shared nationalist ideology.[36] In other words, members of both the FNB and the AIB saw themselves as quintessentially Brazilian and respected each other's claims to civic and racial nationalism. Both groups regarded actively contributing to the modernization of São Paulo—a process that, in the popular imagination, Italian immigrants had monopolized—as the hallmark of national belonging.

And just as Black Brazilians were the primary constituency of the FNB, the AIB's base comprised first- and second-generation Italians like Reale, who sought to assert their identity as Brazilians without shedding or downplaying their ethnicity. It is no coincidence that Reale was one of the principal architects of the organization. Current scholarship on the AIB tends to focus on the party's figurehead, Plínio Salgado. By doing so, it overlooks the fact that Reale—a graduate of the Istituto Medio Italo-Brasiliano Dante Alighieri and a man thoroughly conversant in the New World Italian discourse—penned most of the ideological work behind integralismo, collected in his first book *Estado moderno*. Reale's contemporaries, by contrast, gratefully acknowledged his contributions. For instance, fascist Brazilian commentator Enrico Menzinger, who was tasked with reconnoitering the world of integralism by Italian Foreign Minister Galeazzo Ciano, touted Reale over Salgado as the creative force behind the AIB, praising his crucial contributions to the "development of Fascist propaganda in the bosom of his party."[37] When Italian Ambassador to Rio de Janeiro Roberto Cantalupo wrote an enthusiastic memo to Rome about "the widespread italophilia that permeated some of the integralist leaders, who openly flaunted their admiration for Rome," he almost certainly had Reale in mind.[38]

3. Integrating While Discriminating: O Estado moderno *(1934)*

In addition to children of Italian immigrants, the AIB also appealed to the white-collar middle class that had been left out of elite political circles and longed for political representation. In his 1934 essay collection *O Estado moderno*, Reale places the middle class at the center of his professed integralist revolution. Such centrality is, in turn, reflected in the hierarchical society he envisions for the integralist state, in which white-collar professionals sit at the top. In the AIB's social theory, the middle class is further subdivided into two separate branches: the petite bourgeoisie or small business owners that can achieve success only at the local level, and the professionals—namely doctors, lawyers, intellectuals, and professors—who govern at the national level. The working class, according to Reale, needs the guidance of the middle class and has no way of accessing the higher strata of the social pyramid. This, in turn, means that it is the responsibility of the middle class to "integrating while discriminating."

Reale's notion of "integrating while discriminating" reveals the lie constructed by the ideology that would eventually become known as Brazilian racial democracy, insofar as differences between groups are rigorously maintained and constitute the defining characteristic of the integralist state. Reale believed that "there are in society, besides professional groups, biological, cultural, ethical and religious groups," and he made perfectly clear that these groups did not exist on the same level.[39] This raises the following question: What is the process whereby one decides whom to integrate and, conversely, discriminate against? Here, his broader political project comes to the fore. In fact, a constant concern in Reale's fascist theories—both the one he articulated in 1934 on behalf of the integralist movement and the one he later espoused in defense of the 1964 military coup d'état—was how to reconcile the supposedly revolutionary nature of fascism, on the one hand, and its preservation of the status quo on the other.

Political theorist Marilena Chauí identifies the Brazilian middle class as the audience of this integralist message. This was akin to the situation in Italy, where the middle class also played a crucial role in propping up Mussolini's fascist regime.[40] Both fascism and integralism can be understood, then, largely as middle-class movements performing what literary scholar

Barbara Spackman called a "re-semanticization" of the language of the revolution made popular by the rise of socialist organizations on both sides of the Atlantic.[41] Yet the large presence of the middle class raises some questions as to the presumed revolutionary nature of the movement. The middle class, according to Chauí, is not simply a conservative class; it is "viscerally reactionary."[42] What these constituencies desired was not the overthrow of the existing social order but greater incorporation into it.

Reale's decision to place what social critics Barbara and John Ehrenreich have called "the professional managerial class" or PMC at the center of his revolutionary project shows the degree to which he had internalized and fulfilled the intellectual project of the Institute.[43] His abiding concern for the preservation of the status quo directly mirrors the anxieties about racial and economic superiority that the Italian elite sought to mediate through the school. Reale weaponizes these anxieties by envisioning a state structure in which the professional managerial class produced by places like the Institute would ultimately control who can access "the institutional means of power."[44]

Reale's claim that his "intellectual formation . . . profited from the selected library of the Dante Institute" becomes clear when we turn again to *O Estado moderno*. For example, Reale's belief in the role of the PMC as harbingers of revolutionary change is clearly indebted to Italian economist Vilfredo Pareto's theory of the circulation of elites. The equilibrium of society, according to Pareto, depends upon the velocity with which each nongoverning elite in the higher stratum of society supplants the governing elite. According to Pareto's theory, the circulation of elites happens as a continuous restoration of power: that is, carefully selected individuals from the non-elite who have either a particular "label" or "wealth" will become part of the higher stratum.[45]

But there is a catch: in such a society, social mobility is unlikely to happen, because the ultimate goal of this selected integration is to maintain the power of the elite. Pareto explains that when a revolution is on the horizon, "the members of the lower strata are captained by leaders from the higher strata, because the latter possess the intellectual qualities required for outlining a tactic while lacking the combative tendencies supplied by individuals from the lower strata." Pareto lays the foundation for Reale to envision the marriage between the PMC and what Italian intellectual Giovanni Gentile calls "revolutionary will," namely, that it is the middle class that has the intellectual skills needed to shape the working class's revolutionary desires.[46]

In reading Pareto, Reale not only discovers a way to reconcile the revolutionary nature of integralism with its middle-class—and, hence, inherently conservative—base. He also hits upon a means of maintaining the cohesiveness of the Italian community in São Paulo more broadly, a community riven with class divisions to the degree that, as one political scientist notes, "labor struggles in São Paulo were but an Italian affair."[47] In this way, Italians were a synecdoche and an index of the class conflict in Brazil. Here, it seems, the Italian working class of São Paulo and their revolutionary desires would find capable spokespersons in the Italian PMC trained at the Institute, and, even more concretely, in the AIB. Viewed from this angle, any intraethnic tensions within the Italo-Brazilian community could be transcended, and, by the same token, so too could the class struggle.

Reale's conception of an organic unity that reflected integralism's central imperative of "integrating while discriminating" would ultimately resolve two of his personal struggles. On the one hand, it would allow him to homogenize the Italian community in São Paulo by annihilating class divisions. Under these circumstances, the Italian identity cultivated at the Institute would become hegemonic, normative, and uncontested. On the other hand, as I will explore in the next sections, the idea of "integrating while discriminating" allows Reale to negotiate a compromise between his desire to lay claim to Brazilian nationalism and maintain his commitment to notions of Italian racial and cultural superiority inculcated in him at the Institute. Through integralismo, Reale imagines a way to foreclose the processes of miscegenation and assimilation that, however tentatively and ambivalently, had once seemed axiomatic to the discourse of Italian racial, economic, and cultural superiority in São Paulo. In their place, he inserts a process of discrimination, which allows the New World Italian discourse to continue to generate meaning for Brazilian-born children of upwardly mobile Italian immigrants.

4. *A Middle-Class Revolution:* Imperativos da Revolução de Março *(1964)*

The integralist revolution Reale had originally hoped for and theorized in *O Estado moderno* never materialized. Nonetheless, his moment to take the lead as the intellectual spokesperson of a middle class "revolution" finally occurred with the 1964 military coup d'état in Brazil. Deutsch frames the events of 1964 as a legacy of the integralist movement, and, indeed, the military coup was supported by several of the most prominent integralist figures, including Reale and General Olympio Mourão Filho. Moreover, Plinio Salgado, *chefe* of the AIB, had returned from his exile to form a new party, the Popular Representation Party (PRP), whose "philosophy resembled that of the AIB, although it claimed to support democracy." Historian Odilon Caldeira Neto argues that it is precisely through the PRP that integralism had survived during the democratic period, and that, although integralism had been pushed to the margins, "it could come back in full force with the political currents in support of the military coup of 1964."[48]

As the coup d'état took place, in fact, Miguel Reale—who had likewise long since returned from his Italian exile and become secretary of justice of the State of São Paulo—broadcast a speech on the radio in support of the generals. The military's actions, he said, were democratic and revolutionary. The pieces in the collection *Imperativos da Revolução de Março* (Imperatives of the March Revolution) are for the most part lectures and interviews given in the immediate aftermath of the military takeover. This small book, published by Paulistano publisher Livraria Martins Editora, is currently out of print. The copies circulating in São Paulo are for library use only; some rare copies are available through the secondhand bookstore network. That this extremely controversial set of essays ended up becoming so rare might seem to have benefited Reale's political career. Yet he did not distance himself from these views. In fact, Reale himself includes one of these essays, *Diretrizes Fundamentais* (Fundamental Guidelines), in the appendix of the second volume of his autobiography.

Reale was one of the leading theorists and defenders of the military coup, which he insisted on casting as a revolution. Reale's essays helped create an intellectual discourse regarding the events of 1964 that shaped public opinion at the time. These essays, in fact, simultaneously legitimize the coup and call for an intelligentsia capable of interpreting society in a manner that suited the new constitutional order. According to Reale, the "revolution" was, paradoxically, impulsive *and* calculated, of the people *and* of the governors, democratic *and* militarist. To make his case, Reale drew liberally on the definition of "revolution" detailed by Giovanni Gentile. Just as Gentile understood the fascist takeover as the rightful fulfillment of Giuseppe Mazzini's revolutionary project, Reale interpreted the military coup d'état as "the ultimate phase . . . of a revolutionary process that began to uncoil in the distant year of 1932," the year of the founding of the AIB.[49] Working to legalize the Brazilian coup d'état, then, Reale turned to the works of the Italian philosopher that provided an intellectual framework for Italian fascism. And Reale's familiarity with this conservative tradition of italianità undoubtedly came from his time at the Institute.

Revolution, according to Reale, refers to two different types of events: one actualizes an idea, while the second refers to people's impulses waiting to be crystallized into *concepts*. Referring to the 1964 coup, Reale writes, "[this revolution] contains a governing principle within it, *em germem*, and without the conceptual determination of this governing principle the revolutionary fact ideally would not legitimize itself." Calling it a revolution that expressed the will of the people and their amorphous impulses seemed effective; however, these impulses needed to be shaped into concepts and ideas by figures like Reale himself, figures he refers to as "mentors, men that sensed the moment, alerting the nation" ex post facto. Not only were such men more attuned to the general morale of society, but they were also men entrusted with the *tarefa renovadora* (the task of renewal), since "there isn't a revolution without revolutionaries."[50] Similarly, Gentile argues that an idea is always behind a revolution, which is in keeping with his belief in the simultaneity of thought and action. By contrast, according to Gentile, a revolution without an idea is a negative revolution. Here, the prime example was the Bolshevik Revolution. The idea, which Gentile defined as a "soul that destroys to create," must be transformed into a person, "in one or more determined willpowers that follow determined purposes." Much like Gentile, who, referring both to the Risorgimento and fascism, asserts that a handful of men should be the interpreters of the "revolutionary will," Reale identifies the revolutionaries as men that instantiate the idea of the revolution.[51]

In both Gentile and Reale, the "revolutionary will," which should supposedly bring about a new state, created the conditions under which authoritarian systems of governance could thrive. The first Institutional Act (AI-1), approved on April 9, 1964, by the military junta (called the Comando Supremo da Revolução, or Supreme Command of the Revolution), established indirect presidential elections while brutally suspending the political rights of anybody who was identified as an enemy of the regime. For Reale, the first Institutional Act—not numbered because it was intended to be the only such act—represents the institutionalization of the revolution's true intentions and ideas: "The Institutional Act was, despite indisputable lacunas, the right path found by the revolution. Until this legal decree had been promulgated, the revolution remained suspended and risked witnessing the destruction of its ideas."[52] By imposing political disenfranchisement (*cassações*) on dissidents opposed to the politics implemented by the regime and the military police inquiries (IPM or *inquéritos*), the Institutional Act proved fundamental in helping the military regime execute two main objectives. First, it destroyed the political and intellectual reformist elite who, in years prior, had become something of power bloc. Second, it severed any existing connections between the political and intellectual elite and the popular social movements of the workers and the peasants. In 1968, through the ratification of Institutional Act 5 (AI-5), the Brazilian military government took away the right of habeas corpus, thus actively legitimizing disappearance as a form of political repression. In his 1987 autobiography, Reale says of General Costa e Silva, who signed the AI-5: "he showed uncommon energy and decisiveness . . . so much so that he converted what could have been another coup d'état of a Latin American kind into an authentic revolutionary act." In other words, well after 1964 and the end of the Brazilian military dictatorship, Reale continued to refer to the military coup d'état as a revolution, attributing its success to Costa e Silva. Here again one finds in Reale's apologia echoes of Gentile, who credited Mussolini with fulfilling a revolution that legitimized itself by virtue of its basis in an idea, willpower, and a leader.[53]

Reale's reliance on Italian thinkers and philosophers to find justifications for and make sense of events that occurred in his own Brazilian context clearly derives from his Italian intellectual formation at the Institute, which would have instilled in him a belief in the superiority of Italian culture. Yet when he switches from a polemical style of writing to a more self-consciously literary one, as he does in his autobiography, that superiority is displayed not only by way of his familiarity with Italian political thought. In his *Memórias*, Reale also reveals his intellectual pedigree by adopting a literary persona that evokes classical Italian poetry.

5. An Italian Apologia for Brazilian Fascism: Memórias I & II *(1987)*

In the years Reale composed his autobiography, a spate of testimonial novels by political exiles who had returned to Brazil after the Amnesty Law of 1979—mere "terrorists" according to Reale—had begun to appear in the Brazilian press.[54] Two of the most famous examples of the testimonial literary boom post-amnesty are Fernando Gabeira *O que é isso, companheiro?* (What is this, comrade?) published in 1979 and adapted to film in 1997; and Alfredo Sirkis's *Os Carbonarios* (The Carbonari) published in 1980.[55] Reale clearly wrote his *Memórias* (Memories) with these works in mind. He sought to give voice to the other side of this battle for memory.[56] Reale intended for *Memórias* to be read as an intellectual biography as much as a work of popular literature. This is evidenced partly by the fact that he published it with the well-known Saraiva Press, all but ensuring that it would be marketed to a wide range of readers. His approach also ensured that, amid the repudiation of military action and the celebration of the fight for democracy, including the armed struggle, another kind of revisionist memory would remain part of public discourse. This "restored truth," based on Reale's reappropriation of the ideas of Italian fascist Giovanni Gentile, forcefully averred that the military coup d'état was a democratic revolution.

Reale's involvement in fascist politics—first, with the Ação Integralista Brasileira, and, later, with the military dictatorship—deeply marks the pages of his *Memórias*. Far from showing any regret for his youthful embrace of fascism, Reale uses the pages of his autobiography to exalt his political crusades. Consider, for example, his recollection of his 1938 trip to Italy:

> Italy was living ambiguous moments that would have turned into tragedy not much later. . . . It was easy for me to understand that the Italians did not want war, and especially not a war alongside Nazi Germany, whose orders Mussolini had to obey because of the isolation to which he was condemned by democratic nations. . . . I perceived him as the victim of sclerosis and of corruption, which are the fatal sicknesses of authoritarian regimes of long duration, since they grew more distant from the popular forces that had originally inspired them, a time in which the belief in a *terza via* prevailed, represented by Fascism, [a force] capable of overcoming the disorder in which the Liberal Democracy had drowned and of avoiding the menacing Stalinist oppression.[57]

Exiled from Brazil due to his unwelcome activities with the AIB, Reale originally went to Italy with the hope that Mussolini and the PNF would assist him in his efforts to revive his brainchild. He held the Duce in great esteem, referring to him as a genius. Unencumbered by an Italian society intent on forgetting twenty years of fascist rule as a mere peccadillo, Reale demonstrates in his 1987 autobiography—contrary to what some historians believe—that the propagation of fascist ideas outside of Europe did indeed generate prolific and long-lasting results.[58] Reale's mission was unsuccessful; the situation in Italy proved to be quite different from what he had read and studied at the Istituto Medio Dante Alighieri. Mussolini, in the words of Reale, had become the prey of democratic nations, a victim of the corruption that, to hear him tell it, characterizes all long-term authoritarian regimes. Despite his disappointment, Reale, as late as 1987, long after integralism had disappeared as a political force, continued to laud the capabilities of fascism as a third way: that is, as a method of solving the supposedly irremediable conundrums of socialism and liberalism. Such a long-standing, unwavering faith in fascism hearkens back to Reale's indoctrination at the Institute. The school and its nationalist and later fascist ideology left such a mark on him that in a 1965 essay for a collection dedicated to the 700 years since Dante's birth organized by São Paulo-based Italianist Edoardo Bizzarri, he claims not only that his experiences at the Institute were a "decisive factor in [his] life," but that his encounter with the works of Dante, mediated through the school, shaped his political views. Reale writes that Dante provided him with a model of the "life motto that I ambitiously traced in the preface of my first book, *O Estado moderno*, that is to theorize life and to live theory in an indissoluble unity of thought and action."[59] Reale is tracing here a direct link between his integralist doctrine and Dante Alighieri's political passion, as he calls it. He applies ideas and figures stemming from his Italian heritage and schooling to his particular brand of fascism, revealing how the New World Italian discourse could be weaponized to advance particularly virulent strains of right-wing extremism.

Reale's *Memórias* is belletristic, almost romantic, and emphasizes the individual's life and point of view; yet its content revolves as much around major political events as it does quotidian experience. This tension between style and content creates something more than a traditional autobiography. If autobiography is typically conceived of as a "retrospective prose narrative written by a real person concerning his or her own existence, where the focus is his individual life," then Reale's is a mixed form—part apologia, part narrative history—that never fails to convey a clear sense of self-awareness and tendentiousness.[60] Reale undoubtedly has an audience in mind. In fact, he often resorts to direct address—using the formula *meu caro leitor* (my dear reader)—when dealing with more delicate or controversial subjects, such as the prominent role played by civil society in the coup. The use of the possessive *meu* points to Reale's own insecurity and his need to importune the reader through acts of interpellation, making the reader complicit in his transgressions against democracy. In other instances, Reale's defensiveness is even more palpable, such as when he punctuates his sympathetic account of the military regime with references to his *malicioso* (malicious) readers. In such instances, Reale seems determined to forestall attempts on the part of suspicious readers to scour his autobiography for incriminating evidence.

Although he often engages the reader, Reale does not entertain the possibility of a dialectical, intersubjective exchange with those readers who may oppose his interpretations. Instead, he attempts to frame his recollections and political views as axiomatic by consistently prefacing them with the phrase *ninguém poderá negar* (nobody will be able to deny). This construction only serves to underscore the authoritarian contours of his ideology. Likewise, Reale's prose often affects an overbearing, stentorian tone, which gives the reader the sense of having an ideology foisted on her. This effect is amplified by the autobiographical form itself, which, in Reale's hands, is stridently monological.

While Reale might not have been eager to engage in a constructive dialogue with his less than sympathetic interlocutors in the Brazilian public sphere, he did seek to put himself in conversation with the world of italianità. On top of that, Reale's autobiography is riddled with Italian colloquial expressions and citations of Italian poets. Why does a book that surveys almost a century of Brazilian political history rely so heavily on Italian expressive culture? The answer lies as much in Reale's personal history as it does in the peculiar significance of Italianness in São Paulo. Reale sees his heritage and his education as weapons with which he can deflect criticisms of his fascist past and recast himself as a paradigmatic exponent of that illustrious group that Lombroso Ferrero had depicted as the true colonizers of Brazil.

From the very first pages of the *Memórias*, Reale dedicates lengthy passages to descriptions of his familial pedigree. The purpose of this family history—which covers two chapters—is to show that he was destined to become a jurist. His paternal grandfather, although a doctor, had originally started out studying jurisprudence at the Università Orientale of Naples: "My paternal grandfather, Alfonso Reale, was a doctor and he became a doctor because of love. He had originally started, with success, his studies in Jurisprudence at the University of Naples, following his real vocation. . . . As you can see, the juridical vocation is an old one in my family, despite it being subjected to obstacles and stumbles." His maternal grandfather, on the other hand, was a farmer from Basilicata, who came to Brazil with the hope of finding better economic opportunities: "At twenty years of age, he decided to come to Brazil and tried to live life alongside his brothers. . . . It is clear that, beyond the desire to be with his brothers, what moved him was his entrepreneurial and adventurous spirit." It should not surprise that Reale's grandfather, Michele Chiaradia, "turned out to be the most successful amongst the brothers," and "integrated himself completely to Brazilian life."[61]

These thirty, highly detailed pages of family history depict an idyllic Italian upbringing that perpetuates the myth of the self-made immigrant: the Italian laborer who, by the force of his own will, can achieve great success. Reale also wants his readers to view him as an "exemplary" product of the policies of racial whitening introduced at the turn of the century. Although his family might hail from Southern Italy, which historically conjured images of underdevelopment and miscegenation, Reale can confidently invoke an Italian heritage that not only elides such embarrassing distinctions between Northern and Southern Italy but also offers the best of both worlds. On the one hand, he had grown up in an Italian upper-middle-class family; on the other hand, the rustic roots of his forbears made him a symbol of those industrious Italians who became so central to the rhetoric and iconography of fascist propaganda.

Reale's experience at the Institute occupies a chapter of its own, aptly called "Sob o signo da Dante" (Under the Auspices of the Institute Dante Alighieri).[62] Reale informs us that, during his time there, he grasped the power of education as a means of propaganda and complains that "the preoccupation with italianità was suffocating, it being clear that the desire to transmit the peninsular tradition to the descendants of immigrants was more because of a demand from above, in accordance with the Mussolinian style." But, its "suffocating" nature notwithstanding, the italianità championed by the Institute nonetheless left an indelible mark on Reale's intellectual formation, since, as we saw earlier, it gave him a series of models through which he could understand his own Brazilian reality.[63] While Reale clearly regards himself as a Brazilian nationalist, he is obsessed with asserting his Italian lineage. Indeed, Reale himself attributes his fascist entanglements to his Italian heritage, both literal and figurative. On more than one occasion Reale claims to have modeled his affective and political perspectives along the ones espoused by Dante Alighieri, the most famous poet in the Italian language, emphasizing at once his connection to the classical Italian literary tradition and the eponymous Italo-Brazilian institution he attended at the height of its association with fascism.

However, it is more than simply modeling Dante. Reale goes as far as to compare himself to the *vate*, whose artistic work has been reinterpreted at various historical junctures according to different political agendas.[64] Mussolini, for example, recast the poet as a precursor to the fascist vanguard, a prophet able to foresee the creation of the empire.[65] By finding parallels between his own life and Dante's, Reale seeks to assert the authenticity of his intellectual and ethnic heritage. He first makes this rhetorical gesture when narrating his initial encounter with his future wife, Filomena Pucci (or Nuce), at the Institute:

> The name of the girl with braids was Filomena Pucci. . . . Still very young, I was moved by the sonnets and ballads of Dante's *La Vita Nuova*, which corresponded to my sentimental temperament . . . so filled by the image of Beatrice, I let myself be seduced by the braids I had only seen at a glance.[66]

Reale is so enchanted by the image of Beatrice after reading Dante's *Vita Nuova* that he sees her in Nuce, his future wife, who, like him, is of Italian descent. The origins of their union are thus mediated and sanctioned by Reale's identification with the world of Dante, illustrating how cultural iconography of Italianness could suffuse the most intimate aspects of social reproduction.

Later in *Memórias*, Reale chooses to identify himself with Dante at yet another pivotal moment in his life: when he collaborates with the military regime and serves as the president of the University of São Paulo. A journalist, after hearing rumors that Reale might run for the governorship of São Paulo, published an article portraying him as an opportunist, a man loyal to no one but himself. Reale writes:

> It was the work of a journalist who, naturally, could only misconstrue the situation, presenting me as a politician without scruples, [a] traitor to. . . . Plínio Salgado, Adhemar de Barros, and Getúlio Vargas. . . . In these cases I follow Dante's lesson: "*Non ti curar di loro ma guarda e passa.*"[67]

Reale quotes the popular passage from Canto III of the *Inferno* directly in Italian, which Allen Mandelbaum translates into English as "let us not talk of them but look and pass." It is not a coincidence that Reale would choose to insert this verse here, after referring to efforts to impugn his political integrity. Canto III recounts Dante's encounter with the *ignavi*: those who lived without praise and without blame, oblivious to any political or religious interests. Reale clearly wishes to absolve himself of wrongdoing, and he does so by subtly conjuring up the greater evil of the ignavo. Better to have acted at times irresponsibly or out of self-interest, he seems to suggest, than to have stood on the sidelines and risked nothing. This second invocation of Dante imputes a classical Italian justification to the political crimes Reale committed in a Brazilian context. Citing the *Inferno* represents both an aesthetic and a political appeal to (Italian) authority. When Reale's insistence on his own belonging to a particular type of Italian identity—one that symbolizes racial, cultural, and economic superiority—is considered, the integralist doctrine, particularly its emphasis on *integrar discriminando* (integrating while discriminating), makes much more sense.

With integralism, Reale managed to launch a fascist movement in a nominally democratic and predominantly Black country, while, at the same time, continuing to give primacy to his own Italian heritage. Reale used his knowledge of Italian letters and arts to affirm the superior status of Italians in Brazil. At the same time, he remained faithful to his native land, Brazil, insofar as it offered Italo-Brazilians a space to prosper and affirm their superiority. Counterintuitive as it might seem, Reale's decision to return to Brazil from Italy further emphasizes his commitment to Italianness, for it is only *outside* of Italy that such cultural nationalism can count for anything, especially in terms of political and economic power. Thus, his intervention in the New World Italian discourse instrumentalizes the putative superiority of Italians in relation to Brazil's Black and Indigenous populations but pays lip service to Brazil's racial democracy. His late twentieth-century autobiographical writings shed light on the enduring legacies of Italian cultural imperialism in Brazil while simultaneously providing powerful insight—at times unwittingly, no doubt—into the difficulty of realizing the dream of multiracial democracy.

Indeed, to some extent, the New World Italian discourse elaborated in Reale's political and literary works anticipates thorny questions surrounding citizenship in present-day Italy. For instance, the infamous 1992 Citizenship Law granted citizenship to Italian descendants outside of Italy but deliberately excluded thousands of immigrants who have lived in Italy for decades. By privileging blood lineage over residency, the Italian government has sought to fortify numerically a predominantly "white" imagined community against the incursion of Black bodies that have become all but synonymous with hyper-exploitative, unskilled immigrant labor.[68] And yet those of Italian descent who arrive from Brazil under the auspices of *jus sanguinis* challenge the implicit racial purity endorsed by the Italian citizenship law. Once in Italy, they become racialized as noncitizens and socially ostracized.[69] To the dismay of many, these "new" Italians evoke a demographic reality—one that had to contend with the existence of multiple races and lionized miscegenation, albeit at the expense of Black bodies—vastly different from the prevailing one in Italy. Such a situation reveals how blowback from transnational formations of italianità has called into question who counts as Italian. The New World Italian discourse, despite privileging a nominally white racial identity, diverges in important ways from the Italianness endorsed by the liberal, fascist, and post-fascist Italian national projects. Even in its most conservative and racist expression—exemplified here by Reale—the New World Italian discourse must contend with the impossibility of claiming absolute racial purity of the sort espoused by right-wing extremists in Italy. Not by chance, Reale's Black contemporary José Correia Leite appropriates and subverts this discourse, as we have seen, by pointing to the insurmountable contradictions it inevitably encounters in a country dominated by people of mixed African, European, and Indigenous descent.

In Chapter Five, I turn to yet another Italo-Brazilian writer, Zélia Gattai, and her best-selling memoir, *Anarquistas, graças a Deus*, which appeared in 1979, the same year Brazil's Amnesty Law went into effect. Positioned at the opposite end of the ideological spectrum from Reale, Gattai draws our attention to a constituency that the progenitors of the New World Italian discourse did their best to exclude, namely anarchists. Although critical of this discursive tradition, Gattai nonetheless chooses to reformulate it rather than, as one might expect a leftist to do, jettison it altogether. She does so by depicting a much more fragmented, poorer, and racially ambiguous Italian community than other writers discussed in this book have imagined. By turning to her, we can begin to see how New World Italians have also tried to help transform the myth of racial democracy into a reality.

FIVE

Muito parecida mas completamente diferente

Zélia Gattai, Multidirectionality, and the Italian Anarchists

After reading an early draft of what Zélia Gattai had intended to be a short story, Jorge Amado encouraged Gattai to put her memories on the page. An award-winning Brazilian author as well as Gattai's lifelong partner, Amado remembers that what most caught his attention was not the content of the short story, but the corollary information Gattai had inserted about the "life of a family of Italian immigrants (and anarchists) in São Paulo during the first quarter of the century." He advised her to "throw the short story away and to write [instead] her memories from childhood and adolescence." Amado knew that, once completed, the result "would be a unique book, a singular testimony." He was not wrong. The work she produced turned out to be the most salient literary account of Italians' everyday life in São Paulo during the 1920s and the 1930s and, moreover, achieved fame as a literary record of the city's Italian anarchists at that time. *Anarquistas, graças a Deus* (Anarchists, Thank God) catapulted Gattai to literary stardom and became the quintessential source for understanding the experiences of Italians in São Paulo.[1]

Taken together, Amado's preface, where he discusses the aforementioned circumstances of the book's creation, and the book's title indicate Gattai's twin subjects: Italians *and* anarchists. These two identities were embodied by her parents, Angelina Da Col and Ernesto Gattai, who were both politically active in the anarchist network in São Paulo. For his part, Ernesto was born into anarchism: his father, Francesco, was one of the founders of the legendary experimental socialist commune Colônia Cecília. Angelina, on the other hand, became radicalized in a factory in Brás, the same one she had worked in since she was nine years old. Gattai incorporates in her memoir numerous historical figures—such as the Italian anarchists Oreste Ristori and Angelo Bandoni—and events—such as the trial of the immigrant anarchists Nicola Sacco and Bartolomeo Vanzetti in the United States and the murder of socialist leader Giacomo Matteotti in Italy—making it an important testament to the radicalism animating the Italian community of São Paulo. As historian Angelo Trento has argued, Italian radicals "became the backbone" of São Paulo's labor movement because of the overwhelming presence of Italians among the urban immigrant working class.[2] Gattai's memoir is an ode to that network of Italian radicals concentrated in Brazil's largest metropolis.

At first glance, it may seem that the experiences recollected by Gattai directly contrast with the more conservative narratives of New World Italian discourse analyzed thus far, which reinforce Italians' cultural, racial, and economic superiority in São Paulo. However, that is not necessarily the case. I propose that *Anarquistas* recapitulates all the meanings produced by and through that discourse. The fragmented form of Gattai's memoir allows her to simultaneously represent the (ethnic) Italian experience and the anarchist one, while firmly grounding her as a Brazilian author, one that continues to be read in Brazilian schools. In fact, on multiple occasions in the memoir, Gattai points out that her own sense of belonging hinges on at least three axes of identity: one informed by the ideals of anarchism, one built upon her Italian ethnic origins, and one dependent on her Brazilian upbringing. This chapter explores how Gattai's articulation of the New World Italian discourse exists as the "interaction of different historical memories," whose multiplicity cannot be reduced to a single privative vision of Italianness.

Rather the vision created is a productive one—productive in the sense that, following historian Michael Rothberg's argument about memory's multidirectionality, the New World Italian discourse is informed by a series of dialogical interactions that continuously change its meaning.[3] Hence, this discourse can produce, simultaneously, multiple narratives about Italians in São Paulo, each unfolding in a different direction. Some depict them as settlers and agents of modernization; others portray them as professional elites and fascists; others imagine them as bumpkins and racially ambiguous; and still others paint them as working class and anarchists.

Anarquistas successfully reveals the multidirectional character of the New World Italian discourse not only by making visible the contradictions of its multiple meanings but also by resisting the temptation to transcend them. For example, Gattai's father, while certainly an anarchist, also owned a very lucrative auto shop, making him part of the Italian commercial elite discussed in Chapter Two. At the same time, Angelina, who embodies the self-educated worker, holds racist attitudes toward both Black Brazilians and Southern Italians, partially echoing the exclusionary and discriminatory dimensions of the discourse addressed in Chapters Three and Four. To put it simply, the conservative discourse about race, whiteness, and modernization that accompanied the Italian diaspora to São Paulo rears its head in *Anarquistas*, despite being in obvious tension with the book's nominal subject matter—that is, the Italian tradition of left-wing anarchism.

Gattai rejects any possible way of solving the contradictions embedded within what I have labeled New World Italian discourse. In the Italo-Brazilian lifeworld that she reconstructs, the romantic myths of the anarchists jostle with those surrounding *colonos* of Lombroso Ferrero, the commercial elites of Alcântara Machado, the Carrettas of José Correia Leite, and nationalists like Miguel Reale. In her memoir, painful stories of the Atlantic crossing clash with more glorious tales about brave settlers moving to Brazil in search of a promised land; at the same time, the utopian anarchist dream collides with her parents' bourgeois values and racialized views of the local working class. Gattai puts forward multiple narrative threads that continuously intersect, creating a tapestry that, far from evoking an undifferentiated ethnic mass, constantly seems on the verge of unraveling and, ultimately, fails to cohere.

1. Oreste Ristori, La Battaglia, *and São Paulo's Transnational Italian Anarchist Network*

Labor historians generally divide São Paulo's working class into two competing camps: one reformist, the other revolutionary. Reformers, epitomized by Italian socialists like Antonio Piccarolo, sought to organize workers and understood unions as the means by which the working class could better their material conditions. Revolutionaries were themselves divided into two subgroups: the anarchists, who believed in free association and scoffed at top-down organizing, and the anarcho-syndicalists, who saw the syndicate (that is, the union) as the ideal launching pad for what many of them saw as the only appropriate response to capitalist exploitation—the general strike.

Such divisions existed more in theory than in practice, however. Historian Isabelle Felici points out how the anarchists of São Paulo "welcomed with enthusiasm any popular movement, of any kind, as a victory of the working class, because it showed a class consciousness and solidarity that had not been there before." Moreover, Trento emphasizes that a "shared interest in migration problems helped anarchists and socialists . . . overcome the countless ideological divisions among them, and it made defense of immigrants and denunciation of abuses of immigrant workers a powerful propaganda tool."[4] To be sure, as historian Donna Gabaccia convincingly argues, the ethnic particularism that characterized the Italian transnational working class did not necessarily undermine the internationalism of its various labor movements. She draws a distinction between "ethnic" and "national" bonds and proposes that we understand solidarity within the Italian transnational working class through the lens of the former rather than the latter. Similarly, historian Marcella Bencivenni suggests that the radicalism of the *sovversivi*—literally, "subversives," a term she uses to identify various groups of Italian immigrants engaged in socialist and anarchist activism—in the United States was informed by both ethnic and class allegiances. These two aspects of São Paulo's labor movement—both its enthusiasm for class solidarity and its intense ethnic particularism—find expression in *Anarquistas.* The memoir successfully shows how both aspects shaped the everyday lives of an Italian family directly engaged with the radicalism roiling São Paulo in the first decades of the twentieth century.[5]

Among the many anarchist figures in Gattai's memoir are Oreste Ristori, Angelo Bandoni, Alessandro Cerchiai, Edgard Leuenroth, and José Oiticica—all friends of Zélia's paternal grandfather. Ristori occupies a particularly prominent role in Gattai's life and memoir. She clearly admired him most of all, not least because he served as her mentor, shaping her intellectual development. She writes of him, "he knew about literary novelties, what I should be reading, what would befit me." Not coincidentally, it was Ristori who introduced Gattai to Jorge Amado, by bringing her one of the Brazilian writer's works, "a thin volume, *Cacau*." Her encounter with the man who became her lifelong partner was thus mediated and sanctioned by one of the most active Italian anarchists in all of South America. In fact, he was like other Italian radicals, such as Angelo Badoni and Gigi Damiani, in having spent ample time in Buenos Aires and then Montevideo. In the context of *Anarquistas*, then, Ristori's life trajectory constitutes an excellent example of what historians Carlo Romani and Bruno Corrêa de Sá e Benevides have called "the transnational nature of Italian-Brazilian anarchism rooted in São Paulo" and reveals an additional aspect of the already prismatic New World Italian discourse.[6]

Ristori became radicalized at an early age while living in the Tuscan country town of Empoli during the second half of the nineteenth century. There, dissatisfied daily laborers, artisans, and small business owners joined forces and began advocating an anti-revolutionary, anti-union, and libertarian socialist politics. Ristori's first arrest took place when he was only seventeen years old. The Italian police detained him several other times and even sent him in 1895 to the infamous *domicilio coatto* in the colony of Porto Ercole, in the Argentario. He successfully escaped and wrote a long exposé on the horrific conditions of the prisoners on the island. After the riots of May 1898, Ristori was detained once again and sent to Ponza and then Ustica, where he stayed until 1901. Throughout these years of incarceration, he met other anarchists, such as Luigi Fabbri, and refined his political ideas and projects.[7]

Due to the persecution he suffered in Italy, Ristori ultimately left for Buenos Aires and joined his comrades at the newspaper *L'Avvenire*. In 1902, still newly arrived, he had become one of the most prominent leaders of Buenos Aires's first general strike, which paralyzed the city and its surroundings for a week. The government responded by promulgating the infamous Ley de Residencia, a law allowing for the deportation of foreign undesirables. Among the first ones to suffer its consequences, Ristori was arrested and put on a boat back to Italy in 1903. Nonetheless, he managed to disembark in Montevideo and elude the police. Ristori avoided repatriation two more times, the latter of which, Gattai tells us, cost him the ability to walk properly, since he broke both legs after jumping off a steamship.[8] In Montevideo, where many people deported from Buenos Aires lived, including numerous Italian anarchists, Ristori met Mercedes Gomes, who moved with him to São Paulo in 1904 and ultimately became his partner for life. In his new city, Ristori founded the anarchist weekly *La Battaglia*, which ran without interruption from 1904 to 1913 (changing its name in 1912 to *La Barricata*), publishing up to 5,000 copies a week.

The major question with which *La Battaglia* engaged was that of immigration. Ever conscious of the precarious situation of the colonos in the *fazenda* and wary of the diminishing negotiating power these workers would have in the face of the increasing number of immigrants, the paper's editors vehemently opposed Italian immigration to Brazil. Published mostly in Italian, it functioned first and foremost as an organ for "forming minds."[9] When one studies its pages, it becomes apparent how Ristori and his comrades were somewhat akin to what Antonio Gramsci referred to as "organic intellectuals" whose main purpose was to organize the peasant and working class. The same, Bencivenni remarks, was true for the "radical ethnic brokers" operating in the United States, who "worked to enlighten the minds of Italian immigrant workers, to make them aware of their class interest and rights, and to inspire them toward a more democratic and higher form of human life."[10]

In addition to pursuing its messianic mission, *La Battaglia*—alone among the city's newspapers—routinely reported on the miserable working conditions of the colonos, with sensationally titled articles such as: "Horrors of the Fazenda"; "From the Brazilian Cayennes"; "The Prisons of the Fazenda"; "From the Wretched of the Fazenda"; and "Infamies of the Fazenda." For example, *La Battaglia* condemned Italian socialist Enrico Ferri's visit in 1908, as well as that of Guglielmo Ferrero and Gina Lombroso Ferrero, because the editors saw them as "propagating an imperial myth of the 'greater Italy' to lure immigrants into nationalist thinking and to defend their 'Italian character' at all costs."[11] And Ristori, in an article titled "Le bugie prezzolate della signora Ferrero," (The Corrupt Lies of Mrs. Ferrero) accused Lombroso Ferrero of having lied about the positive conditions of life in the fazenda. Ristori made various trips to the interior of São Paulo in an attempt to proselytize to Italian migrants working in the rural areas of the state, but with little success. Instead, it quickly became clear that *La Battaglia*'s immediate audience was São Paulo's fledgling urban working class, whose largely Italian composition reflected the changing demographics of the city as a whole.

Besides denouncing immigrant working conditions, Oreste Ristori and his colleagues (including Angelo Bandoni, Gigi Damiani, and Alessandro Cerchiai) took aim at Brazilian society at large. Two intertwined phenomena deeply troubled them, and rightly so. The first was police brutality. In 1907, Brazil followed Argentina and passed the Lei Adolfo Gordo, which authorized the expulsion of foreigners who were said to pose a risk to national security. Ristori and his comrades were convinced that the Lei Gordo was nothing but "a government strategy to interrupt the exodus of colonos from the fazendas to the urban centers." In any case, the law further enabled the "exceptional violence" with which police forces in São Paulo, often joined by the military, attacked immigrant workers. *La Battaglia* gave ample space to articles reporting on the Brazilian police, who interrupted weddings and other ceremonies and indiscriminately arrested and detained Italian workers.[12]

Such systemic oppression and repression of dissent continued well into the twentieth century. Consider Ernesto Gattai, Zélia's father, who died in 1940 from the abuse he received while detained by the police forces of Getúlio Vargas's dictatorial regime known as Estado Novo. Likewise, Zélia herself spent years in exile with her husband, Jorge Amado, because of the military dictatorship that was established in 1964 to protect civilians against an alleged communist threat. As explained in Chapter Four, this dictatorship, with the help of fascist intellectuals such as Italo-Brazilian Miguel Reale, disappeared hundreds of political prisoners and forced dissidents to seek political asylum.

The use of violence to contain dissent paralleled the second phenomenon against which *La Battaglia* spoke most vociferously: slavery and its legacies in Brazilian society. In fact, as historian Luigi Biondi has shown, Ristori and the other Italian anarchists behind *La Battaglia* shared a specific ethnocentric vision of Brazilian society. They saw Brazil as "an archaic and poor country" and believed in "the idea of a medieval Brazil," whose primitiveness and corruption derived from the "original sin of Brazilian society: slavery." Consequently, these anarchists essentially saw themselves as superior to local Brazilian workers, who, as Trento explains, "generally held the lowliest of urban jobs and were conscious of the superior attitude of immigrants, who in turn accused natives of scabbing." In fact, he continues, "on those rare occasions when anarchists commented on native Brazilians of African descent, they also did so with timeworn racial epithets, usually referring to the laziness of an African population that was the eternal enemy of fatigue."[13]

To put it simply, the intellectual circle around *La Battaglia* imagined itself as a harbinger of progress. Its anarchist values would eventually deliver Brazil and Brazilians from their backwardness and apathy. Given the Gattais' connections with Ristori, Bandoni, and Cerchiai, we can safely gather that Ernesto and Angelina, Zélia's parents, were familiar with the newspaper and its ideas. Ernesto's father, Francesco Gattai, was on friendly terms with these three influential anarchists and had occasionally contributed to their newspaper. In the comments that Angelina and Ernesto make throughout the memoir, Gattai conveys the sense of moral superiority that inspired *La Battaglia*'s writing about other working-class Brazilians.[14]

Ristori's frustration with the working class in São Paulo, along with his disillusionment with the possibility of a true revolution from below, pushed him to leave the editorial group of *La Battaglia* and to reconsider his own political beliefs. In 1917, he went back to Buenos Aires and began another journalistic enterprise with the newspaper *El Burro*. Two years later, the Argentinian state attempted to repatriate him a third time, with no luck. He found safe harbor in Montevideo, where he resumed publication of *El Burro*. He eventually returned to São Paulo in 1922. There he would stay until his final expulsion and repatriation to Italy in 1936. Ristori was executed by a Nazi firing squad outside of Empoli in 1943, for allegedly having organized a demonstration to celebrate the fall of Mussolini.

Gattai met Ristori during his second stay in São Paulo. By this time, however, Ristori was less an ardent anarchist journalist than an anti-fascist crusader. As she explains:

> A concrete objective brought the old Ristori to our house. He came to invite Mom and Dad to a meeting at the Lega Lombarda: a meeting between anti-fascists and socialists, organized by the São Paulo socialist movement. They would think of a way to commemorate the first anniversary of the death of the great socialist leader Giacomo Matteotti, assassinated by the fascist militias in Rome. Under the pretext of a commemoration, liberals and radicals of São Paulo wanted to reignite the old calling, using Matteotti as the flag of the anti-fascist struggle.[15]

The assassination of Giacomo Matteotti was not the only injustice that Ristori denounced in his second period of Paulistano activity.[16] He also vehemently decried the death sentences of Sacco and Vanzetti and called upon "all anarchists of São Paulo . . . urgently . . . to organize the launching of a national campaign . . . against the heinous crime about to be committed."[17]

Angelina Da Col, Zélia's mother, began working in a factory in São Paulo's Brás neighborhood at nine years old. After becoming literate, she promptly familiarized herself with anarchist and socialist ideas. Zélia remembers how, like Ristori, Angelina also followed the case of Sacco and Vanzetti closely:

> Late at night, when everybody was asleep, Mom woke up from the bed, went back to the dining room, grabbed the newspaper that her husband had tossed, leafed through it looking for something she was very much interested in. With a pair of scissors, she cut out the news about Sacco and Vanzetti: the article by Pietro Nenni and also another one, by another Italian journalist, Umberto Terracini. He, too, was fighting for a reversal of the sentence that had condemned the two innocent men. Mommy would read everything slowly at a calmer hour, reflecting, as she liked to do. Then, she would save them together with the other clippings that she had been putting together for a long time under the mattress.[18]

Angelina's commitment to the anarchist movement calls into question commonly held beliefs about the role of women in the Italian diaspora. Moreover, her intellectual predisposition makes her an example of what Bencivenni calls "one of the most interesting products of the radical movement of the nineteenth century"—that is, the self-educated worker.[19] Angelina's love for literature and art clashed with the demands put on her as a wife, demands that she viscerally disdained and refused to meet seemingly on principle: "She never was a good homemaker, poor thing! A sensible dreamer, she was born for intellectual tasks." At the same time, though, Angelina also "eternally lived enslaved to other people's opinion." The phrase "what would they think" perennially bedeviled her, revealing how she suffered from a lingering bourgeois mentality. Despite what film scholar Rita Antonella Roscilli has called a strained relationship between mother and daughter, Angelina's ideological contradictions—her intellectual and political commitment to an anarchist way of life in contradistinction to her middle-class desires and values—provide the memoir with one of its greatest recurring sources of narrative tension.[20]

Angelina's clippings constitute a de facto archive of the transnational anarchist network and unearth the inner workings of its international solidarity. A small but well-curated collection of books—discolored and battered by abundant use—complete her radical archive. Her collection included an edition of Dante Alighieri's *Divine Comedy* illustrated by Gustave Doré; a collection of anarchist plays by Pietro Gori, or Angelina's "true bible"; two books of anarchist doctrine by Bakunin and Kropotkin; poems by Néry Tanfúcio, "humoristic poet"; Victor Hugo's *Les Misérables* and *The Workers of the Sea*, the former being a "very instructive book" according to Angelina, who read it out loud to her children; and three books by Émile Zola, *Thérèse Raquin*, *Germinal*, and *J'Accuse!* The clandestine manner in which her mother's intellectual labor unfolds in the memoir lends an air of subversiveness to Angelina's actions. Indeed, when the *Estado Novo* secret police searched the Gattai household for evidence of illegal activities, "Mommy's precious archive," along with the "sacred relics" of her books, were seized and used as a pretext for Ernesto's capture and imprisonment, which ultimately led to his death.[21]

Angelina closely safeguarded her books in a locked wardrobe in the bedroom she shared with Ernesto. This lock was the only one in the entire household, symbolizing the value that Angelina placed on her intellectual possessions. Her daughters, however, quickly learned where she kept the key.

They often entertained themselves by flipping through the contents of the wardrobe, and, in this way, they became familiar with most of her books. The most interesting to them was the *Divine Comedy*, which Zélia called "the book with forbidden illustrations." It is no wonder that Gattai uses the word "exploration" to describe her and her sisters' intrusion into Angelina's wardrobe. In doing so, they developed the "habit" of truly scavenging the archive in search of new materials to read or flip through. But, as the result of that practice, their exploration also excavated their own past and their story of migration. In the wardrobe, Angelina's political anarchist archive coexisted with her family's personal story of migration. There, hidden from prying eyes, were carefully collated materials that mapped Angelina and Ernesto's arrivals in Brazil. In that constrained space, internationalism and ethnic particularism coexisted and created space for Gattai to explore the contradictions of the New World Italian discourse.[22]

2. *A Migrant Story: From* Colônia Cecilia *to* Brás

"There, in the back of the wardrobe, we found an old purse, full of documents," Gattai writes. "We had never seen it before."[23] This bag discloses a whole new world for Gattai, who had hitherto been largely unaware of her family's origin story. She writes:

> Wanda was taken aback by this enormous passport, the size of half a newspaper page. It alone occupied a lot of the space in the old purse. At the top, right in the center of the page, above a green and red flag—the Italian flag—the crown of the King of Italy adorned the paper. . . . The Gattai family's immigration passport, opened above the bed, was now read out loud: the family, made up of the husband, wife, and five children, was authorized to travel on the steamship *Città di Roma*, which was set to leave from Genoa with the destination Santos, Brazil, on February 20, 1890.[24]

While reading this passport, Zélia discovers that her father has a younger sister named Hiena (Portuguese for "hyena"). She wonders where that aunt with "the beast name" went, since she has never met her.[25] Such moments of wonderment appear throughout the memoir and account for much of its narrative momentum. Gattai's abundant use of free indirect speech, her oscillation between the first-person and a kind of third-person omniscient ("The Gattai family's immigration passport . . ."), further fastens our attention as we encounter tantalizing clues to the puzzle of her life. Rather than telling her story chronologically, Gattai alternates between multiple threads, each woven around a seemingly stand-alone story, an object, or a relative, which, through their accretion, amounts to a distinctive and poignant personal narrative. As literary scholar Caterina Romeo notes in her study of memoirs by members of the Italian diaspora, "the memory we talk about here . . . is not the medium through which we collect memories but . . . a way through which one creates connections between disparate events and varied subjects."[26] In fact, each thread leads the reader to a discovery, mostly having to do with foundational moments, objects, and symbols of Zélia's Italian upbringing. Gattai recreates for the reader the same experience that she and her sisters had in their mother's bedroom. This exploration of the contents of Angelina's wardrobe had profound consequences. Romeo points out that the transmission of material culture is "fundamental for maintaining contact with the past and for feeling the continuity with one's origin culture."[27] For Gattai, the passport and her curiosity about Hiena would ultimately uncover the tragedy that had marked her family during the trip from Italy to Brazil. It thus opens up the opportunity to relive the trauma of the crossing and the subsequent separation from the life "before."

Through Hiena and her story, the reader learns about the circumstances that brought Gattai's father and his family to Brazil. When pressured by Zélia for information about Hiena, Ernesto, "changing [his] tone, almost stealthily . . . satisfied [Zélia's] curiosity: 'She died of hunger. . . . Here in Brazil, before turning one year old.'" He then begins to recount the story of his family's journey to Brazil, how he lost his sister, and how his mother Argía never recovered from that loss. The story of the Gattais' arrival in Brazil is thus conveyed in Ernesto's voice, as if he were recounting it in real time to the children. This technique, which evokes the mythopoetic qualities of traditional oral storytelling, emphasizes the vernacular underpinnings of the memoir genre. Accordingly, storytelling as such subsequently comes to play a crucial role in unraveling the family tapestry and, from a critical hermeneutic standpoint, making sense of the multidirectionality of Gattai's New World Italian discourse.[28]

In the memoir, Gattai points out that although her grandparents left Italy from Genoa in 1890, their journey had begun two years earlier, in 1888, when Francesco Gattai stumbled upon a pamphlet, *Il comune in riva al mare*, written by a certain Cárdias. This brochure "idealized the foundation of an 'experimental socialist colony' in a Latin American country . . . a society without laws, without religion, without private property, where the family would be established in a more human manner, securing for women the same civil and political rights as men."[29] Cárdias was the pseudonym of Italian anarchist Giovanni Rossi, and the pamphlet in question was, according to fellow Italian anarchist Alessandro Cerchiai, "a true jewel of sociology."[30] Through the story of her paternal grandparents, Gattai introduces the reader to a lesser-known story of Italian immigration to Brazil, that of the experimental socialist colony Colônia Cecília.

Rossi, an agronomist and veterinarian, was a strong proponent of what Felici has called "experimental socialism."[31] In 1873, Rossi—at only seventeen years old—outlined to the International Workingmen's Association in Pisa a project to build a socialist colony in Polynesia. His proposal was rejected, but Rossi's commitment to creating his experimental community did not waver. About five years later, he published the novel *Un comune socialista* (A Socialist Village), which remains one of his better-known works. Therein, Rossi outlines the major principles that would govern his experimental socialist colony: anarchy, love, atheism, and collective ownership of the means of production.[32] In 1886, Rossi began publishing a newspaper, *Lo Sperimentale*, which encouraged Italian workers to form socialist communities. His insistent propaganda drew sharp criticism from other Italian politicians and intellectuals on the Left. Among those who harshly criticized Rossi's ideas and plans were anarchist hard-liner Enrico Malatesta and socialist reformist Filippo Turati. The former found Rossi's enthusiasm infectious but remained skeptical of his plan to realize such a monumental project; the latter judged Rossi a deserter, while also doubting the viability of creating an anarchist regime in a bourgeois society. Undeterred by such criticisms or by the failure of his first experimental socialist colony, Cittadella near Cremona in Northern Italy, Rossi went ahead with his political project.[33]

How Rossi and his fellow dreamers—of whom one of the most committed was Francesco Gattai, grandfather of Zélia—arrived in Paraná, Brazil, constitutes something of a mystery. According to legend, it was Brazilian Emperor Pedro II who granted the land on which they established their experimental socialist Colônia Cecília. Gattai rehearses this story, according to which Giovanni Rossi met Pedro II in Milan, through the famed Brazilian opera composer Carlos Gomes: "Gomes spoke to Giovanni Rossi about his land on the other side of the sea, full of natural beauty and riches," explains Gattai. "Cárdias listened to him, fascinated! This was the land he was looking for, ideal for his experiment. There was no doubt. He immediately put aside the project, still embryonic, to go to Uruguay. Brazil was calling him." As sources for this likely apocryphal story, Gattai cites her father and another important São Paulo writer, socialist Afonso Schmidt, who tells a similar story in his 1958 novel *Colônia Cecília, romance de uma experiência anarquista* (Colônia Cecília, novel of an anarchist experience).[34] Hence, she appeals to the authority of fiction to buttress her claim. At the same, time, the fact that Gattai presents the story as part of her father's own recollection implies that those Italians who took part in Rossi's experimental socialist colony played a role in propagating the myths surrounding its formation.

Whatever the true reason Rossi picked Brazil over Uruguay, and his colony's failure notwithstanding, this self-mythologizing, with its emphasis on the colony's illustrious and enlightened origins, helped foster the notion that its settlers differed from other Italian migrants. In contrast to the exploited colonos of the Brazilian coffee plantations, the migrants who traveled to Paraná did not seek fortune so much as freedom. It mattered little that the departure of Rossi and his followers coincided with the mass exodus of impoverished Italians or that Rossi's ideas about South America had most likely come to him precisely because of the upsurge of Italian migration to the Southern Cone, specifically Brazil, in the last decade of the nineteenth century.[35] To be sure, Rossi himself understood his and his colony's material conditions as similar to those experienced by the colonos departing from Veneto to Brazil.[36] But later representations of the Colônia Cecília tend to leave out how, in many respects, Rossi and his fellow utopian travelers—such as Francesco Gattai and his wife Argía—encountered the same challenges and traumas faced by the other, more benighted colonos.

Gattai cleverly juxtaposes these two origin stories in her text, separating her discussions of them by only a few pages. As the story of Hiena and her death by starvation unfolds and gets repeated, the parallel between Rossi's colonists and the "other" Italian colonos comes into sharper focus. At first glance, her retelling of the story about Pedro II bequeathing the land to Rossi—an act of noblesse oblige that would seem to link anarchism with Brazil's glorious, aristocratic past—seems almost trite and naïve. After all, as one historian writes, despite its questionable veracity, this is "the most well-known story of the Cecilia."[37] But what follows the myth surprises the reader because it strips it of its glory and exposes the ugliness of the crossing. Instead of focusing on the figure of her grandfather Francesco—who, in fact, knew Rossi and remained committed to his utopian vision well after the colony's demise—Gattai draws our attention to the hardships endured by her grandmother Argía, the mother of Hiena.

Gattai describes Argía as a fearless woman, someone who would not "retreat in front of obstacles" and "had no fear of facing the unknown." While Francesco is apprehensive about embarking on the trip to South America with an infant, Argía expresses her confidence that "they didn't need to worry about Hiena" because "never had [Argía] been without milk," and therefore their daughter's food would be guaranteed at least during the crossing. No matter how strong Argía might have been, however, she could not have fathomed what awaited them in the steamship's hold:

> On the second day of travel, there was nowhere to step. Puddles of vomit were scattered all over. The boat tossed around a lot, making the majority of the passengers throw up. Argía Gattai was among those who suffered most. She could not keep anything down; she vomited even what she didn't have in her stomach. As days went on, the Gattais' situation became worse: glued to the breasts of her mother—now one, now the other one—Hiena detached from them only to complain, crying desperately. Where were those fat, full breasts?[38]

Gattai describes what the family had to undergo during the trip as "torments" and aptly compares the steamship to Dante's *Inferno*.[39] But while Dante ultimately leaves the Inferno and ascends to Purgatorio first and Paradiso later, escaping the pains and the horrors of the afterlife, no such fate shines upon the Gattais, who are eventually forced to bury Hiena upon their arrival in Brazil. The Colônia Cecília remembered and invoked in Ernesto's retelling of his family's journey and transposed to the pages of his daughter's memoir helps restore to the historical record some of the human cost that the pursuit of Rossi's grandiose ideals entailed.

The analogy between the colonos of Rossi's utopian society and the colonos who worked as indentured laborers in the coffee fields of Brazil (the fazendas) likewise becomes clearer when Gattai reconstructs the story of her maternal grandfather, Nono Eugênio. "Our story is very similar to that of the Gattais but completely different [*muito parecida mas completamente diferente*]," he muses, when Gattai asks him if he, too, is an anarchist.[40] Moved by her father's origin story, Gattai wants to know how her maternal family came to Brazil as well. Prompted by his granddaughter's questioning, Eugênio narrates in the first-person plural the struggles that he and his wife, Giuseppina, along with their five children, endured during their journey to Brazil. The same emphasis on orality is found here but with greater facticity. For where Ernesto Gattai was in fact too young to recall his family's crossing—making the story he tells Zélia an example of what ethnic studies scholar Agnieszka Bedingfield calls trans-memory—Nono Eugênio remembers the experience as he consciously lived it. He thus represents an important epistemological link between the two shores of the Atlantic.[41] He recalls:

> "We, too, traveled with five little kids and crossed the ocean in the hold of a steamship. We, too, lost a little girl in Brazil, the youngest of the five. Her name was Carolina; she was a bit more than two years old when she died." He stopped and continued with his head lowered: "Only ours died due to lack of resources . . ." Dad gave a hint of a smile when he heard this statement from his father-in-law, for whom it was still hard to admit and still harder to pronounce the phrase: "She died of hunger!"[42]

Eugênio and Giuseppina Da Col had left Pieve di Cadore, a village in Northern Veneto, to work in the coffee fields of the State of São Paulo. Thus, the colonos, having occupied pride of place in the transnational Italian imaginary of the late nineteenth century, reappear here in *Anarquistas*, almost a century later, unearthing those sedimented anxieties related to the material conditions of Italian rural workers in São Paulo that previous exponents of the New World Italian discourse had struggled to bury.

Upon the Da Cols' arrival in Santos, the handlers from the fazenda where they were contracted to work herded them onto a train car, "squeezed like cattle." In Gattai's retelling of her grandparents' migration experiences, their dehumanization becomes the focal point. Their miserable conditions contrast sharply with the bowdlerized accounts that, as we have seen, other writers have deployed to sustain the connection between Italian immigrants and modernization in the Brazilian popular imagination. Just as Argía's "distant eyes saw nothing . . . her cheerfulness, her hope, her enthusiasm remained buried next to her daughter's little body," Eugênio's hopes for a better life for his family dimmed the moment he set foot on the fazenda. Significantly, Gattai conveys her maternal grandfather's story in a manner that emphasizes the similarities between his experience and those of her paternal grandfather—such as through her repetition of the word *também* (too)—even though the former was not an anarchist.[43]

But while Nono Eugênio might not have left Italy with a radical utopian project in mind, he nonetheless believed in a utopia—namely, that of the land of *cuccagna* (Cockaigne). And, not unlike Francesco's, this utopia failed to materialize as its architect had planned. Gattai writes:

> Once he arrived at the fazenda, Eugênio Da Col realized, immediately, that there did not exist that *cuccagna*, that abundance so rumored. All that he had idealized turned out to be a fantasy; the information he had received did not correspond to reality; what was actually there was hard and overtaxing work, beginning before sunrise; men and children followed the same schedule.[44]

As she excavates the indignities that her forebears faced in their relocation to Brazil, however, Gattai also seeks to insinuate a new figure into the New World Italian discourse: that of the Italian radical. Take, for example, this scene at the fazenda, where Eugênio witnesses the public flogging of a Black man at the hands of a foreman determined to teach the colonos their place:

> Suddenly the foreman raised his arm, the long leather whip in the air, ready for the punishment. So, that was it then? Outraged, blind with indignation, the young colono Eugênio Da Col did not resist; it would not be him who would witness this act so savage and cowardly. . . . With a quick jump, he was on top of the executioner, snatching the whip from his hands. Taken by surprise,

> faced with the daring of the Italian, perplexed, the foreman became discouraged. The whip, his weapon, the defense guaranteeing his might, was in the possession of the *carcamano*; was it worth reacting? Outraged, out of himself, roaring against the foreman in his dialect from the Dolomites, the rebel asked his comrades to join him in defending the Black man. All looked at him in silence. . . . A committed Catholic, he was doing what the heart dictated, encouraged by his Christian principles.[45]

Gattai implies that, while Eugênio did not necessarily subscribe to the radical egalitarianism of anarchism, his principles nonetheless still moved him to protest a flagrant injustice. That this injustice was inflicted against a Black man and underwritten by certain unspoken racial codes mattered little to him. Eugênio ostensibly reacted according to his heart, and, revealingly, he does so while others look on "in silence." We are left to assume that the other colonos—whether due to fear, racism, or some incalculable mixture of both—turned a blind eye to the suffering inflicted on the Black man. It is the singularity of Eugênio's behavior that matters here. It establishes him as exceptional in relation to other colonos. But Gattai's decision to focus on her grandfather's heroic act does not simply reflect her disposition toward filiopietism or hagiography. Rather, it also speaks to her desire to redeem men like her grandfather—Catholic, working class—from their perceived complicity in Brazil's fundamentally racist system of oppression. Gattai seeks to convince us that, although such men might not have been doctrinaire leftists, they still possessed an instinctual radicalism that led them to resist the dictates of Brazil's racial hierarchy.[46]

Through her grandparents' experiences of migration, Gattai joins Leite in disrupting the hegemonic discourse of Italian racial, economic, and cultural superiority analyzed in this book. The "torments" of Italian migrants like Eugênio do not accord with the celebratory tone and the story of progressive assimilation embodied by the commercial elites of São Paulo depicted in the work of Alcântara Machado; nor do they fit neatly into the self-aggrandizing narrative Miguel Reale writes about his own family's story of migration. At the same time—again, much like Leite—Gattai reformulates the New World Italian discourse to fit her family's values. If Leite ultimately repurposes it to interpolate São Paulo's Black Brazilians into a system of ethnic pluralism, Gattai reconstructs it to afford a place to the

Italian radicals whose politics, at least on the surface, would appear anathema to such a discourse. In doing so, however, Gattai reveals the limits of her family's ideological beliefs. In fact, her parents, who had absorbed ideas about Brazil disseminated by *La Battaglia*, understood themselves as harbingers of progress vis-à-vis working-class Brazilians, those "nationals" discussed in Chapter Three, and the communities of Southern Italians also living in São Paulo. In other words, in their efforts to articulate an organic Italo-Brazilian radicalism rooted in notions of progress, Gattai's parents and their circle unwittingly ended up reinforcing the link between Italians, whiteness, and modernization that lay at the heart of the very New World Italian discourse which had initially excluded them.[47]

3. Ignorant People: Interracial Relations in the Gattai Household

On more than one occasion, Gattai recounts how her mother explained to her what it would be like to live in a world without money, a world where people unite to fight for a common cause. This is what anarchy means, Angelina patiently explained to her daughter; it did not mean "disorder," as one of Gattai's teachers had implied during a class, a comment that left her quite confused. The problem, according to Angelina, had to do with people's ignorance. Many times, when confronted with an injustice and witnessing her peers' passivity in response to it, Angelina would blame it on their benightedness. However, it so happened that those whom she regarded as ignorant were typically Black Brazilians. Angelina's judgmental and paternalistic comments about lower-class disinterest in joining her political struggle betray her own prejudices about poor Brazilians who were largely Black, mixed-race, or Indigenous (also referred to as nationals). What seems to escape Angelina's attention is that Brazil's racial hierarchy largely impedes these nationals from pursuing the kinds of opportunities for intellectual and socioeconomic advancement that she and her daughters—four white Italian women—have come to enjoy.

Consider, for instance, the exchange between Angelina and Maria Negra, her Black housekeeper, when Angelina learns that the neighborhood cinema planned to break its custom and suspend discounted entrance to women on one Thursday night. The theater owner understood that the actor Ettore Petrolini, starring in that night's feature, *O homem que vendeu a sombra ao diabo* (The Man Who Sold His Shadow to the Devil), would attract more people than usual to the theater; consequently, he decided to reserve this particular Thursday night's screening solely for those who "could afford it." Even infants would have to pay for entry. As Gattai recalls:

> Faced with this last detail, Mommy lost it! She put down the heavy iron so she could better gesticulate. . . . "Vigliacchi, maledetti!" exploded Angelina. ". . . Farabutti, tutti quanti!" added Mommy. "All these capitalists, exploiters of the poor, leeches of the people. Nobody complains, nobody protests against them. . . . They raise the prices of everything when they want, with no regard, without the least consideration. . . . Such impertinent people!"[48]

When she is angry, Angelina often resorts to Italian, if not her Veneto dialect altogether. Her command of Portuguese was never more than mediocre, and, as Gattai points out at the very beginning of the memoir, Angelina uses the adjective *atrevido* (impertinent) to describe a range of things that did not necessarily have anything to do with impertinence. Gattai's emphasis on her mother's poor linguistic abilities and her at times clumsy vacillation between her native tongue and Portuguese gesture toward a long-standing tradition of ethnic autobiographical writing in which, according to Romeo, "languages mixed themselves." As observed by literary scholar Edvige Giunta, "writing with an accent" indicates "a dislocation that is linguistic, cultural, and geographic."[49]

Angelina's rant is cut short by Maria Negra. To avoid becoming a captive audience to yet another one of her employer's political diatribes, the housekeeper—whose crucial role in the upkeep of the household Gattai makes clear earlier in the text by stressing Angelina's ineptness for domestic work—betrays a stubborn nonchalance:

> Maria Negra, who watched the whole thing, wanted to give her two cents. Dona Angelina would not become poorer because of such silliness. Maria Negra preferred, however, to remain quiet. . . . That chitchatting of Dona Angelina would go on for some time. It was not the first time that she had witnessed one of those explosions, and it wouldn't be the last. To each nutcase his own obsession. The obsession her boss had was the most idiotic one:

> wanting to right the world. God forbid! She interrupted the orator in the middle of her speech.[50]

The only time Gattai remarks on Maria Negra's Blackness is when she first introduces her. Perhaps somewhat embarrassed by the nickname the family bestowed upon its housekeeper—her real name is Maria da Conceição—Gattai asserts that "it was certainly not because of racism that they gave her such a nickname [because theirs] was a house of free thinkers, of anarchists."[51] Still, one wonders why the modifier "Black" (Negra in Portuguese) has been appended to her name. Curiously enough, in the Italian edition, the translator Yvonne Giannini chose *not* to translate the appellative "Black," leaving it instead as it appears in the original Portuguese, which creates something of a problem. In the Italian language the word "Negra" holds a decidedly derogatory meaning roughly equivalent to the N-word in English.[52] What is even more puzzling is Giannini's decision to proffer an explanation for Gattai's use of the term "Negra" that does not appear anywhere in the original text. She writes, "la vera ragione è che era nera come il carbone," which translates to "the true reason [for the name] was that she was black as coal."[53] Besides casting suspicion on the translation, this addendum to an already discomfiting addendum further complicates the racial politics that we observed among the Gattais. Whatever the reasoning that lay behind it, the Gattais' decision to interpellate Maria racially is at odds with their adherence to the notions of interracial tolerance and solidarity that circulated in the anarchist and working-class movements in São Paulo. Indeed, it might indicate the cultural limitations of these movements more broadly. As historian George Reid Andrews has shown, interraciality within São Paulo's labor organizations only went so far. Moreover, as we have already seen, Italian anarchists racialized working-class Brazilians, the overwhelming majority of whom were of African descent and Indigenous, by associating them with notions of degeneration and laziness.[54] The appellation "Black" in this context might symbolize the extent to which, for the Gattais, Maria's race naturalized her social status.

The paradox of a Black housekeeper in this anarchist household lays bare the contradictions at the heart of Gattai's memoir. How could the Gattais justify having Maria live with them and do most of the housework given their anti-capitalist ideas? Especially when we consider that Angelina did not have a job? Perhaps Maria's impatience with Angelina's sermonizing about capitalists' exploitation of the people stems from the fact that the irony of this situation was not lost on her. But given that Maria's thoughts come to us in the form of free indirect speech, a technique that erodes the boundary between character and third-person narrator, we might also speculate that these domestic scenes reenact the process through which Gattai herself came to terms with what the presence of Maria, who was also her nanny, meant for her family and its politics. In other words, Maria might ventriloquize Gattai's own anxieties. Certain facts about the trajectory of Gattai's life make such a reading plausible. For instance, after marrying writer Jorge Amado she relocated with him to his native city of Salvador, which, as the undisputed capital of Afro-Brazilian culture, is practically the obverse of São Paulo. Moreover, alongside her husband, she joined the Communist Party Brazil, which was an important platform for the Black Brazilian Movement. In writing her memoir, an older, more mature, and racially sensitive Gattai would have had the opportunity to reflect on her mother's contradictions as well as the class- and race-based power imbalance between these two women.

Angelina's reaction to Maria's dismissal of her speech—which comes across as patronizing and perhaps even somewhat racist—belies this very hierarchical relationship:

> "What an impertinent ragamuffin! Ignorant. This is why the world does not change. Doesn't that other poor devil of Terêncio also disgrace his class by staying on the side of the boss? Unhappy, completely exploited. . . . And he still sides with the boss," she repeated. "Is it really worth it for us [*a gente*] to fight for the poor?"[55]

According to Angelina, Maria is ignorant because she refuses to listen to her boss's speechifying about a worker who submits to his boss. Angelina uses the notion of "ignorance" to blame poor people like the custodian of the cinema and Maria, whom she supposedly wants to free from their enslavement to capitalism, for the perpetuation of their condition. The conflict of interest does not bother Angelina because she imagines that she, Ernesto, and her comrades—the "us" in the quotation (*a gente* in Portuguese)—occupy a higher moral plane. Their commitment to a noble cause absolves them of any blame for social injustice. In this respect, they resemble Rossi's high-minded colonos and Eugênio, who, without hesitation, revolts against the whipping of the Black man on the fazenda. Angelina truly embodies what Bencivenni defines as the "*sovversivi*'s social vision," which, among other things, professed "a disarming idealism and messianic faith in the 'Ideal.'"[56] The condescending attitude Angelina and Ernesto express toward those who do not share that "Ideal"—even if those people are the ones who would stand to benefit the most from it—taints not only the way they see Black and other native-born Brazilians but also their compatriots, specifically those from Southern Italy.

The New World Italian discourse rendered Italians white in São Paulo. Yet when one observes more closely the so-called Italian colony, one notes how not *all* Italians became white, at least not in the eyes of Northern Italians, as Gattai's memoir makes clear. After propping up the heroic figure of the Italian radical, Gattai reveals the insidiousness of Italian anarchists' paternalism first, as we have seen, by exposing their ambivalence toward Black Brazilians. She then debunks the claim that a diasporic nationalism "made Italians abroad"—a proto-version of which we have already encountered in Chapter One, through the work of Gina Lombroso Ferrero—by exploring how the orientalist understanding of "the South" that justified Northern Italian elites' annexation of Southern Italy pervaded the Italo-Paulistano community. Italians may have been seen by Brazilian mainstream society as vectors of whiteness, but within their own ethnic communities, Italians—even anarchist ones—did not always accept each other's claims to assimilable whiteness.

4. Undesirable, Who? Re-Racializing Southern Italians across the Atlantic

Pointed remarks about Southern Italians are found throughout *Anarquistas*. They are conveyed either through Gattai's mother or in the form of narratorial asides that recapitulate stereotypes and thereby betray highly racialized understandings of Southerners. A case in point is the Gattais' relationship with their landlord, Rocco Andretta, a Neapolitan who lives down the street from them with his family. Gattai compares the upbringing of Andretta's daughters to a "slave-like regime," since they do not attend school and could leave their house only with their mother:

> "A woman's place is the house! Our daughter has to learn to take care of her husband, that is right! No school. School is not for women. Women need to know how to read? For what? To send letters to their boyfriends?" asked and affirmed Dona Antonietta, the mother of the Andretta family, also a slave [*escrava*]. The theory by which one would keep their daughters illiterate in order to prevent them from sending correspondence to suitors [was used] by many other neighbors, mostly families from Southern Italy—*meridionais* as they would be called by Northern Italians—to justify the daughters' absence from school.[57]

Gattai's use of the word *escrava* to talk about Antonietta, when the Gattai family had a Black servant working for them, strikes us as especially ironic. Still more risible is the singling out of Southern Italians—calling them *meridionais*, clearly a Portuguese corruption of the Italian *meridionali*—as the only people in the neighborhood who do not send their daughters to school, for fear they might communicate with boys and thus risk bringing dishonor to the family. After all, Ernesto Gattai, despite his more progressive politics, also shared Andretta's fear, for he insists that "the daughters of Gattai had to be virgin on their wedding night." Indeed, far from being only a custom of *meridionali*, concern with chastity, as Trento informs us, often found its way into the pages of the anarchist press. What is more, Ernesto shared Andretta's vision of a woman's societal role. When his eldest daughter, Wanda, offers to find a job to help the family's finances he retorts that "the place of the woman is in the house, learning to cook."[58]

For her part, Angelina holds generally more progressive views of a woman's position in society, even as she echoes Ernesto's beliefs about sexual morality. But her fears were compounded by a latent hostility toward Southern Italians. If Ernesto fears that his daughters might lose their virginity before their wedding night, Angelina fears that this travesty might occur during the celebrations of *Pasquetta* (Pasquélla in Neapolitan dialect) organized by their Neapolitan neighborhoods.

> It was customary of the Italian neighbors—the ones from Southern Italy—to celebrate Pasquélla, the Monday after Easter, by organizing picnics outside of

> the city, with the leftovers from Easter lunch. . . . I always wanted to participate in one of those picnics, but Mommy never accepted the invitations that they extended to me, using any excuse [to decline]. She then would explain to me that these lunches in the middle of the countryside were dangerous, men mixing wine and beer, getting drunk . . . [59]

Angelina prohibits Zélia from mingling with Southern Italians because such people spell danger. To be sure, a mother's desire to avoid putting her daughter in harm's way strikes one as irreproachable. And yet, in this scenario, Zélia would not be among strangers. The same Andrettas whose daughters supposedly live in "slave-like conditions" would be present. Indeed, it is their mother who invites Zélia. Thus, Angelina's fears make sense only if framed within a discourse that understands Southern Italian men as axiomatically dangerous and Southern Italian women as promiscuous and tempestuous.[60]

Such men and women are also linguistically marked in a way that distances them further from Northern Italians like the Gattais. For example, Angelina belittles her neighbor Dona Caropita, a "poorly educated and rowdy woman" who sells goat milk around the neighborhood, by commenting on her "muddled way of speaking," which reflects a combination of Calabrese dialect, Portuguese, and touches of standard Italian. Her alienness is emphasized by the fact that Gattai translates her idiomatic expressions parenthetically. For instance, "*Aggio perso a grappa mia! Aggio perso a grappa mia*" becomes the parenthetical statement "(I lost my goat!)."[61] By contrast, Gattai does not translate any of the standard Italian phrases littered throughout the text—perhaps on the assumption that a Brazilian reader could easily guess their meaning.

A helpful corollary of this appears in the Italian version of *Anarquistas*. Giannini consciously seeks to evoke more of the Southern characters' alien qualities by shifting phrases originally written in standard Portuguese into nonstandard Italian. Thus, instead of having Caropita's husband say "Ti hanno portato la cioccolata," Giannini writes, "T'hanno portato a' cioccolata."[62] The morphological changes clearly reflect a desire to make their speech pattern look and sound more folksy (or to use a term dear to Angelina, ignorant) and, in turn, better render their Southern identity in written form. If we examine another translation from the Portuguese applied to a different Southern Italian woman who appears in the text, Dona Vincenza, we can see how this technique, as in the case of Maria Negra, renders the memoir's racial undertones even more lucidly. In her translation of the Portuguese word *curandeira* (healer), which Gattai uses to describe Dona Vincenza, Giannini opts for *fattucchiera* (witch doctor). Dona Vincenza, we are told, has quite a reputation as an interpreter of dreams, and Angelina often enlists her help in picking a number to play in the infamous *jogo do bicho*. But Ernesto and the young Zélia disdain this Southern woman, whose speech the latter describes as "sharp and sweet at the same time, an unmistakable voice, with a Neapolitan accent."[63] Giannini's choice of the more derogatory *fattucchiera* over the more neutral *guaritrice* (healer) seems in keeping with the overall attitude that the Gattais display toward Southern Italians. If translation is a quintessentially interpretive act, then the use of the term witch doctor here, a word that not only carries a negative connotation but also racializes Dona Vincenza as non-white (an "ignorant" person, as Angelina would put it), speaks to the way the original text calls attention to the Gattai family's racialist anti-Southern attitudes.

Her own poor Portuguese aside, Angelina rightly understood speech patterns as a marker of status.[64] It thus comes as no surprise that, for her, someone who spoke like Dona Caropita, "an ignorant woman," "should be living on Caetano Pinto Street in Bexiga." That is, Caropita and others like her belong together—de facto ghettoized—in Bexiga, a place "infamous for the fights and the daily brawls, [which] would turn [the neighborhood] into a taboo, populated mostly by Italians from Southern Italy—mainly from Calabria—who came looking for fortune in Brazil."[65] The racialized language Angelina uses to describe her compatriots highlights the extent to which the Italo-Brazilian community was riven by intraethnic conflicts. This is not to suggest that Angelina was a stranger to the discourse that I have traced throughout the previous chapters, which seeks to produce a civilized, modern, white Italian subject. On the contrary, Angelina reproduces that discourse here, but she does so to demonstrate that it applies only to certain members of the Italo-Brazilian world: Northern Italian radicals and their offspring. Where conservative figures like Lombroso Ferrero and Reale imagine an undifferentiated Italo-Brazilian mass, Angelina and her circle see a community marked by ethnic, linguistic, and racial distinctions that function as indexes of belonging and worth.

In the pages of *Anarquistas*, the neighborhood of Bexiga reappears not as a paramount example of Italian entrepreneurial spirit, as it does in the work of Alcântara Machado, nor as a space of cross-racial intimacy and political activism, as it was for Leite, but as a highly racialized and segregated urban environment. In fact, Gattai's description of the everyday reality of Bexiga, takes on the tone of an ethnographic study of practices and customs essentially foreign to her. Here she finds "an extremely religious people, deeply patriotic, hot-blooded." Gattai hails from an atheist and cosmopolitan family. Thus, it makes sense that these "extremely religious"—a term of opprobrium that she uses repeatedly—people offer something of an exotic spectacle. Bexiga is, in her words, "picturesque": women compete to see who has the shiniest cookware, which "stayed suspended around the window frame, as if in an exhibit, shining, obfuscating the sight of the passersby." Meanwhile, "from the coal stoves, placed on the sidewalks, smoking pans released smells of sauces and stews," as men played *morra*. This use of the picturesque hearkens back to the literary tradition of depicting the South of Italy, as literary scholar Nelson Moe explains, "as a source of interest and delectation for the civilized observer," becoming both "'Africa' and *terra vergine*, a reservoir of feudal residues, sloth, and squalor on the one hand and of quaint peasants, rustic traditions, and exotica on the other." The way Gattai describes Southern cultural practices; the distance between these realities and hers (notice Gattai's use of the words "a people" and "picturesque"); the stark contrast between her mother's inaptitude for cooking and housekeeping compared with these women's obsession with these occupations—all of this reinforces the "us versus them" paradigm we have seen Angelina adopt in relation to Southern Italians.[66]

Having offered an idyllic depiction of this corner of São Paulo, Gattai quickly amends it, adding that "people from other neighborhoods would hardly spend time in Bexiga, considered a stronghold of backward people, dangerous and hot-blooded." Perhaps recognizing, as she did in the case of the housekeeper Maria's racist appellation, how this statement might betray a certain prejudice, she admits that "probably, there had been some exaggeration in the judgment" given to the community. Indeed, as if to emphasize the exoticness of the inhabitants without overindulging in sensationalism, Gattai judiciously chooses to dwell on the local Southern Italians' devotion to their Catholic saints, who were "celebrated with processions and fireworks," instead of their supposed predilection for violence. Still, this kind of religiosity contrasts sharply with her family's devout secularism and atheism (her maternal grandfather notwithstanding). Thus, even while trying to emphasize what she understands as the more salutary aspects of Southern Italian culture—their devotion moved them to mobilize collectively to build the Achiropita Church in Bexiga, for example—she ends up drawing attention to their backwardness.[67]

Catholicism, rather than class, fostered a sense of solidarity among the inhabitants of Bexiga, their varied regional backgrounds notwithstanding. But these religious celebrations went hand in hand with the ostentatious commemorations organized in honor of Italian civic holidays, undermining yet another tenet of anarchist ideology: its anti-statism and rejection of bourgeois nationalism:

> For the big holidays like, for example, Christmas, New Year, Easter, and for the Italian civic holidays, *they* would enlist the Bersaglieri band, made up of musicians in uniform, showing off elaborate hats with large brims, a green shiny aigrette made of feathers (which looked like the tail of a rooster) bending onto the neck and shoulder. These Bersaglieri were contracted to play in front of houses—*almost always owned by Southern Italians*—and they would do a little concert out front, on the sidewalk. The repertoire of those ostentatious soldiers, made up mostly of old military marches, expanded with the arrival of fascism to include modern hymns, songs of the Duce's glories.[68]

When a neighbor from Calabria asks Ernesto for a contribution for the hiring of a Bersaglieri band, he vehemently refuses: he would not permit them to perform in front of his home for free, much less "bankroll these hymns to Mussolini, Giovinezzas, and other squalors that make [him] smell castor oil."[69] It is perhaps somewhat surprising to learn that Southern Italians participated in celebrations of Italian national holidays, especially in light of the discrimination they faced at the hands of Northern Italian elites in Italy. But such bigotry and exploitation might very well have been what moved them to embrace a state-sponsored form of Italian nationalism. After all, in contrast to white Anglo-Saxon Protestants in North America, who singled out Southern Italian immigrants as mongrelized and undesirable, non-Italian Paulistanos interpellated them as Italians regardless of their regional provenance in the peninsula. If Southern Italians like Gattais' landlord Andretta—as well as Donna Caropita and Vincenza, and the inhabitants of Bexiga—were given to understand that their superior place in the Brazilian racial hierarchy depended on the red, white, and green flag on their passports, then it hardly comes as a surprise that they embraced unequivocally and even vociferously their Italian national identity.

Indeed, it is even less surprising when one considers that Brazilian society embraced more openly Southern-inflected folklorism, whether in the forms of the religious *festas* and their accompanying foodways or of the national hymns played on holidays, than the labor organizing efforts of Italian radicals. When the city of São Paulo was thrown into chaos by the 1917 general strike, organized largely by Italian union organizers, the mainstream media responded in the most inflammatory nativist terms, depicting these immigrants as subversive aliens.[70] In other words, Brazil reversed the hierarchy of Italian identities created in North America, particularly the United States: here Southern Italians embodied a much more desirable iteration of Italianness than did their Northern compatriots, insofar as the latter, as Carlo Romani and Bruno Corrêa de Sá e Benevides have shown, were much more likely to be involved in São Paulo's labor movement.[71] At the same time, much like in the United States, Southern Italian culture has become the signifier for diasporic Italianness in Brazil. One need only consider the stereotypical images of Southern Italians that permeate Gattai's memoir: the women spend their time cooking and shining their pots, the men build churches and play *morra*; all the while, firecrackers crackle and the Bersaglieri play Italian military marches. Such images constitute the doxa of Italianness not only in São Paulo but across the Americas and the other side of the Atlantic Ocean.[72]

5. *Domestication: Whose Roots Are Deeper?*

But while Southern Italians might have indeed been more acceptable because of their presumed political quietism, the fame of *Anarquistas* attests to the fact that, alongside the religious *festas*, Bersaglieri, and superstitions that they despised so much, Italian radicals have been assimilated—co-opted perhaps—into the mainstream discourse surrounding the Italian experience in São Paulo. To a certain extent, Gattai's memoir even documents the Italian anarchists' domestication and cleverly uses her family's discussions over an anarchist allegorical painting to symbolize the fading away of her grandparents' utopia and her father's acceptance of his newly acquired bourgeois status.

As Zélia tells it, Wanda, her older sister, despises the allegorical painting in question, which depicts an "appalling," murderous priest as a symbol of the Inquisition and a naked woman breaking the shackles of capitalist slavery—so much so that on numerous occasions, she attempts to take it down. On one such occasion, Wanda uses Ernesto's lunch date with a German priest who visits his auto shop as a pretext to remove the offending painting. However, Ernesto, "upon walking into the living room and noticing the empty wall, shuddered: almost shouting, he ordered her to immediately return the painting to its place, which [Wanda] did." Wanda's next attempt occurs when it comes time to prepare the house for a party celebrating her marriage to a Portuguese man named José do Rosário Soares. "Your painting," she tells Ernesto, "needs to be removed from where it is—José invited a group of colleagues from the bank . . . noteworthy people." And yet neither this request nor the silent treatment he subsequently receives from his daughter moves Ernesto to take the painting down.[73] Unlike her sister, Zélia grasps the true significance of the painting for her father:

> My sister's impertinence shocked me. . . . Did she not realize that this painting, more so than anything else, was what my father had left of a longtime illusion that sustained our grandparents for many years, in its long and dramatic crossing in a fetid hold of a steamship? The anarchist experience of our ancestors in Colônia Cecília failed but Nono Gattai held onto that painting, a symbol of the anarchist ideal that had brought them to Brazil. He would entrust it to the son before dying, who, since then, has kept it exhibited in a place of importance in the living room. Didn't Wanda understand that the painting was not hung by nails to the walls, but actually by roots? Roots that originated in a distant Italy, the roots of our family?[74]

To avoid having to take down the painting, Ernesto resorts to a bribe: he buys a Zenith radio, making the Gattais the first and only family to possess one of these in the neighborhood. He knows that the "radio . . . would elevate his family's status." To his mind, this resolves the situation: "Wanda did not need to worry anymore, all sorts of noteworthy people could attend her wedding. The allegory would not offend them that much anymore." But his purchase of the radio vitiates the political message of his beloved painting insofar as it acquiesces to bourgeois demands and consumerism. At the same time, by steadfastly refusing to take it down, Ernesto ensures that the anarchist dream—so central to the Italian diasporic experience in São Paulo—remains visible. To put it somewhat differently, the retelling of this story proleptically allegorizes the taming of Italian radicalism in the Brazilian national imaginary, a process that results in a compromise between two competing conceptions of what it means to be a New World Italian. On the one hand, by facilitating Wanda's entry into São Paulo's bourgeoisie with the radio, Ernesto fulfills her desire to assimilate, what Gattai describes as the wish to become "completely Brazilian." On the other hand, by keeping the anarchist allegory on the wall Ernesto insists on the retention of a transnational political and ethnic bond—his "roots," to use Gattai's word. The story allows us to see how ethnic particularism, assimilation, and anarchist internationalism can, however uneasily and tenuously, coexist and how various competing forces, in the words of historians Donna Gabaccia and Fraser Ottanelli, "create and shape Italian national ethnic identities among migrants abroad."[75]

The permanence of the anarchist allegory directly contrasts with the fading of the paintings of Naples that Rocco Andretta, the Gattais' landlord, had commissioned for the exterior walls of their house:

> Rocco, equipped with various postcards, composed the landscape, directing the artist in homage to the distant land—how many years ago had he left Naples? He had lost count. He chose the most spacious part of the exterior wall, the most seen from the street, for Vesuvius, smoke and flames flying out of the crater, blue sky, big birds—which in the nationalist interpretation of Joaquim [the Brazilian artist] became colored parrots, *araras*, and toucans—flying and, down below, at the base, some carts loaded with vegetables and fruits, some others loaded with bricks and construction materials, pulled by donkeys.[76]

When Andretta originally rented the house with the ample garage to the Gattais, he had asked Ernesto, as one of the conditions of the lease, to maintain the murals. When one of Angelina's beloved trees begins to grow a bit thick, obscuring the murals, Andretta shows up with a saw, intending to take it down. Outraged, Ernesto tells him that "since [he] was paying rent on the house, [he] could do whatever he wanted." From this moment, Andretta loses interest in the murals and Ernesto ultimately paints over them. The message is clear: Vesuvius and its flames have stopped exercising their power over the Gattais, who will no longer acquiesce in the face of Andretta's "cockiness."[77]

The divergent fates of these two paintings—Andretta's murals and Ernesto's allegory—imply that Andretta and his stereotypical Neapolitanness *could* become absorbed into the landscape of São Paulo—as the image of the tropical (Brazilian) birds circling over the volcano are clearly meant to suggest—but that the anarchist allegory, with its bloodthirsty priest and its meretricious woman, remain firmly "other" to the city, an exotic—indeed painful—remainder and reminder of an otherwise lost world that had not yet fully succumbed to capitalist imperatives. Or, at least, that is what Gattai would have us believe. With the publication of *Anarquistas*—which promptly became a bestseller and was later transformed into the TV network Globo's first, smash-hit miniseries—Italo-Brazilian radicalism was all but definitively sublimated into the New World Italian discourse, which, by then, was simply the lingua franca of São Paulo.

Coda

Whose Italianness?

In 2017, while visiting the Museu Afro Brasil in São Paulo's Ibirapuera Park, I came across a panel dedicated to the infamous Brazilian activist Carlos Marighella. During the Brazilian military dictatorship (1964–1985), Marighella was a federal congressman from Bahia and a member of the Communist Party Brazil, who founded and led the armed revolutionary group Aliança Nacional Libertadora. He also authored a manual widely circulated among armed revolutionary groups on both sides of the Atlantic, titled *Minimanual do guerrilheiro urbano* (Minimanual of the Urban Guerrilla). In 1969, the secret service police (DOPS) brutally assassinated Marighella outside of his hideout in São Paulo.

A photo of Marighella's battered body occupies half of the panel dedicated to him at the Museu Afro Brasil. The photo is accompanied by a quote from famed literary critic Antonio Candido, as well as a triptych of a young Marighella, his father, and his mother. Despite the panel's detailed account of Marighella's life, not once does it mention that the father of Carlos, Augusto Marighella, was an Italian immigrant from the city of Ferrara in Emilia-Romagna.[1] As historians have noted, Italian anarchists operating in Brazil came largely from the regions of Tuscany and Emilia-Romagna, long-standing sites of intense left-wing radicalism.[2] Accounts of Carlos Marighella's life often elide his ancestral connection with Italy and the ideas about freedom and labor that he inherited from these "red" regions. To be sure, Marighella's ideas widely circulated among radical groups in Italy in the late 1960s and early 1970s. His minimanual had in fact been translated from Spanish into Italian and published in 1968 as part of Feltrinelli's radical series *Documenti della rivoluzione nell'America Latina*. But the preface makes no mention of his Italian origins. Accordingly, critics have failed to consider his connection to a longer, transnational tradition of Italian radical politics across the Atlantic.[3]

A similar erasure, for instance, takes place in the 2019 biopic *Marighella*, whose protagonist is introduced to the audience as the great-grandson of an enslaved Sudanese woman brought to Brazil. Yet again, there is no mention of his Italian father or of the elder Marighella's likely political sympathies. Indeed, the filmmakers cast an actor much darker than the real-life Marighella—the brilliant Seu Jorge—to play him, as if to disavow Marighella's Italian parentage. To be sure, it is easy to see why, in a Brazil plagued by racial inequality and virulent forms of anti-Blackness, many are tempted to emphasize Marighella's African ancestry. And yet, precisely because of the place Italians have occupied in the Brazilian national imaginary, I find the obfuscation of Marighella's direct connection to Italy odd, if not outright suspicious. If Marighella had been recognized as an Italian by the Brazilian or the Italian government, would his fate have been different? Perhaps the Italian government might have intervened on his behalf, as it did in the following decades for numerous other political dissidents and their family members who were disappeared and tortured in Argentina and Chile.[4]

The strange case of Marighella ends this book because I want to highlight how—to Italians who shared Marighella's politics, to the Brazilian military who assassinated him, and to the Italian government so eager to protect the human rights of children and grandchildren of Italians in Argentina—Carlos Marighella ostensibly had nothing to do with Italy. As we saw in

Chapter Three, José Correia Leite wrote of being "too Black" to fully enter São Paulo's Italian community, despite having spent nearly his entire childhood and adolescence ensconced within it. So, too, has Marighella's Blackness—his mother was, in fact, a Black woman from the city of Salvador, in Bahia—prevented him from entering the pantheon of famed Italian radicals, whose rehabilitation as exemplary Italian migrants to South America culminated with the publication of *Anarquistas*.

The exclusion of Marighella's story from the narrative of Italian radicalism in São Paulo further illustrates how, following World War II, the New World Italian discourse co-opted and mythologized the figure of the Italian anarchist. As discussed earlier, the presence of Italian anarcho-syndicalists and socialists in São Paulo initially threatened the project of modernization and whitening that accompanied Italians' arrival in Brazil. Their subversive activities, unsurprisingly, do not appear in the Italian travelogues about Brazil analyzed in Chapter One, nor do they animate the modernist corpus discussed in Chapter Two. However, beginning with the postwar military dictatorship, the Brazilian mainstream media—which had once demonized Italian anarchists and socialists—embraced them as quintessential Italian migrants. The case of Gattai's memoir, adapted into a wildly popular miniseries in 1984, illustrates well how the valences of the Italian anarchist had changed within the New World Italian discourse. Gattai's parents, despite their vulgar Veneto dialect and their utopian anarchist beliefs, posed less of a threat to the assumptions underlying this discourse than the legendary Marighella, the Black revolutionary who taught the world the art of urban guerrilla warfare. Indeed, one measure of this discrepancy is the fact that while *Anarquistas, graças a Deus* became a TV sensation, the 2019 biopic *Marighella* was subjected to a years-long delay in coming to the screen due to alleged interference from the government of Jair Bolsonaro.[5]

Celebrating the story of this endearing Italian family, whose anarchist politics lay safely in the distant past, served a twofold purpose. First, it allowed Brazilian mainstream media, both oppressed by and (at times) complicit in the country's ongoing military dictatorship, to lionize a story of political dissidence, albeit one that did not pose a contemporaneous threat to the status quo. Secondly, Gattai's memoir fostered a more sympathetic narrative about Italians in Brazil, distancing them from the taints of settler colonialism and fascism and, instead, associating them with utopian idealism and victimhood. In so doing, the trope of the Italian anarchist emerged as an ideal mechanism by which to ensure that the New World Italian discourse would remain central to the way Brazilians imagined themselves for years to come.

At the same time, the erasure of Marighella's Italianness, both in the Brazilian and Italian imaginary, reveals the contradictions at the basis of the blood and soil argument that suffuses much of the discourse around who "owns" Italianness.[6] While Marighella's blood lineage makes him Italian, at least according to those who insist on making national belonging a family matter, his phenotype is another matter altogether. As numerous scholars have pointed out, the exemplary "Italian" national subject is tacitly understood to be white.[7] In this sense, Marighella's Blackness would seem to inhibit his recognition as an Italian. At the same time, I also contend that, for as much as emigration informs the making of the Italian nation, certain forms of transnational (Italian) whiteness are not as unambiguously Italian as we might suppose.

One key argument I have advanced throughout this book proposes that Italians became white in São Paulo before they did so anywhere else, not excluding the peninsula. Institutional initiatives alongside travelogues, novels, parodies, pamphlets, and memoirs mediated how Italians functioned as incontrovertible vectors of whiteness in Brazil. In other words, the construction of a distinctively white Italian race occurs within a defined set of social circumstances unique to turn-of-the-century São Paulo. To this day, Paulistanos have a specific conception of who and what the term "Italian" signifies. They have managed to reproduce and, at times, reshape what I have called the New World Italian discourse across time and space. At any given moment, a visitor or resident from Italy going about his or her business in São Paulo is sure to encounter at least one resident who likewise professes to be "Italian." Such people say so with a certain pride—a pride that seems to smack of the *civiltà italiana* so precious to the Italian nationalists and imperialists of the early twentieth century.

While São Paulo residents claim their belonging to a specific national group because their ancestors were Italian immigrants, their understanding of what that Italianness entails has clearly been shaped by the presence of institutions such as the Colégio Dante Alighieri (formerly the Istituto Medio Italo-Brasiliano Dante Alighieri) and by the constant celebration of Italian culture and art in the city. The Bardi power couple—composed of renowned artist Pietro Bardi and perhaps one of the most brilliant architects of the twentieth century, Lina Bo Bardi—offers a potent example of the Italianness projected onto and by São Paulo. So, too, does the fact that the second oldest art biennale after the one in Venice, initiated by none other than Italian industrialist Francesco Matarazzo's nephew Ciccillo, takes place in São Paulo. Ciccillo's indefatigable efforts to secure representation of Brazilian artists in the Italian galleries at the Venice Biennale and to make São Paulo home to the second largest international art exhibition in the world speaks precisely to the ways in which notions of a civiltà italiana shape São Paulo's own Italianness.[8]

The construction of Italian whiteness in São Paulo has relied as much on the city's demographic character, which—thanks to the current laws granting citizenship based on blood lineage—claims the largest number of Italians outside of Italy, as it has on its residents' continuous appeal to those ideals of civiltà italiana that frame Italy as the cradle of Western civilization. In sum, the blood and soil argument alone would not have bestowed upon these Paulistanos the same economic and racial privileges that they have been enjoyed since the arrival of Italians in São Paulo. Authors as diverse as Gina Lombroso Ferrero, Antônio de Alcântara Machado, José Correia Leite, Miguel Reale, and Zélia Gattai all understood that to "own" Italianness one needed to embody both racial *and* cultural traits. The Italian national project not only has coveted what we might refer to as phenotypical whiteness, but also what we might call cultural whiteness—that is, a culture that firmly promotes bourgeois values. In this sense, class also profoundly shapes the construction of Italian whiteness.

But if the examples of José Correia Leite and Carlos Marighella have made the racial limits of the Italian national project quite clear, bringing us back to the United States, where this book started, further reveals which culture and therefore which whiteness determines who can lay claim to *italianità*. While Italian Americans base their own professions to Italianness on generational blood ties, they do not, broadly speaking, interpret their Italianness through the paradigm of civiltà italiana espoused by Paulistanos of

Italian descent and, as I have shown, those city residents with no ancestral ties to Italy. While in the United States Anglo-Saxon Protestant elites believed Italians to be potential agents of racial contamination, their counterparts in São Paulo endorsed the opposite view. That is to say, they not only welcomed Italians with open arms; they also reasoned that the presence of Italians in São Paulo could, by means of miscegenation, if not mere osmosis, transpose the cradle of Western civilization to Brazil.

As I have shown, certain Italian immigrants were able to accrue an impressive amount of cultural and financial capital in São Paulo and thereby turn themselves and their compatriots into paragons of whiteness; however, the same cannot be said of the Italian diasporic experience in North America. Italianness in the US imaginary bears a specific class stigma, which in the past has often taken on overt racial overtones. When contrasted to the New World Italian discourse I have traced in this book, Italian American cultural identity appears to have less to do with civiltà italiana, than with working-class values bound up with notions of family, food, and folklore that serve as a counterpoint to the seemingly bloodless white mainstream. To be sure, in São Paulo too, as I explained in Chapter Five, these more lowbrow, popular manifestations flourished among the Italian ethnic communities of São Paulo and informed their Italianness, but they did not accrue the same fraught connotations, and, more importantly, they were accompanied by a constant search for authenticity reflected in the usage of the Italian language and the inculcation of reverence for Italian canonical artists. In the case of Italian Americans, however, that same search, motivated by deep cultural anxiety over whether they belonged to either the Italian or the American national project, resulted in the glorification of dated stereotypes (or what Robert Viscusi called the "cult of primeval Italy") and a deep attachment to Italian traditions that have lost their original referent.[9] Moreover, these same cultural manifestations index a specific Southern Italianness which, as scholars have noted, simultaneously informs and refutes the Italian national project. Paradoxically, the very cultural practices that ensure Italian Americans' (ethnic) whiteness within the US panorama mark them as *culturally* other to the Italian one. The blood and soil argument that dominates Italian political discourse about national belonging collapses when facing its diasporic iterations.

If descendants of Italians in the Americas have not been historically accepted as "Italian" because of their linguistic and cultural distance from the prototypical Italian citizen, then to what extent can the adoption of these traits ever make one Italian?[10] How far have we come from the days of Leite in Bexiga over a century ago? One way to answer this question would be to take stock of the situation of the children of non-Italian citizens who have grown up in the national school system and whose linguistic and cultural competencies align more directly with those living on the peninsula today. Perhaps, in a post-fascist and post-imperial Italy, these assimilated peninsular Italians are unequivocally "Italian"? But that is also not the case. It seems that neither blood nor culture alone can satisfy the entry requirements of this exclusive club. What, then, does it really mean to be Italian?[11] Are we stuck with the racial nationalist paradigm inherited from the nineteenth century? Is it possible to break the links between Italian citizenship and whiteness, on the one hand, and italianità and civiltà italiana, on the other? By posing the question "Whose Italianness?" I want to suggest that perhaps a more fruitful way of engaging with questions of national belonging might lie in thinking about them in terms of plurality, of not just one "authentic" Italianness but multiple ones of equal validity, which coexist, both nationally and transnationally, and inhere in multiple bodies and languages. This would allow us to acknowledge so much that the historical record has obscured, such as the fact that Carlos Marighella was a Black Brazilian Communist who spoke Portuguese—and also happened to be, in an important sense, Italian.

ACKNOWLEDGMENTS

Studying Modern Languages and Literatures can sometimes take you to places that provide you with another home, one that feels like the place where you truly belong. São Paulo welcomed me with open arms, enveloping me in its chaos and showing me that there are places that accept you with all your flaws. Of course, my encounter with São Paulo would not have been possible without the numerous institutions, advisors, colleagues, friends, and family that have accompanied me throughout this journey.

This book is freely available in an open-access edition thanks to TOME (Toward an Open Monograph Ecosystem)—a collaboration of the Association of American Universities, the Association of University Presses, and the Association of Research Libraries—and the generous support of the University of Michigan College of Literature, Science, and the Arts and the Office of the Vice President for Research. The Italian Scientists and Scholars in North America Foundation recognized the innovation of this book project with their Young Investigator Award in 2021, a prize which came with funds I used to support my research. At the same time, the Modern Languages Association, through the 27th Aldo and Jeanne Scaglione Prize for a Manuscript in Italian Literary Studies, awarded me a generous subvention toward publishing costs. I am grateful to the juries in both awards and to these institutions for financially and intellectually endorsing the book.

At the University of Michigan, the Institute of the Humanities provided me with a faculty writing fellowship during the academic year 2022–2023, which gave me the time and financial support I needed to finish this book on time. The Provost's Early Tenure-Track Faculty Research Support Initiative allowed me to host a book manuscript workshop at the end of my fellowship year. I am especially indebted to Peggy McCraken for taking the helm of the manuscript workshop and for being such a dedicated reader, moderator, and mentor. Pamela Ballinger, Vincenzo Binetti, Dario Gaggio, Victoria Langland, Karla Mallette, and Daniel Nemser offered precious insights and feedback. I want to thank them for taking the time to read the manuscript and for attending the workshop. I am grateful to the outside readers, Christopher Dunn, Claudio Fogu, and Lina Insana, whose careful review of the manuscript helped me transform it into this book. Their guidance throughout this process has been extremely important and helped shape the final product.

My career at the University of Michigan has been struck, like the ones of so many others, by the COVID-19 pandemic. This book should be understood as a product of those years, considering that most of the writing took place against the backdrop of a global pandemic that completely upended our way of life. Thankfully, I found myself in a department that supported and encouraged me every step of the way. Gavin Arnall, David Caron, Nilo Couret, Enrique García Santo-Tómas, Lorenzo García-Amaya, Michèle Hannoosh, Nicholas Henriksen, George Hoffmann, Juli Highfill, Kate Jenckes, Cristina Moreiras, Ana Sabau, Javier Sanjinés, Paolo Squatriti, Gustavo Verdesio, Sergio Villalobos-Ruminott, and Gareth Williams have all taken the time to welcome me into the Department of Romance Languages and Literatures and made me feel that, despite the isolation imposed on us, I was part of a lively intellectual community. I am also grateful to Paulina Alberto, Giorgio Bertellini, Alison Cornish, Walter Cohen, Frieda Ekotto, Lucy Hartley, Aida Levy-Hussain, Marjorie Levinson, Xiomara Santamarina, and Geneviève Zubrzycki for their mentorship, friendship, and advice. The staff in the Department of Romance Languages and Literatures as well as the librarians at the University of Michigan have also been an incredible source of knowledge and support.

I am fortunate to have encountered during this journey colleagues who soon became friends and trusted collaborators, as we each grappled with the research and the writing we were producing under the extraordinary circumstances of the pandemic. This book has benefited from the writing sessions that Swapnil Rai and I have held on Zoom since February 2020. She offered me an incredible example of resilience and industriousness and I am grateful for her comradeship. A special thanks goes to Jason Fitzgerald and Ittai Orr who have provided a space where I could regenerate and feel something akin to familial warmth. Our conversations have enriched this book in many ways, and our road trips helped to keep me going. Hadji Bakara, Adi Saleem, Niloofar Sarlati, and Will Stroebel have provided me with important points of comparison, and I am grateful to have gone through this process alongside them. Milena Magri, Gustavo Scudeller, Eduardo Altheman C. Santos, and Bruna Della Torre made my trips to São Paulo all the more fun; their friendship has accompanied me throughout this very long journey and their brilliant minds have also informed this book in myriad ways.

The conceptualization of *The Italian Colony of São Paulo* also came to fruition thanks to the lively discussions of the Transnational Italian Studies Working Group. The conversations with Serena Bassi, Emma Bond, Evelyn Ferraro, Michele Monserrati, and Loredana Polezzi have especially provided me with a space where I could truly imagine this book. They pushed me to take ownership of my claims and to move forward with the project, despite at times feeling like I was stuck. Thank you for your friendship and encouragement.

Laura E. Ruberto and Nancy Carnevale believed in this project from the very beginning. They welcomed this book in their series and for this I will always be grateful to them. Fred Nachbaur and the entire team at Fordham University Press supported me and ensured that the book moved along the various stages as smoothly as it could. I thank them for their efficiency and professionalism. Kevin Gallin, Lucas Koutsoukos-Chalhoub, Hayden Page-Graves, Ben Platt, Elizabeth Tremmel, and Akiko Yamagata have all contributed to the formatting and editing of this book at different moments. Chapter One contains an expanded version of the article "*Tutto è Italiano*: Gina Lombroso Ferrero, Travel Writing, and the Making of an Italian Empire in São Paulo," which appeared in *Altreitalie: Rivista internazionale di studi sulle migrazioni italiane nel mondo* (no. 68, 2024, 24–44).

I treasure the six years I spent at Duke University with all my heart. They have shaped me into the academic I am today. I had the good fortune to work under the guidance of two brilliant teachers and scholars, Lamonte Aidoo and Roberto Dainotto. Both showed me how to think creatively and critically about the issues that animate much of this book: race, class, culture, and nationalism. I thank them both for the time, the energy, and the support they have given me throughout these many years. I am also grateful to Nancy Armstrong, Deborah Jenson, Jessica Nammakal, and Saskia Ziolkowski for providing me with amazing models of women scholars. David Dulceany, Alyssa Granacki, Ciro Incoronato, and Kasia Stempniak have been constant sources of encouragement, joy, and laughter during and after graduate school. Few academics can say that one of their closest friends and primary collaborators from graduate school has continued on to the same institution. I guess I am one of the lucky ones. Renee Ragin Randall has seen this project grow from a mere idea at Duke University to a fully formed book here at the University of Michigan. This book has benefited tremendously from her feedback and longstanding comradeship.

Valentina Cova and Agnese Selmi have listened to me talk about this book for many years now. Whenever I talked to Agnese, I was reminded of how privileged I was in doing what we always enjoyed doing together: study, learn, write. This book is in many ways a testament to our decades-long intellectual friendship. Valentina is the sister I never had. When we both chose to leave Italy we had no idea what was waiting for us on the other side of the Atlantic. We both knew we wanted something different than what our respective milieus told us to expect. To quote Michela Murgia, "le amicizie pluridecennali . . . sono fonte dell'unica cosa che non si può ripetere: il tempo." Valentina's lust for life and laughter is infectious and has sustained me through some of the hardest moments of this journey.

Chiara Cavazzoni and Giovanni Riccò have been there all along. My mother faced one of the most horrific events that could happen to a young woman with her head held high and she marched through life with a force that moved everything and everyone around her. She taught me to be resilient and to pursue my dreams. It is because of her incessant support, her constant search for freedom, and, to a certain extent, her incorrigible recklessness that this book exists. My brother has helped me to endure the tragedy that befell us, and I hope that I have done the same for him. We have lived it together and our bond is indissoluble. Talking with him always gives me novel ways to interpret events and situations. His creativity and unique worldview reverberate through this book.

The Italian Colony of São Paulo is dedicated to Justin David Mitchell. Over the past ten years he has taught me to be a better thinker, a better writer, and a better person. He is my light and the love of my life, and I wrote this book for him. He knows this. But it feels good to finally write it and read it in print. Thank you Justin for all you have done for me, for all you continue to do.

NOTES

INTRODUCTION. *SÃO PAULO, NOVA YORK DA SUL AMERICA*: ITALIAN IMMIGRANTS IN SÃO PAULO AND THE MAKING OF MODERN BRAZILIAN CULTURE

1. See Jennifer Guglielmo, "Introduction: White Lies, Dark Truths," in *Are Italians White? How Race Is Made in America*, ed. Jennifer Guglielmo and Salvatore Salerno (New York: Routledge, 2003), 1–16; Tatiana Petrovich Njegosh, "Gli italiani sono bianchi? Per una storia culturale della linea del colore in Italia," in *Parlare di Razza: la lingua del colore tra Italia e Stati Uniti*, ed. Tatiana Petrovich Njegosh and Anna Scacchi (Verona: Ombre Corte, 2012), 14. All translations from Italian and Portuguese are mine unless otherwise stated.

2. David R. Roedinger, *The Wages of Whiteness: Race and the Making of the American Working Class* (New York: Verso, 1999); David R. Roedinger, *Working Toward Whiteness: How America's Immigrants Became White: The Strange Journey from Ellis Island to the Suburbs* (New York: Basic Books, 2005), 37; on immigration restrictions, see Danielle Battisti, *Whom Shall We Welcome: Italian Americans and Immigration Reform 1945–1965* (New York: Fordham University Press, 2019).

3. On the race versus color debate, see Thomas A. Guglielmo, *White on Arrival: Italians, Race, Color, and Power in Chicago, 1890–1945* (Oxford: Oxford University Press, 2004); Peter G. Vellon, *A Great Conspiracy against Our Race: Italian Immigrant Newspapers and the Construction of Whiteness in the Early 20th Century* (New York: New York University Press, 2017).

4. Richard Gambino, *Vendetta: The True Story of the Largest Lynching in US History* (Toronto: Guernica Press, 2000).

5. Gary Gerstle, *American Crucible: Race and Nation in the Twentieth Century* (Princeton, NJ: Princeton University Press, 2017), 102, 107; Adolph L. Reed Jr., *The South: Jim Crow and Its Afterlives* (New York: Verso, 2022), 27.

6. Joseph Sciorra offers an invaluable recollection of what it meant for him, an Italian American, to march alongside African Americans holding a sign that read "Italians against Racism." In fact, his sign "called into question the popular notion that joined Italian American identity and racial hatred in some natural and essentialist union." See Joseph Sciorra, "'Italians Against Racism': The Murder of Yusuf Hawkins (R.I.P.) and My March on Bensonhurst," in *Are Italians White? How Race Is Made in America*, ed. Jennifer Guglielmo and Salvatore Salerno (New York: Routledge, 2003), 194.

7. Matthew Frye Jacobson, *Whiteness of a Different Color: European Immigrants and the Alchemy of Race* (Cambridge, MA: Harvard University Press, 1999), 57.

8. See Pierre Bourdieu, *Distinction: A Social Critique of the Judgement of Taste*, trans. Richard Niece (New York: Routledge, 2010 [1986]), 168. Feminist theorist Sara Ahmed speaks of "racialization," and a "racialized body" to "think of the multiple processes whereby bodies come to be seen as 'having' a racial identity." See Sara Ahmed, "Racialized Bodies," in *Real Bodies*, ed. Mary Evans and Ellie Lee (London: Palgrave, 2000), 46.

9. John Gennari describes "the edge and the overlap . . . between Italian American and African American cultures" as "a space of hopeful encounter and wary suspicion, dangerous, sometimes violent collision, and magnificent, joyous collusion." Gennari shows "that the intersections and overlaps of Italian American and African American expressive culture constitute a distinctive space in the American imagination." John Gennari, *Flavor and Soul: Italian America at Its African American Edge* (Chicago: University of Chicago Press, 2017), 8, 12.

10. As anthropologist Valeria Ribeiro Corossacz has noted—channeling James Baldwin's idea that those who can choose to opt into whiteness do so—only those groups who were not perceived as fully white had the "power" to self-define themselves as white. Valeria Ribeiro Corossacz, *Bianchezza e mascolinità in Brasile: Etnografia di un soggetto dominante* (Milano: Mimesis Edizioni, 2015), 21.

11. On the racial debates that accompanied the creation of the Italian nation-state see Aliza Wong, *Race and the Nation in Liberal Italy, 1861–1911: Meridionalism, Empire, and Diaspora* (New York: Palgrave Macmillan, 2006); Lucia Re, "Italians and the Invention of Race: The Poetics and Politics of Difference in the Struggle over Libya, 1890–1913," *California Italian Studies* 1, no. 1 (2010): 1–65; Silvana Patriarca, *Italian Vices: Nation and Character from the Risorgimento to the Republic* (Cambridge: Cambridge University Press, 2010); Rhiannon Noel Welch, *Vital Subjects: Race and Biopolitics in Italy* (Liverpool: Liverpool University Press, 2016).

12. Antonio Gramsci has famously understood the annexation of the southern territories by the Savoy Crown in colonial terms. Pasquale Verdicchio offers an interpretation of this process and its devastating consequences from a diasporic perspective. See Pasquale Verdicchio, *Bound by Distance: Rethinking Nationalism through the Italian Diaspora* (New York: Bordighera Press, 2016), esp. 1-43.

13. On the construction of the *Mezzogiorno* see Jane Schneider, ed., *Italy's "Southern Question": Orientalism in One Country* (New York: Routledge, 1998); John Dickie, *Darkest Italy: The Nation and Stereotypes of the Mezzogiorno, 1860–1900* (New York: Palgrave Macmillan, 1999); Nelson J. Moe, *The View from Vesuvius: Italian Culture and the Southern Question* (Oakland: University of California Press, 2002).

14. Shelleen Greene, in her investigation on race and nation in modern Italian cinema, "looks at the mixed-race as a trope for the country's negotiation of its internal racial heterogeneity that continues to the present day." Shelleen Greene, *Equivocal Subjects: Between Italy and Africa. Constructions of Racial and National Identity in the Italian Cinema* (New York: Continuum, 2012), 3.

15. Historian Nicola Labanca calls this the "heaviest white loss within the entire scramble for Africa." Nicola Labanca, *Oltremare: storia dell'espansione coloniale italiana* (Bologna: Il Mulino, 2007), 82.

16. Fabrizio De Donno offers a detailed analysis of the evolution of Giuseppe Sergi's mediterraneism throughout the fascist *ventennio*. It culminates, in his analysis, in 1926 with the creation of a *razza ario-mediterranea* (Aryan-Mediterranean race) in the aftermath of the occupation of Ethiopia and in conjunction with the alliance with Nazi Germany. See Fabrizio De Donno, "La Razza Ario-Mediterranea. Ideas of Race and Citizenship in Colonial and Fascist Italy, 1885–1941," *Interventions* 8, no. 3 (2007): 405–6.

17. For an in-depth study of the role the Mediterranean has played in the fascist racial imaginary see Gaia Giuliani "Mediterraneità e bianchezza: il razzismo italiano tra fascismo e articolazioni contemporanee (1861–2015)," *Iperstoria–Testi Letterature Linguaggi* 6 (2015): 167–82; for a revaluation of *mediterraneità* and how it ties Italy to Africa see Camilla Hawthorne, *Contesting Race and Citizenship: Youth Politics in the Black Mediterranean* (Ithaca, NY: Cornell University Press, 2022); for the changing valences of the Mediterranean in the Italian national imaginary see Claudio Fogu, *The Fishing Net and the Spider Web: Mediterranean Imaginaries and the Making of Italians* (New York: Palgrave Macmillan, 2020).

18. See Angelica Pesarini, "'Blood Is Thicker than Water': The Materialisation of the Racial Body in Fascist East Africa," *Zapruder World: An International*

Journal for the History of Social Conflict 4 (2017); Angelica Pesarini, "When the Mediterranean Became Black: Diasporic Hopes and (Post)Colonial Traumas," in *The Black Mediterranean: Bodies, Borders, and Citizenship* (London: Palgrave Macmillan, 2021), 31–55.

19. Roberto M. Dainotto, *Europe (in Theory)* (Durham, NC: Duke University Press, 2007).

20. What Sandra Ponzanesi has called Italy's "colonial unconscious," and Caterina Romeo "racial evaporations." See, respectively, Sandra Ponzanesi, "The Postcolonial Turn in Italian Studies: European Perspectives," in *Postcolonial Italy*, ed. Cristina Lombardi-Diop and Caterina Romeo (New York: Palgrave Macmillan, 2012), 52; Caterina Romeo, "Racial Evaporations: Representing Blackness in African Italian Postcolonial Literature," in *Postcolonial Italy*, ed. Cristina Lombardi-Diop and Caterina Romeo (New York: Palgrave Macmillan, 2012), 221.

21. See Alessandro Portelli, "The Problem of the Color Blind: Notes on the Discourse on Race in Italy," in *CrossRoutes: The Meaning of "Race" for the 21st Century*, ed. Paola Boi and Sabine Broeck (Münster: Lit Verlag, 2003), 29–39; Gaia Giuliani and Cristina Lombardi-Diop, *Bianco e nero. Storia dell'identità razziale degli italiani* (Milan: Le Monnier, 2013); Marzia Milazzo, *Colorblind Tools: Global Technologies of Racial Power* (Evanston, IL: Northwestern University Press, 2022).

22. Charles Burdett and Loredana Polezzi, eds., *Transnational Italian Studies* (Liverpool: Liverpool University Press, 2020), 15–16; Emma Bond, "Towards a Trans-National Turn in Italian Studies?," *Italian Studies* 69, no. 3 (2014): 415–24; Teresa Fiore, *Pre-Occupied Spaces: Remapping Italy's Transnational Migrations and Colonial Legacies* (New York: Fordham University Press, 2017).

23. Pamela Ballinger, "Beyond the Italies: Italy as a Mobile Subject?," in *Italian Mobilities*, ed. Ruth Ben-Ghiat and Stephanie Malia Hom (New York: Routledge, 2016), 21; on diaspora studies, see Donna R. Gabaccia, *Italy's Many Diasporas* (Seattle: University of Washington Press, 2000); on mobility studies see Ben-Ghiat and Hom, *Italian Mobilities*; on border studies, see Claudio Fogu, Stephanie Malia Hom, and Laura E. Ruberto, "Italia Senza Frontiere / Borderless Italy," *California Italian Studies* 9, no. 1 (2019): 1–12.

24. Even within the United States, as historian Stefano Luconi has shown, geography matters immensely when studying "the development of Italian Americans' whiteness." Stefano Luconi, "Italian Immigrants, Whiteness, and Race: A Regional Perspective," *Italian American Review* 11, no. 1 (2021): 19.

25. Cristina Lombardi-Diop, "Transoceanic Race: A Postcolonial Approach to Italian American Studies," in *Transcending Borders, Bridging Gaps:*

Italian Americana, Diasporic Studies, and the University Curriculum, ed. Anthony Tamburri and Fred Gardaphé (New York: John D. Calandra Italian-American Institute, 2015), 85.

26. Hawthorne, *Contesting Race and Citizenship*, 193–96.

27. While I am the first to explore this connection in depth, I am not the only one who is familiar with both Italian and Brazilian societies to have intuited this. Corossacz, in her book on whiteness and masculinity in Brazil, mentions in passing that "despite its geographical and cultural specificity," the object of her book "speaks of a reality not too far from the Italian one, in which similar mechanisms, apparently innocuous, sustain the experiences of privilege as invisible structure that keep racism, sexism, and classism in place." Corossacz, *Bianchezza e mascolinità*, 10.

28. Tatiana Petrovich Njegosh, "La finzione della razza: la linea del colore e il meticciato," in *Il colore della nazione*, ed. Gaia Giualiani (Florence: Le Monnier, 2015), 218.

29. "Of the New World receivers, the United States took 4.2 million, or 29 percent of the total; Canada 149,000 or 1 percent; Argentina 1.8 million, or 13 percent; and Brazil 1.4 million or 9 percent." See Walter Nugent, *Crossings: The Great Transatlantic Migrations, 1870–1914* (Bloomington: Indiana University Press, 1992), 95.

30. See Instituto Brasileiro de Geografia e Estatística, *Brasil: 500 anos de povoamento* (Rio de Janeiro: Instituto Brasileiro de Geografia e Estatística, 2000), app. Estatísticas de 500 Anos de Povoamento, 226.

31. John Tofik Karam, *Another Arabesque: Syrian-Lebanese Ethnicity in Neoliberal Brazil* (Philadelphia: Temple University Press, 2007); Oswaldo Truzzi, *Syrian and Lebanese Patricios in Sao Paulo: From the Levant to Brazil* (Champaign: University of Illinois Press, 2018).

32. Lúcia Lippi Oliveira, *Nós e eles: relações culturais entre brasileiros e imigrantes* (São Paulo: FGV, 2006), 44.

33. Very little exists in English on the Italian presence in Brazil. Jeffrey Lesser in a historiographical essay at the end of *Immigration, Ethnicity, and National Identity in Brazil* notes "how little attention is paid to immigration and immigrants to Latin America in the English language academic literature" and lists only two books written in English on Italian immigration to Brazil. Jeffrey Lesser, *Immigration, Ethnicity, and National Identity in Brazil, 1808 to the Present* (New York: Cambridge University Press, 2013), 197; Lesser cites Gloria La Cava, *Italians in Brazil: The Post–World War II Experience* (New York: Peter Lang, 1999); and Warren Dean, *Remittances of Italian Immigrants: From Brazil, Argentina, Uruguay and U.S.A., 1888–1914* (New York: New York University, Ibero-American Language and Area Center, 1974); while not

specifically on Italian migration, I would add to this list Thomas H. Holloway, *Immigrants on the Land: Coffee and Society in São Paulo, 1886–1934* (Chapel Hill: University of North Carolina Press, 1980). More recently, John Starosta Galante's *On the Other Shore: The Atlantic Worlds of Italians in South America during the Great War* (Lincoln: University of Nebraska Press, 2022) stands out as one of the most sophisticated social histories available in English on the Italian experiences in three key South American cities—São Paulo, Montevideo, and Buenos Aires—during World War I.

34. See, respectively, Angelo Trento, *Là dov'è raccolta del caffè. L'emigrazione italiana in Brasile, 1875–1940* (Padua: Editrice Antenore, 1984); Franco Cenni, *Italianos no Brasil: andiamo in 'Merica* (São Paulo: Livraria Martins Editora, 1975); Chiara Vangelista, *Le braccia per la fazenda: immigrati e caipiras nella formazione del mercato del lavoro paulista (1850–1930)* (Turin: Franco Angeli, 1982); Emilio Franzina, *Merica! Merica! Emigrazione e colonizzazione nelle lettere dei contadini veneti e friulani in America Latina (1876–1902)* (Caselle: Cierre Edizioni, 1994); Zuleika Alvim, *Brava gente! Os italianos em São Paulo, 1870–1920* (São Paulo: Brasiliense, 1986).

35. Holloway, *Immigrants on the Land*, 36–42.

36. On Brazilian racial theories and nation-making see Thomas Skidmore, *Black into White: Race and Nationality in Brazilian Thought* (Durham, NC: Duke University Press, 1993); Lilia Moritz Schwarcz, *The Spectacles of the Races: Scientists, Institutions, and the Race Question in Brazil, 1870–1930*, trans. Leland Guyer (New York: Hill and Wang, 1999); Nancy Stepan, *The Hour of Eugenics: Race, Gender, and Nation in Latin America* (Ithaca, NY: Cornell University Press, 1991). On Brazilian race relations see George Reid Andrews, *Blacks and Whites in São Paulo, Brazil 1888–1988* (Madison: University of Wisconsin Press, 1991); Micol Seigel, *Uneven Encounters: Making Race and Nation in Brazil and the United States* (Durham, NC: Duke University Press, 2009); Paulina Alberto, *Terms of Inclusion: Black Intellectuals in Twentieth-Century Brazil* (Chapel Hill: University of North Carolina Press, 2011). For an overview of how "definitions of race have been shaped by processes of nation building" in Latin America more broadly, see Nancy P. Appelbaum, Anne S. Macpherson, and Karin Alejandra Rosemblatt, eds., *Race and Nation in Modern Latin America* (Chapel Hill: University of North Carolina Press, 2003), 9.

37. It is telling that Brazil, represented by João Batista Lacerda, director of the Rio de Janeiro National Museum, was the only South American country invited to present at the First Universal Races Congress in 1911. Lacerda read the paper "Sur lex Métis au Brésil," in which he claimed that in three generations Brazil would "finally" become white. See Lilia Moritz Schwarcz,

Imagens da branquitude: a presença da ausência (São Paulo: Companhia das Letras, 2024), 286–87.

38. Mara Loveman, "Whiteness in Latin America: Measurement and Meaning in National Censuses," *Journal de La Société Des Américanistes* 95, no. 2 (2009): 219, 222–23; for a comparative study on the Italian diaspora to the Americas, see Samuel L. Bailey, *Immigrants in the Land of Promise: Italians in Buenos Aires and New York City, 1870–1914* (Ithaca, NY: Cornell University Press, 2004) and Elizabeth Zanoni, *Migrant Marketplaces: Foods and Italians in North and South America* (Urbana Champaign: University of Illinois, 2018). Ludovico Incisa di Camerana has shown how the nature of Italian migration to Argentina diverged from the one to Brazil in terms of political ideology, push and pull factors, and return rate. See Ludovico Incisa di Camerana, *Il grande esodo: storia delle migrazioni italiane nel mondo* (Milan: Corbaccio, 2003).

39. Patricia de Santana Pinho, "White but Not Quite: Tones and Overtones of Whiteness in Brazil," *Small Axe: A Caribbean Journal of Criticism* 13, no. 2 (2009): 44. Patricia de Santana Pinho also coedited with Hugo Ceron-Anya and Ana Ramos-Zayas a special issue of *Latin American and Caribbean Ethnic Studies* dedicated to the study of whiteness in Latin America. In their introduction they articulate a useful concept, that of "ordinary whiteness," which in turn allows them to "disentangle the subtle Latin American distinction between a whiteness that is never taken for granted or fully neutralized, on the one hand, and that which is, on the other hand, selectively activated, downplayed, and rendered affective or performative." Hugo Ceron-Anaya, Patricia de Santana Pinho, and Ana Ramos-Zayas, "A Conceptual Roadmap for the Study of Whiteness in Latin America," *Latin American and Caribbean Ethnic Studies* 18, no. 2 (2022): 183; on the myth of Brazilian racial democracy, see Paulina L Alberto and Jesse Hoffnung-Garskof, "'Racial Democracy' and Racial Inclusion," in *Afro-Latin American Studies: An Introduction*, by George R. Andrews and Alejandro de la Fuente (New York: Cambridge University Press, 2018).

40. Schwarcz, *Imagens da branquitude*, 58.

41. Warren Dean, *The Industrialization of São Paulo 1880–1945* (Austin: University of Texas Press, 1969), 66.

42. Molly C. Ball, *Navigating Life and Work in Old Republic São Paulo* (Gainesville: University of Florida Press. 2020), 20.

43. Ball, *Navigating Life and Work*, 99.

44. João Fábio Bertonha, "Le rappresentazioni degli italiani in Brasile. Centocinquanta anni di immagini, stereotipi e contraddizioni," *Diacronie* 5, no. 1: Dossier: Italie altre. Immagini e comunità italiane all'estero (2011).

45. Barbara Weinstein, *The Color of Modernity: São Paulo and the Making of Race and Nation in Brazil* (Durham, NC: Duke University Press, 2015), 14.

46. On the myth of backward Italy see John Agnew, "The Myth of Backward Italy in Modern Europe," in *Revisioning Italy: National Identity and Global Culture*, ed. Allen Beverly and Mary Russo (Minneapolis: University of Minnesota Press, 1997), 25–44; on the production of "margins" and the making of the Italian nation-state see David Forgacs, *Italy's Margins: Social Exclusion and Nation Formation since 1861* (Cambridge: Cambridge University Press, 2014).

47. In his extensive study on the Japanese community in Brazil, Lesser reveals that racial mixing in Brazil, especially when it came to immigrants, "was often understood as a joining (rather than mixing) of different identities, as the creation of a multiplicity of hyphenated Brazilians rather than a single, uniform one." (5) In this way, "ethnicity [was] maintained even as its importance was dismissed," (4) which resulted in the hidden hyphen. See Jeffrey Lesser, *Negotiating National Identity: Immigrants, Minorities, and the Struggle for Ethnicity in Brazil* (Durham, NC: Duke University Press, 1999), 4–5.

48. Gabaccia, *Italy's Many Diasporas*, 38. For a discussion on how notions of civilization inform Italians' perceived Europeanness through food and foodways in Argentina, see Zanoni, *Migrant Marketplaces*, 43–72. Ruberto and Sciorra also see the notion of an exportable *civiltà italiana* as a key aspect to the transnational success of Italian artists and artisans, who "as the inheritors and maintainers of European sculptural traditions . . . propagated ideals of the heroic, the triumphant, and the majestic rooted in antiquity and the classics while they supported the modern nation-building of their adopted countries." Laura E. Ruberto and Joseph Sciorra, "Disrupted and Unsettled: An Introduction to Monuments, Memorials, and Italian Migrations," *Italian American Review* 12, no. 1 (2022): 11.

49. Erica Salatini et al., "A presença italiana nas revistas literarias brasileiras da primeira metade do século XX," in *A literatura italiana no Brasil e a literatura brasileira na Itália: sob o olhar da tradução*, ed. Patricia Peterle (Tubarão: Copiart, 2011), 81–100.

50. Gina Lombroso Ferrero, *Nell'America Meridionale (Brasile-Uruguay-Argentina): note e impressioni di Gina Lombroso Ferrero* (Milan: Fratelli Treves, 1908).

51. António de Alcântara Machado, *Novelas paulistanas* (Rio de Janeiro: José Olympio Editora, 1961).

52. José Correia Leite, "E, Apoz a Liberdade," *O Clarim d'Alvorada*, August 30, 1925; "Incorrecto," *O Clarim d'Alvorada*, September 27, 1925; "Naziunale," *O Clarim*, January 6, 1924; "Sempri Avanti!," *O Clarim*, June 1924; "U Clarino," *O Clarim*, April 6, 1924.

53. Miguel Reale, *Obras políticas*, vol. 1, 1931–1937, 2 vols. (Brasília: Editora da Universidade de Brasília, 1983); Miguel Reale, *Imperativos da revolução de março* (São Paulo: Editora Martins, 1964); Miguel Reale, *Memórias*, vol. I:

Destinos cruzados, 2 vols. (São Paulo: Saraiva, 1987); Miguel Reale, *Memórias*, vol. II: A balança e a espada, 2 vols. (São Paulo: Saraiva, 1987).

54. Zelia Gattai, *Anarquistas, graças a Deus* (São Paulo: Companhia das Letras, 2009 [1979]).

CHAPTER ONE. *TUTTO È ITALIANO*: GINA LOMBROSO FERRERO AND THE CULTIVATION OF ITALIAN SÃO PAULO

1. Gina Lombroso Ferrero, *Nell'America Meridionale (Brasile-Uruguay-Argentina): note e impressioni di Gina Lombroso Ferrero* (Milan: Fratelli Treves, 1908), 34 (emphasis mine).

2. Historian Franco Cenni listed nearly thirty-five Italian-owned factories in São Paulo in 1900. See Franco Cenni, *Italianos no Brasil: andiamo in 'Merica* (São Paulo: Livraria Martins Editora, 1975), 204–5.

3. Nelson J. Moe, *The View from Vesuvius: Italian Culture and the Southern Question* (Oakland: University of California Press, 2002); Roberto M. Dainotto, *Europe (in Theory)* (Durham, NC: Duke University Press, 2007).

4. Gina Lombroso Ferrero's account of her travels in Brazil, Uruguay, and Argentina constitutes one of only three Italian travel writings about South America penned by female authors; the others were written by the nun Francesca Saverio Cabrini and novelist Gemma Ferruggia. The former details a journey from Panama to Lima in honor of Saint Rosa, patron of America. The latter narrates the author's travels through the Brazilian Amazon region, where her husband explored possible commercial venues in the booming rubber industry. Lombroso Ferrero is the only Italian woman who visited and witnessed firsthand the Italian settlements, or colonie, of Brazil. See Francesca Saverio Cabrini, *Viaggio delle suore missionarie del S. Cuore nel Pacifico attraverso la Cordigliera e nell'Atlantico* (Rome: Scuola Tip. Salesiana, 1898); Gemma Ferruggia, *Nostra Signora del Mar Dolce (missioni e paesaggi di Amazzonia)* (Milan: Tipografia editrice L.F. Cogliati, 1901).

5. Livio Sansone, "Hiperbólicos italianos: as viagens dos integrantes da escola positiva de antropologia da Itália pela América meridional, 1907–1910," *História, Ciências, Saúde-Manguinhos* 27, no. 1 (2020): 267–70. Emilio Mitre met Guglielmo Ferrero in Paris where Ferrero gave a series of lectures on the history of Rome. Guglielmo Ferrero's magnus opus *Grandezza e decadenza di Roma* (comprising six volumes published over the course of four years) "came to be very popular among intellectuals across all of Latin America." In *Grandezza e decadenza*, Ferrero speculates that "the latin genius could grow and contribute to the success of the young American nations, especially those in South America." Sansone, "Hiperbólicos Italianos," 267–69; on how Mitre and Ferrero met, see Francesco Rotondo,

"Reading a Travel Journal: The Melancholia of Gina Lombroso in Latin America," in *History of Law and Other Humanities*, ed. Virginia Amorosi and Valerio M. Minale (Madrid: Editorial Dykinson, 2019), 419.

6. Mark Choate, *Emigrant Nation: The Making of Italy Abroad* (Cambridge, MA: Harvard University Press, 2008), 32.

7. Rotondo, "Reading a Travel Journal," 419; Sansone, "Hiperbólicos Italianos," 267.

8. Lombroso Ferrero, *Nell'America Meridionale*, 35–36.

9. On Cesare Lombroso's influence in Argentina and Brazil, see Rotondo, "Reading a Travel Journal"; Marcela Varejão, *Il positivismo dall'Italia al Brasile. Sociologia del diritto, giuristi e legislazione (1822–1935)* (Milan: Giuffrè Editore, 2005).

10. On Gina Lombroso Ferrero's degree, see Anna Maria Colaci, "Gina Lombroso: una voce moderata all'interno del movimento emancipazionsita nel primo novecento," *Quaderni Di Intercultura* XI (2019): 173; on the Buenos Aires penitentiary, see Matías Ruíz Díaz, "Europa y América: Guglielmo Ferrero y Gina Lombroso en la Penitenciaría Nacional de Buenos Aires, 1907," *Anales del Instituto de Arte Americano e Investigaciones Estéticas, Mario J. Buschiazzo* 46, no. 1 (June 2016): 77–90.

11. Livio Sansone, *La galassia Lombroso* (Bari: Editori Laterza, 2022).

12. Tullio Pagano, *Italy to Argentina: Travel Writing and Emigrant Colonialism* (Amherst, MA: Amherst College Press, 2023), 152.

13. Delfina Dolza Carrara, *Essere figlie di Lombroso: due donne intellettuali ira '800 e '900* (Milan: Franco Angeli, 1991), 35–36, 42.

14. Carlo A. Gemignani, "Con Gina Lombroso nell'America Meridionale," in *Spazi, segni, parole: percorsi di viaggiatrici italiane*, ed. Federica Frediani, Ricciarda Ricorda, and Luisa Rossi (Milan: Franco Angeli Editore, 2012), 141.

15. Pagano, *Italy to Argentina*, 152.

16. Camilla Cattarulla, "Migrazioni al Río de la Plata e critica letteraria in Italia," *Altre modernità / Otras modernidades / Autres modernités / Other Modernities* 2, no. 10 (2009): 102.

17. Theodore J. Cachey Jr., "An Italian Literary History of Travel," *Annali d'Italianistica* 14 (1996): 55.

18. For example, Polezzi suggests that we read Alberto Moravia's nonfictional essays as belonging to the genre of travel writing. She points out how even literary scholar Mary Louise Pratt, a pioneer in the study of travel writing, uses Moravia as a case study in her work, albeit problematically. Yet in bookstores Moravia's travel writing sits in the shelves dedicated to other genres, such as autobiographical writing or *saggistica*. See Loredana Polezzi, *Translating Travel: Contemporary Italian Travel Writing in English Translation* (London : Routledge, 2001), 17–18.

19. Cattarulla, "Migrazioni al Río de la Plata," 105.

20. For Cattarulla, *scritture letterarie* (literally, "literary writings"), is an "expression that allows [us] to turn toward textual materials of different genres, addressing different goals and desires without having to chain them within the long-standing discussion in Italy about what literature is and is not." See Cattarulla, "Migrazioni al Río de la Plata," 105.

21. This commitment of Cattarulla's—that is, to bring to the fore what she calls a "submerged literature"—is already evidenced in her detailed 1992 bibliography of Italian travel accounts about South America that appeared in print between 1870 and 1914. In her more recent work, however, she notes how—almost two decades later—literary critics had not yet explored most of the critical possibilities that the works listed in her bibliography would open up. Cattarulla, "Migrazioni al Río de la Plata," 105–7.

22. Cachey Jr., "An Italian Literary History of Travel," 56.

23. Cattarulla, "Migrazioni al Río de La Plata," 107. For literary approaches to Italian travel writing, see Polezzi, *Translating Travel*; Charles Burdett and Derek Duncan, eds., *Cultural Encounters: European Travel Writing in the 1930s*: *Remapping Cultural History* (New York: Berghahn Books, 2002); Charles Burdett, *Journeys through Fascism: Italian Travel Writing between the Wars*: *Remapping Cultural History*, v. 7 (New York: Berghahn Books, 2007); Nathalie Hester, *Literature and Identity in Italian Baroque Travel Writing* (Surrey: Ashgate Publishing, Ltd., 2008); Barbara Spackman, *Accidental Orientalists: Modern Italian Travelers in Ottoman Lands* (Liverpool: Liverpool University Press, 2017); and Pagano, *Italy to Argentina*. For more anthropological perspectives, see Cristina Lombardi-Diop, "Gifts, Sex, and Guns: Nineteenth-Century Italian Explorers in Africa," in *A Place in the Sun—Africa in Italian Colonial Culture from Post-Unification to the Present*, ed. Patrizia Palumbo (Berkeley: University of California Press, 2003), 119–37; Barbara Sorgoni, "Diventare antropologo: Alberto Pollera e l'etnografia coloniale," *Quaderni Storici* 37 (February 1, 2002): 55–82; and Federica Frediani, Ricciarda Ricorda, and Luisa Rossi, eds., *Spazi, segni, parole: percorsi di viaggiatrici italiane* (Milan: FrancoAngeli, 2012). Of the aforementioned studies, only one, the excellent book by Tullio Pagano, engages directly with Italian travel writing about Latin America—and focuses mostly on Argentina. Latin Americanist Sebastiano Martelli laments the fact that Italian travel writing about Latin America seems to be the object of historians more so than literary critics. While perhaps there exists in Italy a small group of literary scholars who engage with travel writing about Latin America—such as Martelli himself—they mostly dedicate themselves to Argentina, as is the case of Caterina Cattarulla. When we look at what has critically been done for Italian travel writing about Brazil, Martelli's complaint rings even truer: two

canonical historians of Italian migration to Brazil, Emilio Franzina and Chiara Vangelista seem to have taken upon themselves the duty to fill a gap in literary criticism which this chapter only partially fills. In addition to Franzina and Vangelista, historian David Aliano more recently wrote an essay about Italian travel writing about Brazil during the fascist years. See, Chiara Vangelista, "Vita d'emigrante. Il colono nella piantagione di caffè paulista secondo l'interpretazione dei viaggiatori italiani (1880–1930)," in *Miscellanea di storia delle esplorazioni*, vol. VII, ed. Francesco Surdich (Genoa: Bozzi Editore, 1982); Chiara Vangelista, "Una viaggiatrice italiana di fine ottocento: Gemma Ferruggia in Amazzonia," *Fênix-Revista de História e Estudos Culturais* 13, no. 1 (2016): 1–13; and, more recently, David Aliano, "Brazil through Italian Eyes: The Debate over Emigration to São Paulo during the 1920s," *Altreitalie* 31 (2005): 87–108.

24. Camilla Cattarulla, "Alla 'riscoperta' del Nuovo Mondo 1. Bibliografia dei viaggiatori italiani in America Latina (1870–1914)," *Biblioteche Oggi* 4 (1992): 422, 427.

25. Sandra Ponzanesi, "The Postcolonial Turn in Italian Studies: European Perspectives," in *Postcolonial Italy*, ed. Cristina Lombardi-Diop and Caterina Romeo (New York: Palgrave Macmillan, 2012), 52.

26. Mary Louise Pratt, *Imperial Eyes: Travel Writing and Transculturation* (New York: Routledge, 2008), 3–4.

27. Spackman, *Accidental Orientalists*, 6.

28. Cattarulla, "Migrazioni al Río de la Plata," 117.

29. Choate, *Emigrant Nation*, 3, 23, 29.

30. Nicola Labanca, *Oltremare: storia dell'espansione coloniale italiana* (Bologna: Il Mulino, 2007), 61, 82. In truth, as Giorgio Rochat argues, the battle at Adwa was "lost from the beginning." General Baratieri, who led the attack, had underestimated the size and tenacity of Menelik's army: a mere 16,000 Italian soldiers met roughly 100,000 men, armed with modern weaponry. Moreover, the Italian military had not even bothered to conduct proper reconnaissance of the territory that had lain at the center of their imperial hopes for ten years. See Giorgio Rochat, "Adua: analisi di una sconfitta," in *Adua. Le ragioni di una sconfitta*, ed. Angelo del Boca (Bari: Laterza, 1997), 343–45.

31. Choate, *Emigrant Nation*, 17, 40.

32. Choate, *Emigrant Nation*, 50; Luigi Einaudi, *Un principe mercante; studio sulla espansione coloniale italiana* (Turin: Fratelli Bocca Editore, 1901), 18.

33. Einaudi, *Un principe mercante*, 13.

34. Historian Angelo Trento debunks the myth of the self-made man that *Un principe mercante* popularized. He explains how very few Italians were able to purchase a piece of land in the State of São Paulo and that the modicum of

success Italian craftsmen have enjoyed in the urban centers had less to do with "entrepreneurial flair" than with "the fact that many 'new' activities were alien to the cultural horizons of the local ruling class." To this point, Trento adds that any somewhat successful small business in an urban setting probably resulted from "enormous hardships and sacrifices." See Angelo Trento, "Italianità in Brazil: A Disputed Object of Desire," in *The Columbus People: Perspectives in Italian Immigration to the Americas and Australia*, ed. Lydio F. Tomasi, Piero Gastaldo, and Thomas Row (New York: The Center For Migration Studies of New York, 1994), 254–57; Angelo Trento, *Là dov'è la raccolta del caffè. L'emigrazione italiana in Brasile, 1875–1940* (Padua: Editrice Antenore, 1984), 194.

35. Einaudi, *Un principe mercante*, 14.

36. Einaudi, *Un principe mercante*, 18; Claudio Fogu, *The Fishing Net and the Spider Web: Mediterranean Imaginaries and the Making of Italians* (New York: Palgrave Macmillan, 2020), 92.

37. Teresa Fiore, "The Emigrant Post-'Colonia' in Contemporary Immigrant Italy," in *Postcolonial Italy*, ed. Cristina Lombardi-Diop and Caterina Romeo (New York: Palgrave Macmillan, 2012), 73.

38. Teresa Fiore, *Pre-Occupied Spaces: Remapping Italy's Transnational Migrations and Colonial Legacies* (New York: Fordham University Press, 2017).

39. Ubaldo A. Moriconi, *Nel paese de' macacchi* (Turin: Roux Frassati, 1897), 28 (emphasis mine).

40. For a more detailed overview of Italians in this region, see the authoritative article by Gianfausto Rosoli, "L'emigrazione Italiana nel Rio Grande do Sul, Brasile meridionale," *Altreitalie* 10, no. 2 (1993): 105–22.

41. While there were important Italian settlements in Rio Grande do Sul and Santa Catarina, these regions ultimately became mostly known for their prominent German presence, which was later deemed dangerous. The original preference for this ethnic group had to do with Empress Leopoldina's belief that Germans would have been better at small-scale farming. However, religious differences, the fact that Germans preferred to marry within their own ethnic groups, and the emergence of coffee as the major Brazilian export changed the type of laborers the Brazilian government sought and, consequently, the Italian colono supplanted the German farmer as a more favored immigrant. See Jeffrey Lesser, *Immigration, Ethnicity, and National Identity in Brazil, 1808 to the Present* (New York: Cambridge University Press, 2013), 28–44.

42. Historians Claudio de Majo and Samira Peruchi Moretto have focused on the role that an American grape called Isabella had in the success of Italians in that region, which ultimately allowed them to claim the status of

model colonos. Michele Monserrati proposes a similar argument with regard to the wine-making practices of Italians in California, advancing how viniculture "whitens" Italians. See Claudio De Majo and Samira Peruchi Moreno, "From Slash and Burn to Winemaking: The Historical Trajectory of Italian Colonos in the Uplands of Rio Grande Do Sul, Brazil," *Modern Italy* 26, no. 2 (2021): 141–58; Michele Monserrati, "A Victorian Taste of Italy: Situating the 'Italian-Swiss Colony' in California Wine Culture," *Forum Italicum* 57, no. 2 (2023): 690–713.

43. Vito De Bellis, *Fra l'Italia e Il Brasile* (Rome: Tipografia Nazionale di G. Bertero & C., 1907); Moriconi, *Nel paese de' macacchi*; Alfredo Cusano, *Italia d'oltre mare; impressioni e ricordi dei miei cinque anni di Brasile* (Milan: Stabilimento Tipografico Enrico Reggiani, 1911), 240.

44. The Legge Crispi of 1888 outlawed the figure of the *agente di emigrazione*, turning them into the scapegoats for what was, by all accounts, an acute demographic crisis. For more information on the figure of the agente di emigrazione, see Pietro Brunello, "Agenti di emigrazione, contadini e immagini dell'America nella provincia di Venezia," *Rivista di storia contemporanea* 11, no. 1 (1982): 95–122.

45. For almost two decades, planters exercised complete control over São Paulo's immigration programs and policies, first through the Associação Auxiliadora de Colonização e Imigração and later through the Sociedade Promotora da Imigração (1886) with landowner Martinho Prado Junior at its helm. With the promulgation of the federal constitution in 1891, the Sociedade slowly transitioned to a control-regulated agency, operating under the São Paulo Department of Agriculture. It officially ended its operations in 1895. For a detailed profile of the Sociedade, see also Ivison Poleto Dos Santos, "Sociedade Promotora de Imigração: formação e influência, 1886–1895," *Histórica* 1 (2007): 25.

46. Thomas H. Holloway, *Immigrants on the Land: Coffee and Society in Sao Paulo, 1886–1934* (Chapel Hill: University of North Carolina Press, 1980), 36–42.

47. Historian Micol Seigel notes that "by 1830 coffee dominated the country's export agenda and drove its economic growth. By 1880 Brazil harvested about half of the world's coffee, and by the century's close regularly grew three-quarters of the global harvest." That is, as Mauricio Font explains, the export of coffee coincided with and ignited the capitalist development of Brazil: "the consolidation and transition to industrialization in São Paulo resulted from the capacity of the coffee export elites to concentrate processes of capitalist accumulation in their hands and exercise hegemony over the rest of society." See Micol Seigel, *Uneven Encounters: Making Race and Nation in*

Brazil and the United States (Durham, NC: Duke University Press, 2009), 19; Mauricio Font, *Coffee and Transformation in São Paulo, Brazil* (Plymouth: Lexington Books, 2010), 6.

48. Vangelista, "Vita d'emigrante," 275.

49. Vangelista, "Vita d'emigrante," 302.

50. Moriconi, *Nel paese de' macacchi*, 125, 368.

51. For population figures, see Lesser, *Immigration, Ethnicity and National Identity in Brazil*, 22

52. Labanca, *Oltremare*, 83.

53. Enrico Corradini, *La patria lontana* (Milan: Fratelli Treves, 1910), 60.

54. Choate, *Emigrant Nation*, 192.

55. Ferruccio Macola, *L'Europa alla conquista dell'America Latina* (Venice: Ferdinando Ongania Editore, 1894); Alfonso Lomonaco, *Al Brasile* (Milan: Società Editrice Libreria, 1889).

56. For more on the role that Adwa played in Italo-Brazilian diplomatic relations and Italian literary nationalism, see Giulia Riccò, "'Il segno di Menelik': Enrico Corradini, the *Protocolos*, and the Re-Staging of Adwa in São Paulo," *Italian Culture* 41, no. 1 (2023): 6–24.

57. Adolfo Rossi, *Condizione dei coloni italiani nello stato di San Paolo (Brasile). Relazione e diari* (Bollettino dell'Emigrazione, 1902), 6.

58. Lombroso Ferrero, *Nell'America Meridionale*, 38–39, 55–56.

59. Lombroso Ferrero, *Nell'America Meridionale*, 44,48. It is worth noting the use Lombroso Ferrero makes here of "Europa" as a parallel for "home." In her remapping of Italy thorough Brazil, Italy becomes squarely part of Europe.

60. Lombroso Ferrero, *Nell'America Meridionale*, 42, 43 (emphasis mine).

61. Lombroso Ferrero, *Nell'America Meridionale*, 34.

62. Moriconi, *Nel paese de' macacchi*, 62–63, 105, 138.

63. Cusano, *Italia d'oltre mare*, 240.

64. Lombroso Ferrero, *Nell'America Meridionale*, 37–38 (emphasis mine).

65. See Natalie Hester, "Transnationalism and the Epic Tradition in Baroque Italian Travel Literature," in *Transnational Italian Studies*, ed. Charles Burdett and Loredana Polezzi (Liverpool: Liverpool University Press, 2020), 107–24.

66. Lombroso Ferrero, *Nell'America Meridionale*, v.

67. Lombroso Ferrero, *Nell'America Meridionale*, v, vi.

68. David Atkinson, "Constructing Italian Africa: Geography and Geopolitics," in *Italian Colonialism*, ed. Ruth Ben-Ghiat and Mia Fuller (New York: Palgrave Macmillan, 2018), 16.

69. Lombroso Ferrero, *Nell'America Meridionale*, vii.

70. Lombroso Ferrero, *Nell'America Meridionale*, 8.

71. Pratt, *Imperial Eyes*, 118.

72. Lombroso Ferrero, *Nell'America Meridionale*, 23. Remarkably, Lombroso Ferrero did not travel to Rio Grande Sul, nor to any of the southern states where the Italian capitalist vanguard found its model of "ideal colonization."

73. Coincidentally, most of the later projects of *bonifica* undertaken by fascism, starting with the area near Rome known as the Pontine Marshes are but the remaking of colonie within Italian borders. The same could be said of the Italian South in relation to the North. For more on the Pontine Marshes see Lorenzo Veracini, "Italian Colonialism through a Settler Colonial Studies Lens," *Journal of Colonialism and Colonial History* 19, no. 3 (2018): 16.

74. Lombroso Ferrero, *Nell'America Meridionale*, 24.

75. Lombroso Ferrero, *Nell'America Meridionale*, 27.

76. Lombroso Ferrero, *Nell'America Meridionale*, 28 (emphasis mine).

77. Lombroso Ferrero, *Nell'America Meridionale*, 26, 28. Historian Pietro Brunello's foundational work *Pionieri: gli italiani in Brasile e il mito della frontiera* challenges idealized narratives about the presence of Italians in Southern Brazil and the "myth of the frontier" by documenting, in painstaking detail, encounters between Italians and Indigenous populations. Brunello marshals indisputable evidence that Italians and Indigenous people not only had contact with one another but that these contacts were often violent. More recently, cultural historian Francesco Ricatti in a 2019 special issue for the journal *Altreitalie* extends Brunello's analysis to encompass how Italians in Australia and the Americas have "played an important role in the maintenance of settler colonial structures of power" along these so-called frontiers. See Pietro Brunello, *Pionieri: gli italiani in Brasile e il mito della frontiera* (Rome: Donzelli Editore, 1994); Francesco Ricatti, "Forum. Towards a Decolonial History of Italian Migration to Australia: Introduction," *AltreItalie* 59 (2019): 11.

78. Lombroso Ferrero, *Nell'America Meridionale*, 26 (emphasis mine).

79. Lombroso Ferrero, *Nell'America Meridionale*, 30.

80. Lombroso Ferrero, *Nell'America Meridionale*, 34.

81. Lombroso Ferrero, *Nell'America Meridionale*, 34.

82. For the genealogy behind this expression see Stephanie Malia Hom, "On the Origins of Making Italy: Massimo D'Azeglio and 'Fatta l'Italia Bisogna Fare Gli Italiani,'" *Italian Culture* XXXI, no. 1 (2013): 1–16; for a comprehensive study of how Italians "were made" see Suzanne Stewart-Steinberg, *The Pinocchio Effect: On Making Italians (1860–1920)* (Chicago: University of Chicago Press, 2007).

83. See Benedict Anderson, *Imagined Communities: Reflections on the Origin and Spread of Nationalism* (New York: Verso, 2016).

84. Lombroso Ferrero, *Nell'America Meridionale*, 93.

85. Lombroso Ferrero, *Nell'America Meridionale*, 93, 95, 97.

86. Lombroso Ferrero, *Nell'America Meridionale*, 97.

87. See Hester, "Transnationalism and the Epic Tradition in Baroque Italian Travel Literature," 123–24.

88. Lombroso Ferrero, *Nell'America Meridionale*, 99.

89. Lombroso Ferrero, *Nell'America Meridionale*, 10 (emphasis mine).

90. Lamonte Aidoo, *Slavery Unseen: Sex, Power, and Violence in Brazilian History* (Durham, NC: Duke University Press, 2018), 21–24.

91. Sansone points out how Lombroso Ferrero shows knowledge of the works of Brazilian intellectual José Veríssimo, whose works already address "notions of miscegenation . . . generally associated with Gilberto Freyre." See Sansone, "Hiperbólicos italianos," 270–73.

92. Lombroso Ferrero, *Nell'America Meridionale*, 103–5.

93. Antonio Sérgio Alfredo Guimarães in *Classes, raças, e democracia* traces a nuanced history of the term "racial democracy," focusing specifically on the importance that the word "democracy" plays in this concept. Guimarães explains that when Freyre first adopted this term in his lectures at the University of Indiana in 1944, he originally used "ethnic democracy," and only later, with the visit of the French scholar Roger Bastide, did the adjective "ethnic" become "racial." For Freyre, Guimarães explains, the term democracy itself captured "an esthetic and cultural freedom, based on miscegenated creation and convivium." More so than having to do with specific rights, Guimarães shows that the idea of racial democracy, more an aspiration than a reality itself, functions more as an "ideal norm of behavior," which does not necessarily contrast with or exclude the existence of racial prejudice and discrimination. Antonio Sérgio Alfredo Guimarães, *Classes, raças e democracia* (São Paulo: Editora 34, 2002), 144–48.

94. Aidoo, *Slavery Unseen*, 21. Historian Emília Viotti da Costa finds in the "the system of clientele and patronage" characteristic of pre-independence and imperial Brazil the formalization of racial democracy and in its subsequent "breakdown," which made more apparent the prejudices governing a competitive market, its transformation into myth. Yet despite having been debunked numerous times by Brazilian social scientists since the 1960s it "is not completely dead." Emília Viotti da Costa, *The Brazilian Empire: Myths and Histories* (Chicago: University of Chicago Press, 1985), 243–46.

95. Lombroso Ferrero, *Nell'America Meridionale*, 106.

96. Fogu, *The Fishing Net and the Spider Web*, 104–10.

97. Lombroso Ferrero, *Nell'America Meridionale*, 106, 137.

98. For instance, while Brazil also welcomed large numbers of immigrants from Germany, these people posed a problem for the fledgling state's whiten-

ing project because of their tendency toward endogamy (see for example intellectual Silvio Romero's aptly titled text *O allemanismo no sul do Brasil,seus perigos e meios de os conjurar*). Italians, on the other hand, commonly married outside of their group, a practice that, I contend, won them a more favored place in the country's racial and ethnic imaginary. Trento, "Italianità in Brazil: A Disputed Object of Desire," 259.

99. Lombroso Ferrero, *Nell'America Meridionale*, 119, 123.

100. May E. Bletz, *Immigration and Acculturation in Brazil and Argentina 1890–1929* (New York: Palgrave Macmillan, 2010), 122; Lilia Moritz Schwarcz, *Imagens da branquitude: a presença da ausência* (São Paulo: Companhia das Letras, 2024), 284.

101. Bletz, *Immigration and Acculturation*, 122–23.

CHAPTER TWO. *CIDADÃO ITALIANO RESIDENTE EM SÃO PAULO*: MODERNISM, CANNIBALISM, AND THE ITALIANS OF SÃO PAULO

1. António de Alcântara Machado, *Novelas paulistanas* (Rio de Janeiro: José Olympio Editora, 1961), 56. In 1845, C. F. von Martius, a Bavarian scientist, published in the *Revista do Instituto Histórico e Geográfico Brasileiro* a piece in which he argued that in order to understand how race operated in Brazil, one should understand the three races that made up the country—which will later become the three "sad races"—as three rivers, of different sizes and importance, whose waters would reunite into a singular, purified river: the white one. Later, as sociologist Renato Ortiz observes, Parnassian poet Olavo Bilac, a figure despised by Brazilian modernists, recapitulated in his poetry von Martius's by then widespread racial theory and coined the phrase *três raças tristes* (three sad races) to describe the national character of Brazil. In literary critic David Haberly's analysis of Bilac, he explains how for the poet the Portuguese, the first race, "sang songs filled with nostalgia for the homeland they had left behind. The Indian joined in to mourn what the white man had taken from them. The African, brought to Brazil in chains, wept for the freedom they lost." Interestingly, Paulo Prado, a scion of São Paulo and artistic sponsor of the modernist activities in São Paulo, argues along similar lines in his *Retrato do Brasil* (1928). According to him, *saudade*, a specific variation of sadness, is the most inherent quality of the Brazilian people, the result of miscegenation and of the settlers' actions driven by lust and greed, which were met by the Indigenous people's sensuality and the African captives' sadness. It makes sense that Alcântara Machado would contrast the Italian race to the Brazilian people's "sadness" by using the adjective "jovial" to describe the recently arrived immigrants. For modernists in search of the

quintessential national identity, thinking about Brazilian culture as an amalgamation of a specific set of characteristics—whether it was lust, greed, or sadness—allows them to mask racial conflicts while allowing for the assimilation of new cultures to the national paradigm by keeping them distinct but united under the banner of Brazilianness. See Lilia Moritz Schwarcz, *Imagens da branquitude: a presença da ausência* (São Paulo: Companhia das Letras, 2024), 255–56; David Haberly, *Three Sad Races: Racial Identity and National Consciousness in Brazilian Literature* (Cambridge: Cambridge University Press, 1983), 1; Renato Ortiz, *Cultura brasileira e identidade nacional* (São Paulo: Brasiliense, 1985), 19, 44; Paulo Prado, *Retrato do Brasil: ensaio sobre a tristeza brasileira* (São Paulo: Duprat-Mayença, 1928).

2. Alcântara Machado, *Novelas paulistanas*, 56; May E. Bletz, *Immigration and Acculturation in Brazil and Argentina 1890–1929* (New York: Palgrave Macmillan, 2010), 144.

3. A note on terminology: *Paulistano* refers to residents of the city of São Paulo or a characteristic proper of the city; *Paulista* describes someone who lives in the State of São Paulo or a trait defining the state of São Paulo more broadly.

4. Barbara Weinstein, *The Color of Modernity: São Paulo and the Making of Race and Nation in Brazil* (Durham, NC: Duke University Press, 2015), 4, 23.

5. Haroldo de Campos, "Da razão antropofágica: diálogo e diferença na cultura brasileira," in *Metalinguagem & outras metas: ensaios de teoria e crítica literária* (São Paulo: Perspectiva, 1992), 231–56; Randal Johnson, "Tupy or Not Tupy: Cannibalism and Nationalism in Contemporary Brazilian Literature and Culture," in *On Modern Latin American Fiction*, ed. John King (New York: Hill and Wang, 1987), 41–59; Bendito Nunes, *A utopia antropofágica: a antropofagia ao alcance de todos* (São Paulo: Globo, 1990)

6. Sara Castro-Klarén, "A Genealogy for the 'Manifesto Antropófago,' or the Struggle between Socrates and the Caraïbe," *Nepantla: Views from the South* 1, no. 2 (2000): 295–322.

7. Castro-Klarén, "A Genealogy for the 'Manifesto Antropófago,'" 312; Isabel C. Gómez, *Cannibal Translation: Literary Reciprocity in Contemporary Latin America* (Evanston, IL: Northwestern University Press, 2023), 5; Zita Nunes, *Cannibal Democracy in the Literature of the Americas* (Minneapolis: University of Minnesota Press, 2008), xvii–xix, 13.

8. Ruth Ben-Ghiat, *Fascist Modernities: Italy 1922–1945* (Berkeley: University of California Press, 2001), 29; Mia Fuller, *Moderns Abroad: Architecture, Cities and Italian Imperialism* (Abingdon: Routledge, 2010), 6.

9. According to what Rafael Cardoso calls the "mythic narrative" of Paulistano modernism, it was Andrade who brought the Futurist Manifesto

back from Paris to Brazil in 1912. Others have noted, however, that a translation of the manifesto had already appeared in a Natal-based newspaper, *A République*, in 1909 without much fanfare. See Rafael Cardoso, *Modernity in Black and White: Art and Image, Race and Identity in Brazil, 1890–1945* (Cambridge: Cambridge University Press, 2021), 6.

10. Mario Carelli, *Carcamanos e comendadores: os italianos de São Paulo: da realidade à ficção (1919–1930)* (São Paulo: Editora Ática, 1985), 119; Maurício Martins do Carmo, *Paulicéia scugliambada, paulicéia desvairada. Juó Bananére e a imagem do italiano na literatura brasileira* (Niterói: Editora da Universidade Federal Fluminense, 1998), 35. Interestingly, the Black journalist José Correia Leite, who, in 1924, also wrote under the Italian pseudonym "Juó Carretta," has received far less critical attention than Marcondes. And yet, thanks to his upbringing in the largely Italian neighborhood of Bexiga, Leite had a much more profound knowledge of the Italians of São Paulo and their language than Marcondes, as I show in Chapter Three. Thus his "italianado," as Leite dubs it, hews more closely to the Italian dialect in São Paulo than the one Marcondes created for his cultured, upper-middle-class readership.

11. Johnson, "Tupy or Not Tupy," 195.

12. Carmo, *Paulicéia scugliambada, paulicéia desvairada*, 55.

13. Carelli, *Carcamanos e comendadores*, 106; Nelson Endebo Shuchmacher, "'A Invençó do Brasile': Juó Bananére and Non-Italian Literature," *California Italian Studies* 9, no. 1 (2019): 8.

14. Lucia Helena, *Uma literatura antropofágica* (Rio de Janeiro: Livraria Editora Catedra, 1982), 104–5.

15. Carelli, *Carcamanos e comendadores*, 121–22.

16. António de Alcântara Machado, *Cavaquinho e saxofone 1926–1935* (Rio de Janeiro: José Olympio Editora, 1940), 254, 258.

17. Ugo Serani, "Nella letteratura brasiliana," in *Storia dell' emigrazione italiana*, ed. Piero Bevilacqua, Andreina De Clementi, and Emilio Franzina, vol. II: Arrivi (Rome: Donzelli Editore, 2009), 667; Rubens Ricupero, "Introduzione," in *Notizie di São Paulo: racconti*, by Antônio de Alcântara Machado, trans. Giuliano Macchi (Milan: All'insegna del pesce d'oro, 1981), 11; Carlos Eduardo Schmidt Capela, "Italianos na ficção brasileira: modernidade em processo," *Fragmentos* 21 (2001): 150.

18. Roch Duval, "Antonio de Alcântara Machado's Brás, Bexiga e Barra Funda as a Translation of São Paulo during Brazilian Modernism," in *Speaking of Memory: How Translation Shapes City Life*, ed. Sherry Simon (Montreal: McGill-Queen's University Press, 2016), 214; Alfredo Bosi, *História concisa da literatura brasileira* (São Paulo: Editora Cultrix, 1994), 375.

19. That same year also marked the one-hundredth anniversary of Brazil's peculiar proclamation of independence from Portugal. It is peculiar because,

in contrast to other South American countries, it was neither the result of nor the catalyst for a brutal war of independence. In 1808, Brazil experienced a singular event compared to other European colonies: the Portuguese court, threatened by the Napoleonic invasion, moved to Rio de Janeiro. Here the center becomes periphery, and for the first—and only—time, there is an inversion of the colonial pact. The king also proclaimed the kingdom of Brazil. Thus, Brazil had been a colony, a kingdom, and an empire before it was conceptualized as nation. When the constitutionalist wave spread across Europe, the king was asked to return to Portugal and left his son Pedro in charge of Brazil. Finally, Pedro, disobeying his father's order to return to Lisbon, proclaimed Brazilian independence from Portugal, thus becoming Pedro I of Brazil. For an account of these events, see Emília Viotti da Costa, *The Brazilian Empire: Myths and Histories* (Chicago: University of Chicago Press, 1985), 1–23.

20. Antônio de Alcântara Machado, "O que eu disse a um comediógrafo nacional," *Novíssima* (December 1924).

21. The contentious relationship between Rio de Janeiro and São Paulo helps to explain why Paulistano modernists have poured so much energy into making São Paulo the headquarters for all things modernist. For example, art historian Rafael Cardoso debunks the myth surrounding São Paulo's 1922 Week of Modern Art by showing that Rio de Janeiro was once the cultural center of the nation and that, contrary to popular belief, it was modern earlier and in a different way that was more attuned to Black popular culture than São Paulo. See more in Cardoso, *Modernity in Black and White*. For a detailed summary of the São Paulo–Rio de Janeiro rivalry, see Weinstein, *The Color of Modernity*, 6.

22. Andrade's first manifesto, *Manifesto da Poesia Pau-Brasil* (Manifesto of Brazilwood Poetry), dated 1924, turns toward the Indigenous and African cultures of Brazil as the sources from which to imagine a modern Brazilian poetry. Authenticity becomes the key shibboleth of this poetry for export. But this was an authenticity that still imagined itself as being consumed *outside* of Brazil—just like brazilwood, the raw material that the Portuguese originally extracted from the country and to which Brazil owes its name. For more on *Manifesto da Poesia Pau-Brasil* see Christopher Dunn, *Brutality Garden: Tropicália and the Emergence of a Brazilian Counterculture* (Chapel Hill: UNC Press, 2001), 15–17.

23. Bosi, *História concisa da literatura brasileira*, 355; Ilan Rachum, "Antropofagia against Verdeamarelo," *Latin American Literary Review* 4, no. 8 (1976): 75.

24. Johnson, "Tupy or Not Tupy," 204; Castro-Klarén, "A Genealogy for the 'Manifesto Antropófago,'" 312.

25. Carelli, *Carcamanos e comendadores*, 129. For an analysis of Menotti del Picchia's autobiography see Giulia Riccò, "Navigating between Italianità and Brasilidade: The Case of Menotti del Picchia," *Literatura da (i)migração no Brasil*, ed. Wail Hassan and Rogério Lima (Rio de Janeiro: Edições Makunaima, 2020), 100–121.

26. Menotti del Picchia, "A Questão Racial," *Correio Paulistano*, May 10, 1921; Plínio Salgado, *O Estrangeiro* (Rio de Janeiro: José Olympio, 1972), 151.

27. Rafael Cardoso insists on how both splinters from the Group of '22 discuss the Indigenous figure in a manner that is controversial. Cardoso takes issue with the "entitlement with which many of the Semana group appropriated African and Amerindian heritage," because, for him, it "betrays a sense of prerogative not too distant from the way European colonial authorities regarded the 'native' under their 'protection.'" *Modernity in Black and White*, 14.

28. Carelli, *Carcamanos e comendadores*, 136. Reading *Paulicéia*, Oswald praised Mário (in an article published in *Jornal do Comércio* in 1921) as "my futurist poet." But in reply, Mário declared, "I am not a Futurist (of Marinetti). I said it and I repeat it. I have points of contact with Futurism. Oswald de Andrade, calling me a Futurist, missed the mark." The adjective "futurist" in Brazil, whose use gained momentum in the 1920s as a way to identify the crop of young artists involved with the Week, had "little to do with the meaning of the Italian movement" started in Paris by Filippo Tommaso Marinetti in 1909. See Lucia Helena, "Brazilian Modernism and the Modern Art Week: The Influence of the European Twentieth-Century Vanguards," in *Brazilian Literature as World Literature*, ed. Eduardo F. Coutinho (New York: Bloomsbury, 2018), 148. On the reasons why Mário de Andrade wanted to distance himself from Marinetti, and on the latter's trip to Brazil, see Jeffrey T. Schnapp and João Cezar de Castro Rocha's excellent article, "Brazilian Velocities: On Marinetti's 1926 Trip to South America," *South Central Review* 13, no. 2/3, Futurism and Avant-Garde (1996): 105–56.

29. Mário de Andrade, *Macunaíma: o herói sem nenhum caráter* (Rio de Janeiro: Nova Fronteira, 2012), 48. Zita Nunes astutely points out that Macunaíma "turns white before entering the city of São Paulo, where he participates in the technologically advanced civilization." It is "only when he [Macunaíma] is white that he is a cannibal." For Nunes's close reading of *Macunaíma*, see Nunes, *Cannibal Democracy in the Literature of the Americas*, 41–57.

30. Bletz, *Immigration and Acculturation in Brazil and Argentina 1890–1929*, 140; Carelli, *Carcamanos e Comendadores*, 159.

31. Alcântara Machado, *Novelas paulistanas*, 63–65.

32. Alcântara Machado, *Novelas paulistanas*, 63, 68.

33. Alcântara Machado, *Novelas paulistanas*, 77.

34. Alcântara Machado, *Novelas paulistanas*, 63.

35. These real estate developments, an early take on popular housing, were known as "workers' villas" and became extremely popular in the first two decades of the twentieth century in São Paulo. Historian Molly C. Ball explains that there were actual real estate laws that were created to benefit developers and industrialists who designed these worker housing compounds. Their availability and subsidized rents were contingent upon working in the factory and, at any sign of any labor unrest, employers could forcibly evict the tenants. Molly C. Ball, *Navigating Life and Work in Old Republic São Paulo* (Gainesville: University of Florida Press, 2020), 59, 135.

36. Alcântara Machado, *Novelas paulistanas*, 77, 80.

37. Alcântara Machado, *Novelas paulistanas*, 80.

38. Alcântara Machado, *Novelas paulistanas*, 81.

39. Alcântara Machado, *Novelas paulistanas*, 100–103.

40. Alcântara Machado, *Novelas paulistanas*, 100, 104.

41. Alcântara Machado, *Novelas paulistanas*, 93.

42. Carelli, *Carcamanos e comendadores*, 186; Joseph Pecorelli, "Constructing a Community: The Italian Press in São Paulo from 1880 to 1920," *Italica* 97, no. 2 (2020): 264–82.

43. Alcântara Machado, *Novelas paulistanas*, 106.

44. Vittorio Cappelli, "Pequenas pátrias, a pátria, outras pátrias: as complexas identidades dos italianos no Brasil e na América Latina," *Naveg@ mérica* 13 (2014): 6.

45. That the wife embodies the manager of the family's resources aligns with the overall pattern in gender roles within the Italian diaspora, observed by historians such as Donna Gabaccia and Franca Iacovetta. Donna R. Gabaccia and Franca Iacovetta, *Women, Gender and Transnational Lives: Italian Workers of the World* (Toronto: University of Toronto Press, 2002).

46. Alcântara Machado, *Novelas paulistanas*, 107–8.

47. Alcântara Machado, *Novelas paulistanas*, 55.

48. Carelli, *Carcamanos e comendadores*, 159.

49. Maggie Dunn and Ann Morris, *The Composite Novel: The Short Story Cycle in Transition* (New York: Twayne Publishers, 1995), 2, 15–16.

50. Dunn and Morris, *The Composite Novel*,15.

51. Barbara Foley, *Telling the Truth: The Theory and Practice of Documentary Fiction* (Ithaca, NY: Cornell University Press, 1986), 25–26.

52. Alcântara Machado, *Novelas paulistanas*, 57; Foley, *Telling the Truth*, 36.

53. Dunn and Morris, *The Composite Novel*, 19.

54. Pantaleone Sergi, "Funzioni pedagogiche, etniche, e politiche della stampa italiana in Brasile," in *Italiani in Brasile: rotte migratorie e percorsi*

culturali, ed. Vittorio Cappelli and Alexandre Hecker (Soveria Mannelli: Rubbettino Editore, 2010), 15, 17, 24.

55. Pecorelli, "Constructing a Community," 281; Samuel L. Bailey, "The Role of Two Newspapers in the Assimilation of Italians in Buenos Aires and São Paulo, 1893–1913," *The International Migration Review* 12, no. 3 (1978): 330.

56. Bailey, "The Role of Two Newspapers," 331, 333, 337.

57. Duval, "Antonio de Alcântara Machado's Brás, Bexiga e Barra Funda," 211.

58. Alcântara Machado, *Novelas paulistanas*, 88.

59. Note how the author's travelogue of Europe is titled *Pathé Baby*. This is the name of an actual home projector, launched by French entrepreneur Charles Pathé in 1922, which became very popular in Europe. Indeed, numerous films were made to be played on these projectors, including "Pathé magazines," which were less polished versions of newsreels. It is likely that Alcântara Machado became familiar with these Pathé magazines while in Europe and decided to emulate them through his writing, much like the "Camera Eye" sections of Dos Passos's *USA Trilogy*.

60. Alcântara Machado, *Novelas paulistanas*, 87.

61. Alcântara Machado, *Novelas paulistanas*, 96.

62. Lilia Moritz Schwarcz interprets the presence (or absence) of shoes and socks as symbols of freedom in post-abolition Brazil. The fact that the feet of the Black woman in the short story are visible hints at her lower social status, while also pointing back to a time when it was commonplace to represent Black Brazilians barefoot. *Imagens da branquitude*, 23–28.

CHAPTER THREE. *I PERCHÈ NU SO NAZIUNALE?*: JOSÉ CORREIA LEITE, BLACKNESS, AND NEW WORLD ITALIANS

1. In later columns, the second "t" is dropped, and the name appears as Carreta. Throughout this chapter, I employ the original spelling of the name. Maintaining the double dental consonant, a feature of Italian that distinguishes it typographically and aurally from Portuguese, helps to make clear the column's original satirical intent.

2. With the expression "Black Brazilian Movement," I am referring to what historian Regina Pahim Pinto identified as the Afro-Brazilian struggle "to be recognized as a full citizen of the country." Pinto identifies the realm of education, "whether because of the importance that was attributed to it as a means to achieve full integration in society, or whether because of the critiques against education about its omissions when it came to the necessities and specificities of Black people," as the axis upon which this struggle rested

throughout the twentieth and twenty-first centuries. See Regina Pahim Pinto, *O movimento negro em São Paulo: luta e identidade* (Ponta Grossa: Editora UEPG, 2013), 21.

3. Homi Bhaba, *The Location of Culture* (New York: Routledge, 1994), 2; Graziella Parati, *Migration Italy: The Art of Talking Back in a Destination Culture* (Toronto: University of Toronto Press, 2005), 29.

4. Thomas Ferraro, *Feeling Italian: The Art of Ethnicity in America* (New York: NYU Press, 2005).

5. Vetri Nathan, "Mimic-Nation, Mimic-Men," in *National Belongings: Hybridity in Italian Colonial and Postcolonial Cultures*, ed. Jacqueline Andall and Derek Duncan (Bern: Peter Lang, 2010), 51.

6. Kim Butler, *Freedoms Given, Freedoms Won: Afro-Brazilians in Post-Abolition São Paulo and Salvador* (Newark, NJ: Rutgers University Press, 2000). Literary scholar Rubens Ricupero, in his introduction to the Italian translation of António de Alcântara Machado's stories discussed in Chapter Two, explains that the lack of "homogenous ghettoes such as the 'Little Italy' of New York and of other American cities," had to do with the heightened social mobility of Italians in São Paulo, which prompted them to move "horizontally . . . in their moves toward more desirable neighborhoods." See Rubens Ricupero, "Introduzione," in *Notizie di São Paulo: racconti*, by Antônio de Alcântara Machado, trans. Giuliano Macchi (Milan: All'insegna del pesce d'oro, 1981), 19.

7. Butler, *Freedoms Given, Freedoms Won*, 65.

8. Carlos José Ferreira dos Santos, *Nem tudo era italiano: São Paulo e pobreza (1890–1915)* (São Paulo: Annablume Editora, 1998), 40, 42.

9. Barbara Weinstein, *The Color of Modernity: São Paulo and the Making of Race and Nation in Brazil* (Durham, NC: Duke University Press, 2015), 14. On the racialized discourse about Southern Italy see also John Dickie, *Darkest Italy: The Nation and Stereotypes of the Mezzogiorno, 1860–1900* (New York: Palgrave Macmillan, 1999); Nelson J. Moe, *The View from Vesuvius: Italian Culture and the Southern Question* (Oakland: University of California Press, 2002). Weinstein too highlights the similarities between the Italian South and the Brazilian Northeast in her introduction by drawing on economist Albert O. Hirschman's notion of dualistic development.

10. Cited in Santos, *Nem tudo era italiano*, 31.

11. Santos, *Nem tudo era italiano*, 35.

12. Molly C. Ball, *Navigating Life and Work in Old Republic São Paulo* (Gainesville: University of Florida Press. 2020), 42; Butler, *Freedoms Given, Freedoms Won*, 67, 69, 73.

13. Butler, *Freedoms Given, Freedoms Won*, 73.

14. Santos, *Nem tudo era Italiano*, 52.

15. George Reid Andrews, *Blacks and Whites in São Paulo, Brazil 1888–1988* (Madison: University of Wisconsin Press, 1991); Paulina Alberto, *Terms of Inclusion: Black Intellectuals in Twentieth-Century Brazil* (Chapel Hill: University of North Carolina Press, 2011), 6.

16. Butler, *Freedoms Given, Freedoms Won*, 73–74. Gennari regards as hopeful the "edge and overlap" in the US popular imaginary between Italian American and African American cultural expressions. See John Gennari, *Flavor and Soul: Italian America at Its African American Edge* (Chicago: University of Chicago Press, 2017), 8.

17. Butler, *Freedoms Given, Freedoms Won*, 13.

18. José Correia Leite and Cuti, . . . *E disse o velho militante José Correia Leite* (São Paulo: Secretaria Municipal de Cultura, 1992), 20.

19. Butler, *Freedoms Given, Freedoms Won*, 57, 60; Alberto, *Terms of Inclusion*, 57.

20. Alberto, *Terms of Inclusion*, 57

21. At the same time, Zanin also acknowledges that "calling Blacks by the name of the Ethiopian monarch who had repeatedly beaten the Italians makes visible the perception of the subversive force of the Black Brazilian people, [a force] that Italians had been able to observe during the abolitionist campaign." See Valter Zanin, "O'Menelik eroe dei due mondi," *Il Manifesto*, March 25, 1996.

22. Leite and Cuti, *E disse*, 23.

23. Butler, *Freedoms Given, Freedoms Won*, 97.

24. Butler, *Freedoms Given, Freedoms Won*, 65. As historian Oswaldo Truzzi writes, the blossoming of Italian societies of mutual aid resulted directly from the complete neglect of these migrants by both Italian and Brazilian governmental institutions. In fact, no public health plan existed that safeguarded Italians arriving to São Paulo, an absence reflected in these associations' primary insistence on mutual aid. See Oswaldo Truzzi, *Italianidade no interior paulista: percurso e descaminhos de uma identidade étnica (1880–1950)* (São Paulo: Editora UNESP, 2015), 87.

25. Leite and Cuti, *E disse*, 25.

26. Leite's case anticipates, to a certain extent, the current debate in Italy about the *jus culturae*, or the granting of Italian citizenship to children of immigrants born in Italy that have completed a set number of years in an Italian school.

27. Leite and Cuti, *E disse*, 52.

28. For more on *madamato* see Sandra Ponzanesi, "The Color of Love: *Madamismo* and Interracial Relationships in the Italian Colonies," *Research in African Literatures* 43, no. 2 (2012): 155–72; Angelica Pesarini, "'Blood Is Thicker than Water': The Materialisation of the Racial Body in Fascist East

Africa," *Zapruder World: An International Journal for the History of Social Conflict* 4 (2017). For more on the *ascari* see Tekeste Negash, *Italian Colonialism in Eritrea 1882–1941: Policies, Praxis and Impact* (Uppsala: Uppsala University Press, 1987).

29. Étienne Balibar and Immanuel Wallerstein, *Race, Nation, Class: Ambiguous Identities* (London: Verso, 2011), 96; Pesarini, "Blood Is Thicker than Water."

30. Micol Seigel, *Uneven Encounters: Making Race and Nation in Brazil and the United States* (Durham, NC: Duke University Press, 2009), 195.

31. Leite and Cuti, *E disse*, 26, 52–53. Truzzi, referring mostly to the interior of São Paulo, also makes a similar point with regard to the fact that Italians assimilated white Brazilians' racial bias. See Truzzi, *Italianidade no interior paulista*, 39.

32. Leite and Cuti, *E disse*, 27, 29.

33. Benedict Anderson, *Imagined Communities: Reflections on the Origin and Spread of Nationalism*, 2nd ed. (London: Verso, 2006).

34. Butler, *Freedoms Given, Freedoms Won*, 58; Alberto, *Terms of Inclusion*, 18. In their edited collection *Voices of the Race*, Alberto, Andrews, and Hoffnung-Garskof highlight how the Black press in Latin America developed for the most part in cities with white majorities—São Paulo, but also Buenos Aires, Montevideo, and Havana. They explain how "for Black writers and readers, the role of race in shaping opportunities and inclusion in these cities was sharply evident and racial identities were highly salient." See Paulina Laura Alberto, George Reid Andrews, and Jesse Hoffnung-Garskof, *Voices of the Race: Black Newspapers in Latin America, 1870–1960* (Cambridge: Cambridge University Press, 2022), 14.

35. Michael Mitchell, "Racial Consciousness and the Political Attitudes and Behavior of Blacks in São Paulo, Brazil," PhD Dissertation (Bloomington, Indiana University, 1977), 159; Butler, *Freedoms Given, Freedoms Won*, 90. Scholars have pointed out how the Brazilian Black press reflected the interest and sensibilities of Black elites. But as Alberto has put it, "despite their apparent relative privilege, their stories can help us understand how and why a society like Brazil, where few people identified as *preto* or *negro* could have produced a vocal minority of people who not only identified as such but worked to make blackness or Africanness fundamental to Brazilian identity." It is also important to note how José Correia Leite's story diverges from other Black intellectual experiences due to his humble upbringing and his illiteracy. See Alberto, *Terms of Inclusion*, 20–21; Mitchell, "Racial Consciousness," 159.

36. By the same token, the Black press of São Paulo at first disavowed any associations with Africa. This was due in no small part to Black writers' desire to be seen as integral to the modernization and civilizationalist discourse

surrounding the development of São Paulo. From their perspective, Black intellectuals could not afford to identify too closely with Africa, for if "Italian Brazilians were not really Brazilians," as Alberto explains, then Black intellectuals "had little stomach for the idea that they themselves were African Brazilians" (64). Despite their similar experiences with modernity and European immigrants, members of the Black Brazilian press were also wary of expressing solidarity with Black Americans, as the visit of African American journalist Richard Abbott to Brazil in 1923 makes clear. For a more detailed description of Abbott's visit see Seigel, *Uneven Encounters*, 187, 179–205.

37. Alberto, *Terms of Inclusion*, 56.

38. José Correia Leite, "Naziunale," *O Clarim*, January 6, 1924.

39. Leite was not the first one to employ such a linguistic strategy. As discussed in Chapter Two, Alexandre Ribeiro Marcondes Machado, who wrote under the pseudonym Juó Bananére, also blended Italian and Portuguese in his columns and poems. However, Bananére's use of Italo-Brazilian dialect has received much more attention from scholars than Leite's.

40. Alberto, *Terms of Inclusion*, 63.

41. Nancy C. Carnevale, *A New Language, A New World: Italian Immigrants in the United States, 1890–1945* (Champaign: University of Illinois Press, 2009), 23.

42. Paola Gambarota, *Irresistible Signs: The Genius of Language and Italian National Identity* (Toronto: University of Toronto Press, 2011), 5.

43. Carnevale, *A New Language*, 22, 32.

44. Carnevale, *A New Language*, 36.

45. Carnevale, *A New Language*, 38.

46. With regard to the Italian nation-state and language planning, Totaro-Genevois explains that while during the liberal period in Italy the preferred language policy had mostly to do with "status planning" or "the spread of the national language among Italians themselves," during the fascist era language planning took the form of "corpus planning" and the enforcement of a "ban on the use of foreign words in order to avoid pollution of the pure Italian language." See Mariella Totaro-Genevois, *Cultural and Linguistic Policy Abroad: The Italian Experience* (Bristol: Multilingual Matters, 2005), 47.

47. Gambarota, *Irresistible Signs*, 6.

48. Carnevale, *A New Language*, 35.

49. Butler, *Freedoms Given, Freedoms Won*, 74.

50. Donna R. Gabaccia, *Italy's Many Diasporas* (Seattle: University of Washington Press, 2000), 65.

51. Butler, *Freedoms Given, Freedoms Won*, 18.

52. Warren Dean, *The Industrialization of São Paulo 1880–1945* (Austin: University of Texas Press, 1969), 66; Angelo Trento, *Là dov'è la raccolta del*

caffè. L'emigrazione italiana in Brasile, 1875–1940 (Padua: Editrice Antenore, 1984).

53. José Correia Leite, "U Clarino . . . ," *O Clarim*, April 6, 1924.

54. Butler, *Freedoms Given, Freedoms Won*, 79–81.

55. Andrews, *Blacks and Whites*, 81.

56. Historians have long noted the ideological construction of certain foodways, from pasta to pizza, as uniquely Italian. Ironically, it was emigration, historian Simone Cinotto explains, that precipitated the production of durum wheat pasta, which, unlike fresh pasta, could be shipped and stored for longer periods of time. Contrary to popular belief, Italians in the peninsula did not begin to consume pasta until the early 1900s. See Simone Cinotto, *The Italian American Table: Food, Family and Community in New York City* (Champaign: University of Illinois Press, 2013), 5, 118; see also Elizabeth Zanoni, *Migrant Marketplaces: Foods and Italians in North and South America* (Champaign: University of Illinois Press, 2018).

57. Leite's quasi-prescient understanding of the relationship between samba, Italianness, and São Paulo's urban working class comes to life in the figure of Adoniran Barbosa—whose real name was João Rubinato, and who was himself the child of Italian immigrants—who in 1935 won a prize sponsored by the city of São Paulo for the best Carnaval song. Adoniran Barbosa's most famous song is perhaps precisely "Samba Italiano," with a melody that follows samba rhythmic and with lyrics that resemble the *italianado* of Leite. In 1975, foremost Brazilian literary critic Antonio Candido wrote for the cover of one of Barbosa's records: "I have already commented on the fact that he uses a mixture of Italian and Portuguese . . . Adoniran . . . has performed a radically Brazilian operation, in which the better cadences of samba and of popular songs . . . aligned naturally with the deformation of Brazilian Portuguese, in which Ernesto becomes Arnesto. Just as in the entire country, in São Paulo, today, Italian exists between the lines." Cited in Maria Izilda Santos de Matos, "Un sambista italiano a São Paulo: Adoniran Barbosa," in *Italiani in Brasile. Rotte migratorie e percorsi culturali*, ed. Vittorio Cappelli and Alexandre Hecker (Soveria Mannelli: Rubbettino Editore, 2010), 73.

58. Gary Gerstle, *American Crucible. Race and Nation in the Twentieth Century* (Princeton, NJ: Princeton University Press, 2017), 102, 107; on exchanges between the Black Press in the US and Brazil, see Seigel, *Uneven Encounters*, 180, 224.

59. Lucy Riall, "Men at War: Masculinity and Military Ideals in the Risorgimento," in *The Risorgimento Revisited*, ed. Silvana Patriarca and Lucy Riall (London: Palgrave Macmillan, 2012), 158. For a detailed overview of the role occupied by Giuseppe Garibaldi in the national imaginary of Italians in

South America see Heather Sottong, "'Hero of Two Worlds': The Equestrian Monument to Giuseppe Garibaldi in Buenos Aires, Argentina," *Italian American Review* 12, no. 1 (2022): 36–60.

60. José Correia Leite, "Sempri Avanti!," *O Clarim*, June 1924.

61. James Sanders, *The Vanguard of the Atlantic World. Creating Modernity, Nation, and Democracy in Nineteenth Century Latin America* (Durham, NC: Duke University Press, 2014), 26.

62. One of the most successful campaigns launched by the "new" *O Clarim* was the institution of "Dia da Mãe Preta," literally the "Day of the Black Mother," to celebrate the childrearing labor of formerly captive Black women. On this, see Seigel, *Uneven Encounters*, 206–34; Alberto, *Terms of Inclusion*, 69–109.

63. José Correia Leite, "E, apoz a liberdade . . . ," *O Clarim d'Alvorada*, August 30, 1925.

64. Pinto, *O movimento negro em São Paulo*, 156.

65. Butler, *Freedoms Given, Freedoms Won*, 103.

66. The *Frente*'s somewhat paradoxical ideological positioning comes to the fore most flagrantly in its support for Mussolini's invasion of Ethiopia. See Pinto, *O movimento negro em São Paulo*, 141. For his part, José Correia Leite, who had already distanced himself from the FNB due to Arlindo Veiga dos Santos's flirtations with fascism, vehemently condemned the Italian occupation.

67. Jessica Lynn Graham, *Shifting the Meaning of Democracy: Race, Politics, and Culture in the United States and Brazil* (Berkeley: University of California Press, 2019), 122–23, 126. Graham points out that Santos took a particular interest in Nazi Germany: "Arlindo Veiga dos Santos even favorably portrayed Nazism as an undemocratic nationalist paradigm that could promote racial equity in Brazil more effectively than the Brazilian system of government." (122)

68. Butler, *Freedoms Given, Freedoms Won*, 123.

69. Graham, *Shifting the Meaning of Democracy*, 125.

CHAPTER FOUR. *SOB O SIGNO DA DANTE*: MIGUEL REALE, ITALIANNESS, AND FASCISM

1. Alessandro Dell'Aira, *Lungo studio grande amore: Rodolfo Crespi e l'Istituto Medio Italo-Brasiliano "Dante Alighieri" di San Paolo* (Soveria Mannelli: Rubbettino Editore, 2012), 43.

2. Savoia, as cited in Patricia Salvetti, *Immagine nazionale ed emigrazione nella Società "Dante Alighieri"* (Rome: Bonacci Editore, 1995), 75.

3. Michael Mitchell, "Miguel Reale and the Impact of Conservative Modernization on Brazilian Race Relations," in *Racial Politics in Contemporary Brazil*, ed. Michael Hanchard (Durham, NC: Duke University Press, 1999), 119.

4. Salvetti, *Immagine nazionale*," 75. Salvetti's claim needs further clarification. While many other examples of successful Dante Alighieri Society schools exist across the Italian empire, especially in the Mediterranean, the São Paulo's Institute is unique in regard to the type of funding it received from the local Italian elite of São Paulo and the Brazilian elite who sent their own children to school there. Additionally, the secondary level of the school and the fact that it granted an Italian diploma (as well as a Brazilian one) made the school quite different from other schools set up by the Dante Alighieri Society. For more on other successful Dante Alighieri Society schools, see Valerie McGuire, *Italy's Sea: Empire and Nation in the Mediterranean, 1895–1945* (Liverpool: Liverpool University Press, 2020), 151–53.

5. Mitchell, "Miguel Reale," 123. See also Thomas Skidmore, *Black into White: Race and Nationality in Brazilian Thought* (Durham, NC: Duke University Press, 1993); George Reid Andrews, *Blacks and Whites in São Paulo, Brazil 1888–1988* (Madison: University of Wisconsin Press, 1991).

6. Mark Choate, "Italy at Home and Abroad After 150 Years: The Legacy of Emigration and the Future of Italianità," *Italian Culture* XXX, no. 1 (2012): 53; Federico Finchelstein, *Transatlantic Fascism: Ideology, Violence, and the Sacred in Argentina and Italy, 1919–1945* (Durham, NC: Duke University Press, 2010), 8.

7. Mitchell, "Miguel Reale," 123. Mitchell highlights the importance that Gilberto Freyre's *Casa grande e senzala* (1934) has had on this tradition of conservative thinking. Freyre argues that "race did not have to be viewed as a drag on the elite's project of modernization," proposing a different, but no less problematic, way of understanding the relationship between race and modernization in Brazil. For Freyre, "Brazil had actually produced a singular solution to the question of racial conflict that had troubled so many other multiracial societies." It is precisely this point that many critics have recognized as central to the myth of Brazilian "racial democracy." See Mitchell, "Miguel Reale," 124, 129.

8. Miguel Reale, *Obras políticas*, vol. 1, 1931–1937 (Brasília: Editora da Universidade de Brasília, 1983), 132.

9. The Dante Alighieri Society was especially concerned with the preservation of *italianità* among Italian citizens living in the Austrian territories known as *terre irridente*. Due to this "secret" interest, Tamara van Kessel, in her comparative study of Dante's French, German, and British counterparts,

suggests that the Dante Alighieri Society bears a closer resemblance to the Allgemeiner Deutscher Schulverein than its more obvious competitor in the Mediterranean basin, the Alliance Française. See Tamara van Kessel, *Foreign Cultural Policy in the Interbellum: The Italian Dante Alighieri Society and the British Council Contesting the Mediterranean* (Amsterdam: Amsterdam University Press, 2016), 36.

10. Patrizia Salvetti, "Le scuole italiane all'estero," in *Storia dell' emigrazione italiana*, ed. Piero Bevilacqua, Andreina De Clementi, and Emilio Franzina, vol. II: Arrivi (Rome: Donzelli Editore, 2009), 535.

11. Kessel, *Foreign Cultural Policy in the Interbellum*, 38.

12. Choate, "Italy at Home and Abroad," 60.

13. See Mark Choate, *Emigrant Nation: The Making of Italy Abroad* (Cambridge, MA: Harvard University Press, 2008), 192. The situation differed dramatically in the US, where "Italy was not allowed to establish state schools, so the state relied entirely upon proxy groups, including Catholic Church schools, subsidized after 1901 through the Emigration Fund." Choate, "Italy at Home and Abroad," 60.

14. See Andrews, *Blacks and Whites*, 62.

15. Savoia, as cited in Salvetti, *Immagine nazionale*, 75.

16. Dell'Aira, *Lungo studio grande amore*, 48. As Dell'Aira finds, "in addition to [Crespi's £10,000], there were the four shares from the Puglisi-Carboni brothers, the two from Francesco Matarazzo and then the shares, one each, from Enrico Maggi, Nicola Serricchio, Luigi Pucci, the Banco Commerciale Italo-Brasiliano, Antonio de Camillis, Egidio Pinotti-Gamba, Luigi Minervino-Napolitano, the brothers Falchi, the brothers Secchi, the engineer Giulio Micheli, Giuseppe Martinelli and from the Società per l'Esportazione e per l'Industria italo-americana." Dell'Aira, *Lungo studio grande amore*, 71.

17. Dell'Aira, *Lungo studio grande amore*, 73.

18. On July 9, 2011, the Colégio Dante Alighieri of São Paulo celebrated its one hundredth anniversary. The centerpiece of the celebrations was a time capsule containing artifacts, books, and testimonials that tracked the numerous changes the school had undergone throughout the twentieth century. The school still celebrates some of the most important Italian holidays, such as the *Festa della Repubblica* on June 2nd, and also publishes its own magazine, which frequently highlights famous alumni and exalts the Italian history of São Paulo.

19. Fernanda Franchini, "Entre Vargas e Mussolini: A nacionalização do Instituto Médio Ítalo-Brasileiro 'Dante Alighieri,'" Master's Dissertation (Universidade de São Paulo, 2015), 24, 43.

20. For example, Bertonha tells us that professors Isoldi and Tripoli were purged from the faculty as early as 1927. João Bertonha, *O fascismo e os imigrantes italianos no Brasil* (Porto Alegre: EDIPUCRS, 2001), 153.

21. Angelo Trento, "'Dovunque è un italiano, là è il tricolore': la penetrazione del fascismo tra gli immigrati in Brasile," in *Fascisti in Sud America*, ed. Eugenia Scarzanella (Florence: Le Lettere, 2005), 10–11; Bertonha, *O fascismo*, 171; On the school's fascist sympathies, see Franchini, "Entre Vargas e Mussolini," 43.

22. Philip V. Cannistraro, "Mussolini's Cultural Revolution: Fascist or Nationalist," in *Fascism: Critical Concepts in Political Science*, vol. 2, ed. Roger Griffin and Matthew Feldman (New York: Routledge, 2004), 198.

23. Kessel, *Foreign Cultural Policy in the Interbellum*, 42–43. For a more detailed study of the relationship between the Dante Alighieri Society and the fascist regime see Beatrice Pisa, *Nazione e politica nella "Società Dante Alighieri"* (Rome: Bonacci Editore, 1995). Regarding the Institute, I should note, however, that Alessandro Dell'Aira, a former diplomat in São Paulo who wrote the only exhaustive history of the school, suggests that it resisted directives from Italy in those years, albeit unsuccessfully. Salvetti, too, in her work on the impact of the Dante Alighieri Society abroad, briefly mentions how in a memo to Rome Sergio Mazzolini, then the Italian consul in São Paulo, complained of the "problematic and needy situation" at the Institute engendered by the presence of anti-fascists among its faculty. See Dell'Aira, *Lungo studio grande amore*, 194; Salvetti, *Immagine nazionale*, 254. See also Bertonha, *O fascismo*, 141–47.

24. Gianni Scipione Rossi, *Mussolini e il diplomatico: la vita e i diari di Serafino Mazzolini, un monarchico a salò* (Soveria Mannelli: Rubbettino Editore, 2005), xx; Barbara Weinstein, *The Color of Modernity: São Paulo and the Making of Race and Nation in Brazil* (Durham, NC: Duke University Press, 2015), 124–26. For an authoritative history of Italian fascism in São Paulo see Bertonha, *O Fascismo*; see also Trento, "Dovunque è un italiano."

25. Emilio Gentile, "I Fasci Italiani All'Estero, The 'Foreign Policy' of the Fascist Party," in *Fascism Outside Europe: The European Impulse against Domestic Conditions in the Diffusion of Global Fascism*, ed. Stein Ugelvik Larsen (Boulder, CO: Social Science Monographs, 2001), 95.

26. Bertonha, *O fascismo*, 101. Bertonha reports that in the early 1940s the files of the São Paulo Secret Police list between 3,000 and 5,000 citizens associated with the fasci all'estero, to whom should be added the 2,300 members of the Gioventù Italiana del Littorio all'Estero.

27. Bertonha, *O fascismo*, 45.

28. Bertonha, *O fascismo*, 71. Brazil, of course, was not the only South American country in Mussolini's crosshairs. For an in-depth look at Italian fascism in Argentina, see Finchelstein's *Transatlantic Fascism* and David Aliano, *Mussolini's National Project in Argentina* (Madison, NJ: Fairleigh Dickinson University Press, 2012). For a comparative analysis, see Michael

Goebel, "Italian Fascism and Diasporic Nationalisms in Argentina, Brazil, and Uruguay" in Nicola Foote and Michael Goebel, *Immigration and National Identities in Latin America* (Gainesville, FL: University Press of Florida, 2014), 234–54.

29. Angelo Trento, "I fasci in Brasile," in *Il fascismo e gli emigrati: la parabola dei fasci italiani all'estero*, ed. Emilio Franzina and Matteo Sanfilippo (Bari: Laterza, 2003), 154.

30. Bertonha, *O fascismo*, 327.

31. Ricardo Silva Seitenfus, "Ideology and Diplomacy: Italian Fascism and Brazil (1935–1938)," *Hispanic American Historical Review* 64, no. 3 (1984): 591, 607. This is an exhaustive article on the relationship between the fascist party and the integralists.

32. This supposed planned coup was called, with just a hint of antisemitism, "Operation Cohen." Despite the falsity of such a plan, Vargas's fears were somewhat founded since only two years prior in 1935, Luis Carlos Prestes led a communist insurrection against the Vargas government known as *Intentona*.

33. Helgio Trindade, *Integralismo: o fascismo brasileiro da década de 30* (São Paulo: Difel, 1974), 12.

34. For a detailed biography of Arlindo Veiga dos Santos please see Teresa Malatian, *O Cavaleiro Negro: Arlindo Veiga dos Santos e a Frente Negra Brasileira* (São Paulo: Alameda Editorial, 2015).

35. Jessica Lynn Graham, *Shifting the Meaning of Democracy: Race, Politics, and Culture in the United States and Brazil* (Berkeley: University of California Press, 2019), 114.

36. Andrews, *Blacks and Whites*, 153–54; Sandra McGee Deutsch, *Las Derechas: The Extreme Right in Argentina, Brazil, and Chile, 1890–1939* (Stanford, CA: Stanford University Press, 1999), 281.

37. Menzinger, as cited in Seitenfus, "Ideology and Diplomacy," 591.

38. Marco Mugnaini, *L'America Latina e Mussolini: Brasile e Argentina nella politica estera dell'Italia (1919–1943)* (Milan: Franco Angeli, 2008), 113.

39. Reale, *Obras políticas*, 154. On the history of the concept of "racial democracy," see Paulina L. Alberto and Jesse Hoffnung-Garskof, "'Racial Democracy' and Racial Inclusion," in *Afro-Latin American Studies: An Introduction*, by George R Andrews and Alejandro de la Fuente (New York: Cambridge University Press, 2018).

40. Marilena Chauí and Maria Sylvia Carvalho Franco, *Ideologia e mobilização popular* (Rio de Janeiro: Paz e Terra, 1978). Following Luigi Salvatorelli's hypothesis, historian Renzo de Felice stresses that in order to fully comprehend the fascist phenomenon, it is necessary to understand the important role

played by the petite bourgeoisie, for it is among this group and the middle class in general that fascism found its most ardent supporters. This group encompasses bureaucrats, office managers, accountants, and salaried intellectuals, who, according to De Felice, "lacked personal autonomy [and] were only slightly integrated" without "adequate instruments for collective bargaining and in a situation of steady loss of social and economic status." Luigi Salvatorelli, *Nazionalfascismo* (Turin: Einaudi, 1977 [1923]); Renzo de Felice, *Interpretations of Fascism*, trans. Brenda Huff Everett (Cambridge, MA: Harvard University Press, 1977), 176–77.

41. Barbara Spackman, *Fascist Virilities: Rhetoric, Ideology, and Social Fantasy in Italy* (Minneapolis: University of Minnesota Press, 1996), 131.

42. Chauí and Franco, *Ideologia e mobilização popular*, 59.

43. Barbara and John Ehrenreich, "The New Left and the Professional Managerial Class," *Radical America* 11, no. 3 (May–June 1977): 7–24.

44. C. Wright Mills, *The Power Elite* (Oxford: Oxford University Press, 1968 [1956]), 9.

45. Miguel Reale, *Memórias*, vol. I: Destinos cruzados (São Paulo: Saraiva, 1987), 34. See Vilfredo Pareto, *The Mind and Society*, vol. 3 (New York: Harcourt, Brace and Company, 1935). American sociologist C. Wright Mills, another follower of Pareto, highlights how "there is a kind of mutual attraction among those 'who sit on the same terrace.'" "The overlapping 'crowds' and intricately connected cliques" constitute a defining feature of what Mills calls "the power elite." Observing the post–World War II era United States, Mills discerns an oligarchical structure of governance in which a group of men, the power elite, "are in positions to make decisions having major consequences." These men stand at the helm of what Mills identifies as "the major institutions of modern society," which fall under three categories: the economic, political, and military. For Mills, the key is not simply financial capital but also who has "access to the command of major institutions." Where Mills imagined white-collar workers as fundamentally weak and subordinate to the power elite, Reale insists that only the professional managerial class can tap into the "institutional means of power" Mills so aptly describes and use them to bring about change. See Mills, *The Power Elite*, 4–5, 9, 11.

46. Pareto, *The Mind and Society*, 555; Giovanni Gentile, *Origini e dottrina del fascismo* (Rome: Libreria del Littorio, 1929), 30.

47. Ludovico Incisa di Camerana, "San Paolo, Italia," *Limes: Rivista Italiana di Geopolitica* 6: Dossier: Brasile la Stella del Sud (2007).

48. Deutsch, *Las Derechas*, 322–23; Odilon Caldeira Neto, *Sob o signo do sigma: integralismo, neointegralismo, antissemitismo* (Maringá: Editora da Universidade Estadual de Maringá, 2014), 69.

49. Miguel Reale, *Imperativos da revolução de março* (São Paulo: Editora Martins, 1964), 112.

50. Reale, *Imperativos da revolução de março*, 12, 16, 47.

51. Gentile, *Origini e dottrina del fascismo*, 9, 30–31.

52. Reale, *Imperativos da revolução de março*, 101.

53. Miguel Reale, *Memórias*, vol. II: A balança e a espada (São Paulo: Saraiva, 1987), 124–25; Gentile, *Origini e dottrina del fascismo*, 32.

54. Reale, *Memórias*, II, 137.

55. The 1979 Amnesty Law was the product of a long-planned transition to democracy that started in 1974 with the shift in power from the hard-liner Emílio Médici to the more moderate Ernesto Geisel. The law gave military personnel the possibility of safeguarding themselves from future prosecutions and framed this provision as a step toward a more democratic government. For more on testimonial literature in Brazil see Rebecca Atencio's chapter "Testimonies and the Amnesty Law," in *Memory's Turn: Reckoning with Dictatorship in Brazil* (Madison: University of Wisconsin Press, 2014), 28–58.

56. In 2006, former general and Chief of Secret Services Carlo Alberto Brilhante Ustra also wrote a testimonial novel about his time as chief torturer during the military regime. See Carlos Alberto Brilhante Ustra, *A verdade sufocada: a história que a esquerda não quer que o Brasil conheça* (São Paulo: Editora Ser, 2006).

57. Reale, *Memórias*, I, 138–39.

58. Reale, *Obras políticas*, 121; on the propagation of fascist ideas outside of Europe see Stanley G. Payne, *Fascism: Comparison and Definition* (Madison: University of Wisconsin Press, 1980), 175.

59. Miguel Reale, "Meu Dante," in *O Meu Dante*, ed. Maria Cecilia Casini. (Cotia, SP: Atelie Editorial, 2024), 105.

60. Philippe Lejeune, *On Autobiography*, trans. Katherine M. Leary (Minneapolis: University of Minnesota Press, 1989), 4.

61. Reale, *Memórias*, I, 2–3, 9.

62. I am translating "Sob o signo da Dante" as "Under the Auspices of the Institute Dante Alighieri" because Reale uses the Portuguese construction *de + a= da* before Dante, referring with the determinative, feminine article to the *escola*, or school.

63. Reale, *Memórias*, I, 30–32.

64. In a recent essay titled "Dante and the Transnational Turn," Tristan Kay reads Dante's oeuvre as a model for thinking about "forms of allegiance and identity that transcend the modern borders and territories." Such a

quintessential transnational approach to reading Dante is perhaps even more visible in the provocative piece by Simone Brioni and Lorenzo Mari, who show how "references to the *Commedia*" in the works of two Somali writers "can be interpreted as an anti-colonial critique since they challenge the use of Dante's work to promote colonialism and its racial policies." Yet another example of Dante's transnational reception can be found in Dennis Looney's *Freedom Readers*. Such is the breadth of Dante's political valences: his work has inspired everyone from Italo-Brazilian fascists to champions of the African American civil rights movement. See Tristan Kay, "Dante and the Transnational Turn," in *Transnational Italian Studies*, ed. Charles Burdett and Loredana Polezzi (Liverpool: Liverpool University Press, 2020), 296; Simoni Brioni and Lorenzo Mari, "Postcolonial Dante: Reading the *Commedia* in Mogadishu," in *Dante's Worlds: Echoes, Places, Questions*, ed. Peter Carravetta (Rome: L'Erma di Bretschneider, 2019), 114; Dennis Looney, *Freedom Readers: The African American Reception of Dante Alighieri and the Divine Comedy* (South Bend, IN: University of Notre Dame Press, 2011).

65. In *Dante's Bones*, an exhaustive journey through the transformations of Dante across the centuries, literary scholar Guy Raffa dedicates an entire chapter to Dante and Mussolini. "A masterful demagogue," Raffa writes, "Mussolini easily grasped the advantage of claiming the poet for his cause, just as D'Annunzio had for irredentism and, before that, Mazzini had for the Risorgimento. In a famous speech at the Augusteo Theater in Rome on November 8, 1921. . . . Mussolini identified the poet as the inspiration not just for Italian nationhood but specifically for fascism." See Guy P. Raffa, *Dante's Bones: How a Poet Invented Italy* (Cambridge, MA: Harvard University Press, 2020), 210. On Dante and fascism see also Stefano Albertini, "Dante in camicia nera: uso e abuso del divino poeta nell'Italia fascista," *The Italianist* 16, no. 1 (1996): 117–42.

66. Reale, *Memórias*, I, 30.

67. Reale, *Memórias*, II, 216.

68. Policy analyst Guido Tintori has written extensively about the consequences of the legislation on citizenship; see for example his article on "Latin America Italians" and the formation of "a potentially massive transnational political subject entitled to claim Italian citizenship." See Guido Tintori, "The Transnational Political Practices of 'Latin American Italians,'" *International Migration* 49, no. 3 (2011): 173.

69. Teresa Fiore, "The Emigrant Post-'Colonia' in Contemporary Immigrant Italy," in *Postcolonial Italy*, ed. Cristina Lombardi-Diop and Caterina Romeo (New York: Palgrave Macmillan, 2012), 74–79.

CHAPTER FIVE. *MUITO PARECIDA MAS COMPLETAMENTE DIFERENTE*: ZÉLIA GATTAI, MULTIDIRECTIONALITY, AND THE ITALIAN ANARCHISTS

1. Jorge Amado, "O Livro de Zélia," in *Anarquistas, graças a Deus*, by Zélia Gattai (São Paulo: Companhia das Letras, 2009), 9–10. Note that *Anarquistas* has been reprinted six times since 1979 by major Brazilian press Companhia das Letras, while the two-volume autobiography of conservative Italo-Brazilian politician Miguel Reale (discussed in Chapter Four), although originally published by an important trade press, has long since gone out of print.

2. Angelo Trento, "'Wherever We Work, The Land Is Ours': The Italian Anarchist Press and Working-Class Solidarity," in *Italian Workers of the World: Labor Migration and the Formation of Multiethnic States*, ed. Donna R. Gabaccia and Fraser Ottanelli (Champaign: University of Illinois Press, 2001), 102. Trento informs us that between 1890 and 1920, Italians constituted between 50 and 80 percent of the workers in industry, crafts, and transportation.

3. Michael Rothberg, *Multidirectional Memory: Remembering the Holocaust in the Age of Decolonization* (Stanford, CA: Stanford University Press, 2009), 3.

4. Isabelle Felici, "Gli anarchici italiani di São Paulo e il problema dell'organizzazione operaia," in *La riscoperta delle americhe: lavoratori e sindacato nell'emigrazione italiana in America Latina 1870–1970*, ed. Vanni Blengino, Emilio Franzina, and Adolfo Pepe (Milan: Teti Editore, 1999), 332; Trento, "Wherever We Work, the Land Is Ours," 107.

5. Donna R. Gabaccia, "Worker Internationalism and Italian Labor Migration, 1870–1914," *International Labor and Working-Class History*, no. 45 (1994): 63–79. I follow historian Marcella Bencivenni's understanding of terms such as "radicalism" and "radicals," insofar as they "encompass the whole range of class-based ideologies associated with the European political left: anarchism, socialism, syndicalism, and communism." See Marcella Bencivenni, *Italian Immigrant Radical Culture: The Idealism of the* Sovversivi *in the United States 1890–1940* (New York: New York University Press, 2011), 2.

6. Zélia Gattai, *Anarquistas, graças a Deus* (São Paulo: Companhia das Letras, 2009), 206–7, 243; Carlo Romani and Bruno Corrêa de Sá e Benevides, "The Italian Anarchists' Network in São Paulo at the Beginning of the Twentieth Century," in *In Transatlantic Radicalism: Socialist and Anarchist Exchanges in the 19th and 20th Centuries*, ed. Frank Jacob and Mario Keßler (Liverpool: Liverpool University Press, 2021), 71.

7. I have collected and rephrased all the biographical details summarized here from Carlo Romani, *Oreste ristori: vita avventurosa di un anarchico tra Toscana e Sudamerica* (Ghezzano: BFS Edizioni, 2015).

8. Gattai, *Anarquistas, graças a Deus*, 243.

9. Luigi Biondi, "Anarquistas italianos em São Paulo: o grupo do jornal anarquista 'La Battaglia' e a aua visão da sociedade brasileira: o embate entre imaginários libertários e etnocêntricos," *Cadernos AEL* 8/9 (1998): 118; Felici, "Gli anarchici italiani di São Paulo e il problema dell'organizzazione operaia," 326.

10. Bencivenni, *Italian Immigrant Radical Culture*, 39. For "radical ethnic brokers," see Elisabetta Vezzosi, "Radical Ethnic Brokers: Immigrant Socialist Leaders in the United States between Ethnic Community and Larger Society," in *Italian Workers of the World: Labor Migration and the Formation of Multiethnic States*, ed. Donna R. Gabaccia and Fraser Ottanelli (Champaign: University of Illinois Press, 2001), 121–38.

11. Trento, "Wherever We Work, the Land Is Ours," 112–14.

12. Biondi, "Anarquistas italianos em São Paulo," 120, 134–38.

13. Biondi, "Anarquistas italianos em São Paulo," 120, 125; Trento, "Wherever We Work, the Land Is Ours," 111.

14. Similarly, Patricia Galvão in her canonical novel of proletarian literature *Parque industrial* (first published in 1933) glorifies the immigrant as the quintessential militant and "good" worker and stigmatizes the native (Black) Brazilians. See Patrícia Galvão, *Parque industrial* (São Paulo: Companhia das Letras, 2022).

15. Gattai, *Anarquistas, graças a Deus*, 241.

16. Giacomo Matteotti was an Italian congressman and socialist politician who openly spoke against Mussolini and fascist violence only to be brutally murdered on June 10, 1924.

17. Gattai, *Anarquistas, graças a Deus*, 197. Sacco and Vanzetti were executed on August 23, 1927. The allegations against them remain dubious. For more on the trial, see Paul Avrich, "Sacco and Vanzetti's Revenge," in *The Lost World of Italian American Radicalism: Politics, Labor, and Culture*, ed. Philip V. Cannistraro and Gerald Meyer (New York: Bloomsbury, 2003), 167.

18. Gattai, *Anarquistas, graças a Deus*, 96.

19. Donna R. Gabaccia and Franca Iacovetta, *Women, Gender and Transnational Lives: Italian Workers of the World* (Toronto: University of Toronto Press, 2002); Bencivenni, *Italian Immigrant Radical Culture*, 43.

20. Gattai, *Anarquistas, graças a Deus*, 133, 193; Rita Antonella Roscilli, *Da palavra à imagem em* Anarquistas, graças a Deus *de Zélia Gattai* (Salvador: EDUFBA, 2011), 42.

21. Gattai, *Anarquistas, graças a Deus*, 150–51, 284.

22. Gattai, *Anarquistas, graças a Deus*, 147.

23. Gattai, *Anarquistas, graças a Deus*, 152.

24. Gattai, *Anarquistas, graças a Deus*, 152–53.

25. Gattai, *Anarquistas, graças a Deus*, 153.

26. Caterina Romeo, *Narrative tra due sponde: memoir d'italiane d'America* (Rome: Carrocci Editore, 2005), 53.

27. Romeo, *Narrative tra due sponde*, 116.

28. Gattai, *Anarquistas, graças a Deus*, 177.

29. Gattai, *Anarquistas, graças a Deus*, 178.

30. Cerchiai, as cited in Isabelle Felici, "La colonia Cecilia: fra leggenda e realtà," *Rivista Storica Dell'anarchismo* a. III, no. 2 (1996): 2.

31. Felici, "La Colonia Cecilia," 3.

32. A subsequent 1884 edition of the novel, one of many, carries a preface by none other than Italian anarchist Andrea Costa. While Costa had broken with the Italian anarchist movement by that time and would subsequently move on to create his Socialist Revolutionary Party, Rossi saw in his preface, which would cater to those whose beliefs fell more in Costa's camp, a way to garner more support for the project. See José Antônio Vasconcelos, "Giovanni Rossi and His Anarchist Utopia in Nineteenth Century Brazil," *Anarchist Studies* 24, no. 2 (2016): 63.

33. Felici, "La Colonia Cecilia," 3–4; Vasconcelos, "Giovanni Rossi and His Anarchist Utopia," 63. Two interlinked factors contributed to the collapse of Cittadella, which, before Rossi's arrival, was an association of agricultural workers: first, the workers' goal was to become landowners, a desire incompatible with Rossi's anarchist ideals; second, the workers did not share Rossi's utopian ideas. Still, such a setback did not stop Rossi. Instead, it allowed him to see that, in addition to suitable land, his experimental socialist colony needed men and women who shared both his ideals and his fervor to see those ideals reflected in concrete reality.

34. Gattai, *Anarquistas, graças a Deus*, 180, 188.

35. Vasconcelos, "Giovanni Rossi and His Anarchist Utopia," 64.

36. Felici, "La Colonia Cecilia," 8.

37. Felici, "La Colonia Cecilia," 1.

38. Gattai, *Anarquistas, graças a Deus*, 182.

39. Gattai, *Anarquistas, graças a Deus*, 183.

40. Gattai, *Anarquistas, graças a Deus*, 188.

41. Agnieszka Bedingfield, "Trans-Memory and Diaspora: Memories of Europe and Asia in American Immigrant Narratives," in *Sites of Ethnicity: Europe and the Americas*, ed. William Boelhower, Rocío G. Davis, and Carmen Birkle (Heidelberg: Universitätsverlag Winter, 2004), 333–46. Evelyn Ferraro has reformulated this concept through the lenses of the transnational, "whereby memories are reworked in the present from one generation to the next, contingent upon specific geographies of relations and belonging that

invite engagement across difference." See Evelyn Ferraro, "Place and Trans-memory in California Italian American Literary Narratives: Dorothy Bryant's *Miss Giardino*," *Forum Italicum* 57, no. 2 (2023): 616.

42. Gattai, *Anarquistas, graças a Deus*, 188.

43. Gattai, *Anarquistas, graças a Deus*, 185, 189.

44. Gattai, *Anarquistas, graças a Deus*, 190.

45. Gattai, *Anarquistas, graças a Deus*, 190–91.

46. For more on the question of Catholicism and how it plays out in the memoir see Francesca Miller's analysis of *Anarquistas*. "Anarquistas, Graças a Deus! 'Italy' in South America," in *Revisioning Italy: National Identity and Global Culture*, ed. Beverly Allen and Mary Russo (Minneapolis: University of Minnesota Press, 1997), 213–32.

47. Gattai, *Anarquistas, graças a Deus*, 223.

48. Gattai, *Anarquistas, graças a Deus*, 36–37.

49. Romeo, *Narrative fra due sponde*, 44; Edvige Giunta, *Writing with an Accent: Contemporary Italian American Women Authors* (New York: Palgrave MacMillan, 2002), 4.

50. Gattai, *Anarquistas, graças a Deus*, 37.

51. Gattai, *Anarquistas, graças a Deus*, 26.

52. As I explained in Chapter Three, the word *negro* or *negra* in Brazilian Portuguese does not have an inherently negative connotation. On the contrary, it holds the same meaning as "Black" in English. The equivalent of these terms in Italian would be *nero* or *nera*.

53. Zélia Gattai, *Anarchici, grazie a Dio*, trans. Yvonne Giannini (Milano: Sperling & Kupfer Editori, 1992), 17.

54. George Reid Andrews, *Blacks and Whites in São Paulo, Brazil 1888–1988* (Madison: University of Wisconsin Press, 1991), 64–65; Trento, "Wherever We Work, the Land Is Ours," 39, 75.

55. Gattai, *Anarquistas, graças a Deus*, 37–38.

56. Bencivenni, *Italian Immigrant Radical Culture*, 43.

57. Gattai, *Anarquistas, graças a Deus*, 55.

58. Gattai, *Anarquistas, graças a Deus*, 56, 217, 247; Trento, "Wherever We Work, the Land Is Ours," 112.

59. Gattai, *Anarquistas, graças a Deus*, 309.

60. For a historical and literary analysis of the racializing discourses plaguing the Italian kingdom at the time of unification (and later), see Aliza Wong, *Race and the Nation in Liberal Italy, 1861–1911: Meridionalism, Empire, and Diaspora* (New York: Palgrave Macmillan, 2006); Rhiannon Noel Welch, *Vital Subjects: Race and Biopolitics in Italy* (Liverpool: Liverpool University Press, 2016).

61. Gattai, *Anarquistas, graças a Deus*, 97, 100.

62. Gattai, *Anarquistas, graças a Deus*, 99; Gattai, *Anarchici, grazie a Dio*, 82.

63. Gattai, *Anarquistas, graças a Deus*, 62.

64. On linguistic abilities as a marker of status, see Nancy C. Carnevale, *A New Language, A New World: Italian Immigrants in the United States, 1890–1945* (Champaign: University of Illinois Press, 2009), 35.

65. Gattai, *Anarquistas, graças a Deus*, 101–2.

66. Gattai, *Anarquistas, graças a Deus*, 102–3; Nelson J. Moe, *The View from Vesuvius: Italian Culture and the Southern Question* (Berkeley: University of California Press, 2002), 3.

67. Gattai, *Anarquistas, graças a Deus*, 103. Lorenzo Aristodemo has written in great detail about the tradition of the Nossa Senhora da Achiropita, including how and when it traveled from Rossano Calabro to São Paulo, where it is still celebrated in August. Aristodemo explains that "the icon is strongly marked by the presence of the sea, understood not as a barrier between distant worlds, but as the nexus between them." It is likely that someone from Rossano crossed the Atlantic and brought with them the iconography. The earliest reports of its celebration in São Paulo date back to 1908. Between 1908 and 1926, the festa was used to collect money to buy the lot for a chapel dedicated to the Madonna. Today the festa is one of the largest in São Paulo. See Lorenzo Aristodemo, "La Madonna Divorata. La festa della Nossa Senhora da Achiropita un culto calabro-bizantino," in *Italiani in Brasile: rotte migratorie e percorsi culturali*, ed. Vittorio Cappelli and Alexandre Hecker (Soveria Mannelli: Rubbettino Editore, 2010), 51.

68. Gattai, *Anarquistas, graças a Deus*, 104 (emphasis mine).

69. Gattai, *Anarquistas, graças a Deus*, 104.

70. Andrews, *Blacks and Whites*, 62.

71. Romani and Corrêa de Sá e Benevides, "The Italian Anarchists' Network in São Paulo at the Beginning of the Twentieth Century," 71.

72. On the role of Southern Italian culture in forming a specific ethnicity in the US and Canada, see Pasquale Verdicchio, *Bound by Distance: Rethinking Nationalism through the Italian Diaspora* (New York: Bordighera Press, 2016), esp. 102–68. On the creation of a "Neapolitan synecdoche," that is, the practice of reducing all Italians to Neapolitans or Southerners within the Italian diaspora in the United States, see Giuliana Muscio, *Napoli/New York/Hollywood: Film between Italy and the United States* (New York: Fordham University Press, 2018). With regard to "the other side of the Atlantic," one need only take a look at a recent *The Economist*'s cover, in which Liz Truss, dressed up as Britannia, forcefully clasps a fork with spaghetti instead of the trident, while her other hand proudly holds a shield with a British flag that not only looks like a pizza, but whose colors have transformed into the red, white,

and green of the Italian *tricolore*, representing, respectively, tomato sauce, cheese, and basil. Before *The Economist*'s "Britaly," there was the infamous *Der Spiegel*'s cover of 1977, "Pistole auf spaghetti," where a black pistol was laid upon a heaping plate of spaghetti on a checkered tablecloth, in front of a window with three bullet holes. The sensationalist title "Urlaubsland ITALIEN: Entführung, Erpressung, Straßenraub" [Destination Italy: Kidnapping, Blackmail, Street Robberies] filled in the gaps for those unsure of the image's meanings. In the introduction I cowrote with Loredana Polezzi and Serena Bassi for the *Forum Italicum* special issue, "Critical Issues in Transnational Italian Studies," in which we analyze these images in depth, we point out how "*The Economist*'s cover exists as part of a global network of circulation in which specific stereotyped images of Italy are constantly re-elaborated and re-worked according to the distinctive needs of each locality. The transnational circulation of the sign Italy across the Channel and its echoing back within the confines of the nation-state, ensured that whoever saw the image of Britaly caught its references." Bassi et al. "Introduction," *Forum Italicum* 57, no. 2 (2023): 275–76.

73. Gattai, *Anarquistas, graças a Deus*, 195, 298.

74. Gattai, *Anarquistas, graças a Deus*, 298.

75. Gattai, *Anarquistas, graças a Deus*, 200, 302; Donna R. Gabaccia and Fraser Ottanelli, "Introduction," in *Italian Workers of the World: Labor Migration and the Formation of Multiethnic Studies* (Champaign: University of Illinois Press, 2001), 3.

76. Gattai, *Anarquistas, graças a Deus*, 19.

77. Gattai, *Anarquistas, graças a Deus*, 22.

CODA: WHOSE ITALIANNESS?

1. Mário Magalhães, *Marighella: O guerrilheiro que incendiou o mundo* (São Paulo: Companhia das Letras, 2012), 33–34.

2. Carlo Romani and Bruno Corrêa de Sá e Benevides, "The Italian Anarchists' Network in São Paulo at the Beginning of the Twentieth Century," in *Transatlantic Radicalism: Socialist and Anarchist Exchanges in the 19th and 20th Centuries*, ed. Frank Jacob and Mario Keßler (Liverpool: Liverpool University Press, 2021), 71.

3. While perhaps not relevant to Feltrinelli's goals with the series (literary scholar Neelam Srivastava explains that Feltrinelli's involvement in the Italian armed struggle was influenced by his own reading and absorption of the Tricontinental message), it seems curious that nowhere in the secondary work about Marighella in Italian does his Italian parentage receive mention. Marighella's manual has recently been reissued by the conservative publishing

house Passaggio al Bosco, whose name refers ominously to Ernst Junger's essay "The Forest Passage." See Neelam Srivastava, "Publishing the Resistance: Third-Worldist Writing in Cold War Italy," in *The Form of Ideology and the Ideology of Form: Cold War, Decolonization and Third World Print Cultures*, ed. Francesca Orsini, Neelam Srivastava, and Laetitia Zecchini (Cambridge: Open Book Publishers, 2022), 171; Carlos Marighella, *Piccolo manuale della guerriglia urbana* (Florence: Passaggio al Bosco, 2022).

4. See for example the testimonies collected as part of the impressive journalistic project *Archivio Desaparecido* curated by Elena Basso, Marco Mastrandrea, and Alfredo Sproveri, published in 2021 by Nova Delphi and also accessible online here: https://www.archiviodesaparecido.com/.

5. The distributor of the film, Ancine, postponed the film's theatrical release for almost two years. The movie was shown at the Berlin Festival in 2019 and screened in Brazilian cinemas only in 2021. While Ancine attributed this delay to issues with their backlog, some came to suspect that it had something to do with comments made by former President Bolsonaro about the company and the need to impose restrictions on the film industry. See "'Marighella' estreia em novembro após adiamentos e problemas com a Ancine," *Folha de S. Paulo*, October 4, 2021.

6. The obfuscation of his Italianness could and should also be understood within what scholars Stefano Bellin and Guido Bartolini have called "multidimensional forgetting," or "how political power, cultural hegemony, and entrenched social and discursive structures have actively shaped distorted and problematic narratives of the Italian past." Stefano Bellin and Guido Bartolini, "Italy's Multidimensional Forgetting: Narratives, Contested Memories, and Solidarity," in "Italian Amnesias: Multidimensional Forgetting in Contemporary Italy," special issue, *Italian Culture* XLII, no. 2 (September 2024), 92.

7. I am thinking here of the following works: Alessandro Portelli, "The Problem of the Color Blind: Notes on the Discourse on Race in Italy," in *CrossRoutes: The Meaning of "Race" for the 21st Century*, ed. Paola Boi and Sabine Broeck (Münster: Lit Verlag, 2003), 29–39; Tatiana Petrovich Njegosh, "Gli italiani sono bianchi? Per una storia culturale della linea del colore in Italia," in *Parlare di razza: la lingua del colore tra Italia e Stati Uniti*, ed. Tatiana Petrovich Njegosh and Anna Scacchi (Verona: Ombre Corte, 2012), 13–45; Gaia Giuliani and Cristina Lombardi-Diop, *Bianco e nero: storia dell'identità razziale degli italiani* (Milan: Le Monnier, 2013); Gaia Giuliani, "Mediterraneità e bianchezza: il razzismo italiano tra fascismo e articolazioni contemporanee (1861–2015)," *Iperstoria–Testi Letterature Linguaggi* 6 (2015): 167–82; Angelica Pesarini, "'Blood Is Thicker than Water': The Materialisation of the Racial Body in Fascist East Africa," *Zapruder World: An International Journal*

for the History of Social Conflict 4 (2017); Camilla Hawthorne, *Contesting Race and Citizenship: Youth Politics in the Black Mediterranean* (Ithaca, NY: Cornell University Press, 2022), to name but a few.

8. For a detailed account of how Ciccillo founded the São Paulo Biennale, see Laura Iamurri, "Modernity Abroad: Italy at the Bienal de São Paulo, the Early Years," in *Voyages Between Brazil and Italy* (35th CIHA World Congress: Motion, São Paulo, 2021), 1805–19. In 2024, perhaps as a testament to these exchanges, the Brazilian Adriano Pedrosa became the first non-Western artistic director of the Venice Biennale.

9. Robert Viscusi, "The Future of Italianità: The Italian Commonwealth," in *The Columbus People: Perspectives in Italian Immigration to the Americas and Australia*, ed. Lydia F. Tomasi, Piero Gastaldo, and Thomas Row (New York: Center for Migration Studies, 1994), 485. One of the best studies of this is Tom Ferraro, *Feeling Italian: the Art of Ethnicity in America* (New York: New York University Press, 2005); for a study of the construction of white ethnicities in post–WWII America see Gary Gerstle, *American Crucible: Race and Nation in the Twentieth Century*, Second Edition (Princeton, NJ: Princeton University Press, 2017); and Matthew Frye Jacobson, *Roots Too: White Ethnic Revival in Post-Civil Rights America* (Cambridge, MA: Harvard University Press, 2008).

10. As literary scholar Martino Marazzi has pointed out in *Italexit*, such exclusion cannot be more visible than in the absence (and outright snobbism) within the Italian literary canon of the rich literature produced by diasporic Italians. Marazzi here is thinking in unison with two fundamental thinkers of Italian American Studies, Robert Viscusi and Francesco Durante. Viscusi has consistently advocated for rethinking approaches to Italian Studies that consider it as distinct from its diaspora, explaining that such an approach already depends on the inextricable global network in which Italy and its cultures had existed. At the same time, Durante has been similarly consistent in highlighting the absence of sustained scholarship on the phenomenon of Italian literature of the diaspora; his work is underwritten by a suspicion that this lacuna derives from a shared collective shame vis-a-vis the migration that marked the Italian national project. See Martino Marazzi, *Italexit: Saggi su risorgimento e disunione nazionale* (Florence: Franco Cesati Editore, 2019); Robert Viscusi, "The Future of Italianità: The Italian Commonwealth"; Francesco Durante, "Italy and the Literature of Immigration," trans. Antony Shugaar, in *Words Without Borders*. Online at, https://wordswithoutborders.org/read/article/2016-09/september-2016-italy-the-literature-of-immigration-francesco-durante/.

11. Literary scholar Anthony J. Tamburri rightly understands that migrant writers who write in Italian, Italian-language writers who live outside of Italy,

and Italian American writers are all trafficking within the "ur-sign" Italy (199). Following this logic, he envisions an "expansion of this new 'Italian' group of writers . . . within Italian studies" which in turn "validates the existence of a more fertile field of study of the transnational discourse in which these 'Italians' engage but that, from a hegemonic point of view, are not recognized" (200). He then continues, "the insistence on a limited and . . . limiting group of artists of all sorts restricted to Italy-born, -bred, and -residential can only stifle the critical voice that wishes to make the evident connections that indeed exist under a more broad umbrella that we can, and might, still readily call 'Italian'" (200). With this book I hope to have shown the necessity and urgency to critically engage with this expanded idea of who counts as an "Italian writer," and thus who should be studied and included in our scholarship. See Anthony Julian Tamburri, "Afterword: Rethinking Labels: The Italian Writer as Exemplar or Distinct Categories as Quixotic," in *New Italian Migrations to the United States: Vol. 2: Art and Culture Since 1945*, ed. Laura E Ruberto and Joseph Sciorra (Champaign: Illinois University Press, 2017), 193–202.

BIBLIOGRAPHY

Agnew, John. "The Myth of Backward Italy in Modern Europe." In *Revisioning Italy: National Identity and Global Culture*, edited by Allen Beverly and Mary Russo, 25–44. Minneapolis: University of Minnesota Press, 1997.

Ahmed, Sara. "Racialized Bodies." In *Real Bodies*, edited by Mary Evans and Ellie Lee, 46–63. London: Palgrave, 2000.

Aidoo, Lamonte. *Slavery Unseen: Sex, Power, and Violence in Brazilian History*. Durham, NC: Duke University Press, 2018.

Albertini, Stefano. "Dante in camicia nera: uso e abuso del divino poeta nell'Italia fascista." *The Italianist* 16, no. 1 (1996): 117–42.

Alberto, Paulina L. *Terms of Inclusion: Black Intellectuals in Twentieth-Century Brazil*. Chapel Hill: University of North Carolina Press, 2011.

Alberto, Paulina L., George Reid Andrews, and Jesse Hoffnung-Garskof. *Voices of the Race: Black Newspapers in Latin America, 1870–1960*. Cambridge: Cambridge University Press, 2022.

Alberto, Paulina L., and Jesse Hoffnung-Garskof, "'Racial Democracy' and Racial Inclusion." In *Afro-Latin American Studies: An Introduction*, edited by George R. Andrews and Alejandro de la Fuente. New York: Cambridge University Press, 2018.

Aliano, David. "Brazil through Italian Eyes: The Debate over Emigration to São Paulo during the 1920s." *Altreitalie* 31 (2005): 87–108.

———. *Mussolini's National Project in Argentina*. Teaneck, NJ: Farleigh Dickinson University Press, 2012.

Alvim, Zuleika. *Brava gente! Os italianos em São Paulo, 1870–1920*. São Paulo: Brasiliense, 1986.

Amado, Jorge. "O Livro de Zélia." In *Anarquistas, graças a Deus*, by Zelia Gattai, 9–13. São Paulo: Companhia das Letras, 2009.

Anderson, Benedict. *Imagined Communities: Reflections on the Origin and Spread of Nationalism*. New York: Verso, 2016.

Andrade, Mario de. *Macunaíma: o herói sem nenhum caráter.* Rio de Janeiro: Nova Fronteira, 2012.
Andrews, George Reid. *Blacks and Whites in São Paulo, Brazil 1888–1988.* Madison: University of Wisconsin Press, 1991.
Appelbaum, Nancy P., Anne S. MacPherson, and Karin A. Rosenblatt. "Introduction: Racial Nations." In *Race and Nation in Modern Latin America*, 1–31. Chapel Hill: University of North Carolina Press, 2003.
Aristodemo, Lorenzo. "La Madonna divorata: la festa della Nossa Senhora da Achiropita un culto calabro-bizantino." In *Italiani in Brasile: rotte migratorie e percorsi culturali*, edited by Vittorio Cappelli and Alexandre Hecker, 49–72. Soveria Mannelli: Rubbettino Editore, 2010.
Atencio, Rebecca J. *Memory's Turn: Reckoning with Dictatorship in Brazil.* Madison: University of Wisconsin Press, 2014.
Atkinson, David. "Constructing Italian Africa: Geography and Geopolitics." In *Italian Colonialism*, edited by Ruth Ben-Ghiat and Mia Fuller, 15–26. New York: Palgrave Macmillan, 2018.
Avrich, Paul. "Sacco and Vanzetti's Revenge." In *The Lost World of Italian American Radicalism: Politics, Labor, and Culture*, edited by Philip V. Cannistraro and Gerald Meyer, 163–69. New York: Bloomsbury, 2003.
Bailey, Samuel L. *Immigrants in the Land of Promise: Italians in Buenos Aires and New York City, 1870–1914.* Ithaca, NY: Cornell University Press, 2004.
———. "The Role of Two Newspapers in the Assimilation of Italians in Buenos Aires and São Paulo, 1893–1913." *The International Migration Review* 12, no. 3 (1978): 321–40.
Balibar, Étienne, and Immanuel Wallerstein. *Race, Nation, Class: Ambiguous Identities.* London: Verso, 2011.
Ball, Molly C. *Navigating Life and Work in Old Republic São Paulo.* Gainesville: University of Florida Press, 2020.
Ballinger, Pamela. "Beyond the Italies: Italy as a Mobile Subject?" In *Italian Mobilities*, edited by Ruth Ben-Ghiat and Stephanie Malia Hom, 20–45. New York: Routledge, 2016.
Bassi, Serena, Loredana Polezzi, and Giulia Riccò. "Introduction: Critical Issues in Transnational Italian Studies." *Forum Italicum*, 57, no. 2 (2023): 273–88.
Battisti, Danielle. *Whom Shall We Welcome: Italian Americans and Immigration Reform 1945–1965.* New York: Fordham University Press, 2019.
Bedingfield, Agnieszka. "Trans-Memory and Diaspora: Memories of Europe and Asia in American Immigrant Narratives." In *Sites of Ethnicity: Europe and the Americas*, edited by William Boelhower, Rocío G. Davis, and Carmen Birkle, 333–46. Heidelberg: Universitätsverlag Winter, 2004.

Bellin, Stefano, and Guido Bartolini. "Italy's Multidimensional Forgetting: Narratives, Contested Memories, and Solidarity." *Italian Culture* 42, no. 2 (2024): 91–108.

Bencivenni, Marcella. *Italian Immigrant Radical Culture: The Idealism of the* Sovversivi *in the United States 1890–1940*. New York: New York University Press, 2011.

Ben-Ghiat, Ruth. *Fascist Modernities. Italy 1922–1945*. Berkeley: University of California Press, 2001.

Ben-Ghiat, Ruth, and Stephanie Hom, eds. *Italian Mobilities*. New York: Routledge, 2019.

Bertonha, João Fábio. "Le rappresentazioni degli italiani in Brasile: centocinquanta anni di immagini, stereotipi e contraddizioni." *Diacronie* 5, no. 1: Dossier: Italie altre. Immagini e comunità italiane all'estero (2011).

———. *O fascismo e os imigrantes italianos no Brasil*. Porto Alegre: EDIPUCRS, 2001.

Bhaba, Homi. *The Location of Culture*. New York: Routledge, 1994.

Biondi, Luigi. "Anarquistas italianos em São Paulo: o grupo do jornal anarquista 'La Battaglia' e a sua visão da sociedade brasileira: o embate entre imaginários libertários e etnocêntricos." *Cadernos AEL* 8/9 (1998): 117–47.

Bletz, May E. *Immigration and Acculturation in Brazil and Argentina 1890–1929*. New York: Palgrave Macmillan, 2010.

Bond, Emma. "Towards a Trans-National Turn in Italian Studies?" *Italian Studies* 69, no. 3 (2014): 415–24.

Bosi, Alfredo. *História concisa da literatura brasileira*. São Paulo: Editora Cultrix, 1994.

Bourdieu, Pierre. *Distinction: A Social Critique of the Judgement of Taste*. Translated by Richard Niece. New York: Routledge, 2010.

Brioni, Simone, and Lorenzo Mari. "Postcolonial Dante: Reading the Commedia in Mogadishu." In *Dante's Worlds: Echoes, Places, Questions*, edited by Peter Carravetta, 113–29. Rome: L'Erma di Bretschneider, 2019.

Brunello, Pietro. "Agenti di emigrazione, contadini e immagini dell'America nella provincia di Venezia." *Rivista di Storia Contemporanea* 11, no. 1 (1982): 95–122.

———. *Pionieri: gli Italiani in Brasile e il mito della frontiera*. Rome: Donzelli Editore, 1994.

Burdett, Charles. *Journeys through Fascism: Italian Travel Writing between the Wars*. Remapping Cultural History, v. 7. New York: Berghahn Books, 2007.

Burdett, Charles, and Derek Duncan, eds. *Cultural Encounters: European Travel Writing in the 1930s*. Remapping Cultural History. New York: Berghahn Books, 2002.

Burdett, Charles, and Loredana Polezzi, eds. *Transnational Italian Studies.* Liverpool: Liverpool University Press, 2020.

Butler, Kim. *Freedoms Given, Freedoms Won: Afro-Brazilians in Post-Abolition São Paulo and Salvador.* Newark, NJ: Rutgers University Press, 2000.

Cabrini, Francesca Saverio. *Viaggio delle suore missionarie del S. Cuore nel Pacifico attraverso la Cordigliera e nell'Atlantico.* Rome: Scuola Tip. Salesiana, 1898.

Cachey, Theodore J., Jr. "An Italian Literary History of Travel." *Annali d'Italianistica* 14 (1996): 55–64.

Campos, Haroldo de. "Da razão antropofágica: diálogo e diferença na cultura brasileira." In *Metalinguagem & outras metas: ensaios de teoria e crítica literária*, 231–56. São Paulo: Perspectiva, 1992.

Cannistraro, Philip V. "Mussolini's Cultural Revolution: Fascist or Nationalist." In *Fascism: Critical Concepts in Political Science*, edited by Roger Griffin and Matthew Feldman, 2, 183–203. New York: Routledge, 2004.

Capela, Carlos Eduardo Schmidt. "Italianos na ficção brasileira: modernidade em processo." *Fragmentos* 21 (2001): 147–64.

Cappelli, Vittorio. "Pequenas pátrias, a pátria, outras pátrias: as complexas identidades dos italianos no Brasil e na América Latina." *Naveg@mérica* 13 (2014).

Cardoso, Rafael. *Modernity in Black and White: Art and Image, Race and Identity in Brazil, 1890–1945.* Cambridge: Cambridge University Press, 2021.

Carelli, Mario. *Carcamanos e comendadores: os italianos de São Paulo: da realidade à ficção (1919–1930).* São Paulo: Editora Ática, 1985.

Carmo, Maurício Martins do. *Paulicéia scugliambada, Paulicéia desvairada: Juó Bananére e a imagem do italiano na literatura brasileira.* Niterói: Editora da Universidade Federal Fluminense, 1998.

Carnevale, Nancy C. *A New Language, A New World: Italian Immigrants in the United States, 1890–1945.* Champaign: University of Illinois Press, 2009.

Castro-Klarén, Sara. "A Genealogy for the 'Manifesto Antropófago,' or the Struggle between Socrates and the Caraïbe." *Nepantla: Views from the South* 1, no. 2 (2000): 295–322.

Cattarulla, Camilla. "Alla 'riscoperta' del Nuovo Mondo 1. Bibliografia dei viaggiatori italiani in America Latina (1870–1914)." *Biblioteche Oggi* 4 (1992): 419–45.

———. "Alla 'riscoperta' del Nuovo Mondo 2. La seconda parte della bibliografia dei viaggiatori italiani in America Latina (1870–1914)." *Biblioteche Oggi* 5 (1992): 545–62.

———. "Migrazioni al Río de La Plata e critica letteraria in Italia." *Altre Modernità / Otras Modernidades / Autres Modernités / Other Modernities* 2, no. 10 (2009): 100–22.

Cenni, Franco. *Italianos no Brasil: andiamo in 'Merica.* São Paulo: Livraria Martins Editora, 1975.

Ceron-Anaya, Hugo, Patricia de Santana Pinho, and Ana Ramos-Zayas. "A Conceptual Roadmap for the Study of Whiteness in Latin America." *Latin American and Caribbean Ethnic Studies* 18, no. 2 (2023): 177–99.

Chauí, Marilena, and Maria Sylvia Carvalho Franco. *Ideologia e mobilização popular.* Rio de Janeiro: Paz e Terra, 1978.

Choate, Mark. *Emigrant Nation: The Making of Italy Abroad.* Cambridge, MA: Harvard University Press, 2008.

———. "Italy at Home and Abroad After 150 Years: The Legacy of Emigration and the Future of Italianità." *Italian Culture* XXX, no. 1 (2012): 21–67.

Cinotto, Simone. *The Italian American Table: Food, Family and Community in New York City.* Champaign: University of Illinois Press, 2013.

Colaci, Anna Maria. "Gina Lombroso: una voce moderata all'interno del movimento emancipazionista nel primo novecento." *Quaderni di Intercultura* XI (2019): 167–79.

Corossacz, Valeria Ribeiro. *Bianchezza e mascolinità in Brasile: Etnografia di un soggetto dominante.* Milano: Mimesis Edizioni, 2015.

Corradini, Enrico. *La patria lontana.* Milan: Fratelli Treves, 1910.

Cusano, Alfredo. *Italia d'oltre mare; impressioni e ricordi dei miei cinque anni di Brasile.* Milan: Stabilimento Tipografico Enrico Reggiani, 1911.

Dainotto, Roberto M. *Europe (in Theory).* Durham, NC: Duke University Press, 2007.

De Bellis, Vito. *Fra l'Italia e il Brasile.* Rome: Tipografia Nazionale di G. Bertero & C., 1907.

De Donno, Fabrizio. "La Razza Ario-Mediterranea. Ideas of Race and Citizenship in Colonial and Fascist Italy, 1885–1941." *Interventions* 8, no. 3 (2007): 394–412.

De Majo, Claudio, and Samira Peruchi Moreno. "From Slash and Burn to Winemaking: The Historical Trajectory of Italian Colonos in the Uplands of Rio Grande Do Sul, Brazil." *Modern Italy* 26, no. 2 (2021): 141–58.

Dean, Warren. *Remittances of Italian Immigrants: From Brazil, Argentina, Uruguay and U.S.A., 1888–1914.* New York: New York University, Ibero-American Language and Area Center, 1974.

———. *The Industrialization of São Paulo 1880–1945.* Austin: University of Texas Press, 1969.

Dell'Aira, Alessandro. *Lungo studio grande amore: Rodolfo Crespi e l'Istituto Medio Italo-Brasiliano 'Dante Alighieri' di San Paolo.* Soveria Mannelli: Rubbettino Editore, 2012.

Deutsch, Sandra McGee. *Las Derechas: The Extreme Right in Argentina, Brazil, and Chile, 1890–1939.* Stanford, CA: Stanford University Press, 1999.

Dickie, John. *Darkest Italy: The Nation and Stereotypes of the Mezzogiorno, 1860–1900.* New York: Palgrave Macmillan, 1999.

Dolza Carrara, Delfina. *Essere figlie di Lombroso: due donne intellettuali Tra'800 e '900*. Milan: Franco Angeli, 1991.

Dos Santos, Ivison Poleto. "Sociedade promotora de imigração: formação e influência, 1886–1895." *Histórica* 1 (2007): 25.

Dunn, Christopher. *Brutality Garden: Tropicália and the Emergence of a Brazilian Counterculture*. Chapel Hill: University of North Carolina Press, 2001.

Dunn, Maggie, and Ann Morris. *The Composite Novel: The Short Story Cycle in Transition*. New York: Twayne Publishers, 1995.

Durante, Francesco. "Italy and the Literature of Immigration." Translated by Antony Shugaar. In *Words Without Borders*. 2016. Online. https://wordswithoutborders.org/read/article/2016-09/september-2016-italy-the-literature-of-immigration-francesco-durante/.

Duval, Roch. "Antonio de Alcântara Machado's Brás, Bexiga e Barra Funda as a Translation of São Paulo during Brazilian Modernism." In *Speaking of Memory: How Translation Shapes City Life*, edited by Sherry Simon, 205–19. Montreal: McGill-Quenn's University Press, 2016.

Ehrenreich, Barbara, and John Ehrenreich. "The New Left and the Professional Managerial Class." *Radical America* 11, no. 3 (May–June 1977): 7–24.

Einaudi, Luigi. *Un principe mercante; studio sulla espansione coloniale italiana*. Turin: Fratelli Bocca Editore, 1901.

Felice, Renzo de. *Interpretations of Fascism*. Translated by Brenda Huff Everett. Cambridge, MA: Harvard University Press, 1977.

Felici, Isabelle. "Gli anarchici italiani di São Paulo e il problema dell'organizzazione operaia." In *La riscoperta delle Americhe: lavoratori e sindacato nell'emigrazione Italiana in America Latina 1870–1970*, edited by Vanni Blengino, Emilio Franzina, and Adolfo Pepe, 326–38. Milan: Teti Editore, 1999.

———. "La Colonia Cecilia: fra leggenda e realtà." *Rivista Storica dell'anarchismo* a.III, no. 2 (1996): 103–9.

Ferraro, Evelin. "Place and Transmemory in California Italian American Literary Narratives: Dorothy Bryant's *Miss Giardino*." *Forum Italicum* 57, no. 2 (2023): 612–40.

Ferraro, Thomas J. *Feeling Italian: The Art of Ethnicity in America*. New York: New York University Press, 2005.

Ferruggia, Gemma. *Nostra signora del mar dolce (missioni e paesaggi di Amazzonia)*. Milan: Tipografia editrice L.F. Cogliati, 1901.

Finchelstein, Frederico. *Transatlantic Fascism: Ideology, Violence, and the Sacred in Argentina and Italy, 1919–1945*. Durham, NC: Duke University Press, 2010.

Fiore, Teresa. *Pre-Occupied Spaces: Remapping Italy's Transnational Migrations and Colonial Legacies*. New York: Fordham University Press, 2017.

———. "The Emigrant Post-'Colonia' in Contemporary Immigrant Italy." In *Postcolonial Italy*, edited by Cristina Lombardi-Diop and Caterina Romeo, 71–82. New York: Palgrave Macmillan, 2012.

Fogu, Claudio. *The Fishing Net and the Spider Web: Mediterranean Imaginaries and the Making of Italians*. New York: Palgrave Macmillan, 2020.

Fogu, Claudio, Stephanie Malia Hom, and Laura E. Ruberto. "Italia Senza Frontiere/Borderless Italy." *California Italian Studies* 9, no. 1 (2019): 1–12.

Foley, Barbara. *Telling the Truth: The Theory and Practice of Documentary Fiction*. Ithaca, NY: Cornell University Press, 1986.

Font, Mauricio. *Coffee and Transformation in São Paulo, Brazil*. Plymouth: Lexington Books, 2010.

Forgacs, David. *Italy's Margins: Social Exclusion and Nation Formation since 1861*. Cambridge: Cambridge University Press, 2014.

Franchini, Fernanda. "Entre Vargas e Mussolini: a nacionalização do Instituto Médio Ítalo-Brasileiro 'Dante Alighieri.'" Master's Dissertation. Universidade de São Paulo, 2015.

Franzina, Emilio. *Dall'arcadia in America: attività letteraria ed emigrazione transoceanica in Italia (1850–1940)*. Turin: Fondazione Giovanni Agnelli, 1996.

———. *Merica! Merica! Emigrazione e colonizzazione nelle lettere dei contadini veneti e friulani in America Latina (1876–1902)*. Caselle: Cierre Edizioni, 1994.

Frediani, Federica, Ricciarda Ricorda, and Luisa Rossi, eds. *Spazi, segni, parole: percorsi di viaggiatrici italiane*. Milan: FrancoAngeli, 2012.

Fuller, Mia. *Moderns Abroad: Architecture, Cities and Italian Imperialism*. Abingdon: Routledge, 2010.

Gabaccia, Donna R. *Italy's Many Diasporas*. Seattle: University of Washington Press, 2000.

———. "Worker Internationalism and Italian Labor Migration, 1870–1914." *International Labor and Working-Class History*, no. 45 (1994): 63–79.

Gabaccia, Donna R., and Franca Iacovetta. *Women, Gender and Transnational Lives: Italian Workers Of the World*. Toronto: University of Toronto Press, 2002.

Gabaccia, Donna R., and Fraser Ottanelli. "Introduction." In *Italian Workers of the World: Labor Migration and the Formation of Multiethnic Studies*, 1–20. Champaign: University of Illinois Press, 2001.

Galante, John Starosta. *On the Other Shores: The Atlantic Worlds of Italian in South America during the Great War*. Lincoln: University of Nebraska Press, 2022.

Galvão, Patrícia. *Parque industrial*. São Paulo: Companhia das Letras, 2022.

Gambarota, Paola. *Irresistible Signs: The Genius of Language and Italian National Identity*. Toronto: University of Toronto Press, 2011.

Gambino, Richard. *Vendetta: The True Story of the Largest Lynching in US History.* Toronto: Guernica Press, 2000.

Gattai, Zelia. *Anarchici, grazie a Dio.* Translated by Yvonne Giannini. Milan: Sperling & Kupfer Editori, 1992.

———. *Anarquistas, graças a Deus.* São Paulo: Companhia das Letras, 2009.

Gemignani, Carlo A. "Con Gina Lombroso nell'America meridionale." In *Spazi, segni, parole: percorsi di viaggiatrici italiane*, edited by F. Frediani, R. Ricorda, and L. Rossi, 127–44. Milan: Franco Angeli Editore, 2012.

Gennari, John. *Flavor and Soul: Italian America at Its African American Edge.* Chicago: University of Chicago Press, 2017.

Gentile, Emilio. "I Fasci Italiani All'Estero, The 'Foreign Policy' of the Fascist Party." In *Fascism Outside Europe: The European Impulse against Domestic Conditions in the Diffusion of Global Fascism*, edited by Stein Ugelvik Larsen, 95–115. Boulder, CO: Social Science Monographs, 2001.

Gentile, Giovanni. *Origini e dottrina del fascismo.* Rome: Libreria del Littorio, 1929.

Gerstle, Gary. *American Crucible: Race and Nation in the Twentieth Century.* Princeton, NJ: Princeton University Press, 2017.

Giuliani, Gaia. "Mediterraneità e bianchezza: il razzismo italiano tra fascismo e articolazioni contemporanee (1861–2015)." *Iperstoria–Testi Letterature Linguaggi* 6 (2015): 167–82.

Giuliani, Gaia, and Cristina Lombardi-Diop. *Bianco e nero: storia dell'identità razziale degli italiani.* Milan: Le Monnier, 2013.

Giunta, Edvige. *Writing with an Accent: Contemporary Italian American Women Authors.* New York: Palgrave MacMillan, 2002.

Goebel, Michael. "Italian Fascism and Diasporic Nationalisms in Argentina, Brazil, and Uruguay." In *Immigration and National Identity in Latin America*, edited by Nicola Foote and Michael Goebel, 234–55. Gainesville: University Press of Florida, 2014.

Gómez, Isabel C. *Cannibal Translation: Literary Reciprocity in Contemporary Latin America.* Evanston, IL: Northwestern University Press, 2023.

Graham, Jessica Lynn. *Shifting the Meaning of Democracy: Race, Politics, and Culture in the United States and Brazil.* Berkeley: University of California Press, 2019.

Greene, Shelleen. *Equivocal Subjects: Between Italy and Africa. Constructions of Racial and National Identity in the Italian Cinema.* New York: Continuum, 2012.

Guglielmo, Jennifer. "Introduction: White Lies, Dark Truths." In *Are Italians White? How Race Is Made in America*, edited by Jennifer Guglielmo and Salvatore Salerno, 1–16. New York: Routledge, 2003.

Guglielmo, Thomas A. *White on Arrival: Italians, Race, Color, and Power in Chicago, 1890–1945*. Oxford: Oxford University Press, 2004.

Guimarães, Antônio S. A. *Classes, raças e democracia*. São Paulo: Editora 34, 2002.

Haberly, David. *Three Sad Races: Racial Identity and National Consciousness in Brazilian Literature*. Cambridge: Cambridge University Press, 1983.

Hawthorne, Camilla. *Contesting Race and Citizenship: Youth Politics in the Black Mediterranean*. Ithaca, NY: Cornell University Press, 2022.

Helena, Lucia. "Brazilian Modernism and the Modern Art Week: The Influence of the European Twentieth-Century Vanguards." In *Brazilian Literature as World Literature*, edited by Eduardo F. Coutinho, 137–64. New York: Bloomsbury, 2018.

———. *Uma literatura antropofágica*. Rio de Janeiro: Livraria Editora Catedra, 1982.

Hester, Natalie. *Literature and Identity in Italian Baroque Travel Writing*. Surrey: Ashgate Publishing, 2008.

———. "Transnationalism and the Epic Tradition in Baroque Italian Travel Literature." In *Transnational Italian Studies*, edited by Charles Burdett and Loredana Polezzi, 107–24. Liverpool: Liverpool University Press, 2020.

Holloway, Thomas H. *Immigrants on The Land: Coffee and Society in São Paulo, 1886–1934*. Chapel Hill: University of North Carolina Press, 1980.

Hom, Stephanie Malia. "On the Origins of Making Italy: Massimo D'Azeglio and 'Fatta l'Italia Bisogna Fare Gli Italiani.'" *Italian Culture* XXXI, no. 1 (2013): 1–16.

Iamurri, Laura. "Modernity Abroad: Italy at the *Bienal de São Paulo*, the Early Years." In *Voyages Between Brazil and Italy, Motion: Migrations* (35th CIHA World Congress), edited by Claudia Mattos Avolese, 1805–19. São Paulo: Vasto Edições, 2023.

Incisa di Camerana, Ludovico. *Il grande esodo: storia delle migrazioni italiane nel mondo*. Milan: Corbaccio, 2003.

———. "San Paolo, Italia." *Limes: Rivista Italiana di Geopolitica* 6: Dossier: Brasile la Stella del Sud, 2007.

Instituto Brasileiro de Geografia e Estatística. *Brasil: 500 anos de povoamento*. Rio de Janeiro: Instituto Brasileiro de Geografia e Estatística, 2000.

Jacobson, Matthew Frye. *Roots Too: White Ethnic Revival in Post-Civil Rights America*. Cambridge, MA: Harvard University Press, 2008.

———. *Whiteness of a Different Color: European Immigrants and the Alchemy of Race*. Cambridge, MA: Harvard University Press, 1999.

Johnson, Randal. "Brazilian Modernism: An Idea Out of Place?" In *Modernism and Its Margins. Reinscribing Cultural Modernity from Spain and Latin*

America, edited by Anthony Geist and José B. Monleón, 186–214. New York: Routledge, 1999.

———. "Tupy or Not Tupy: Cannibalism and Nationalism in Contemporary Brazilian Literature and Culture." In *On Modern Latin American Fiction*, edited by John King, 41–59. New York: Hill and Wang, 1987.

Karam, John Tofik. *Another Arabesque: Syrian-Lebanese Ethnicity in Neoliberal Brazil.* Philadelphia: Temple University Press, 2007.

Kay, Tristan. "Dante and the Transnational Turn." In *Transnational Italian Studies*, edited by Charles Burdett and Loredana Polezzi, 291–308. Liverpool: Liverpool University Press, 2020.

Kessel, Tamara van. *Foreign Cultural Policy in the Interbellum: The Italian Dante Alighieri Society and the British Council Contesting the Mediterranean.* Amsterdam: Amsterdam University Press, 2016.

Labanca, Nicola. *Oltremare: storia dell'espansione coloniale italiana.* Bologna: Il Mulino, 2007.

Leite, José Correia. "E, Apoz a Liberdade." *O Clarim d'Alvorada*, August 30, 1925.

———. "Incorrecto." *O Clarim d'Alvorada*, September 27, 1925.

———. "Naziunale." *O Clarim*, January 6, 1924.

———. "Sempri Avanti!" *O Clarim*, June 1924.

———. "U Clarino." *O Clarim*, April 6, 1924.

Leite, José Correia, and Cuti. . . . *E disse o velho militante José Correia Leite.* São Paulo: Secretaria Municipal de Cultura, 1992.

Lejeune, Philippe. *On Autobiography.* Translated by Katherine M. Leary. Minneapolis: University of Minnesota Press, 1989.

Lesser, Jeffrey. *Immigration, Ethnicity, and National Identity in Brazil, 1808 to the Present.* New York: Cambridge University Press, 2013.

———. *Negotiating National Identity: Immigrants, Minorities, and the Struggle for Ethnicity in Brazil.* Durham, NC: Duke University Press, 1999.

Lombardi-Diop, Cristina. "Gifts, Sex, and Guns: Nineteenth-Century Italian Explorers in Africa." In *A Place in the Sun–Africa in Italian Colonial Culture from Post-Unification to the Present*, edited by Patrizia Palumbo, 119–37. Berkeley: University of California Press, 2003.

———. "Transoceanic Race: A Postcolonial Approach to Italian American Studies." In *Transcending Borders, Bridging Gaps: Italian Americana, Diasporic Studies, and the University Curriculum*, edited by Anthony Tamburri and Fred Gardaphé, 83–95. New York: John D. Calandra Italian American Institute, 2015.

Lombroso Ferrero, Gina. *Nell'America Meridionale (Brasile-Uruguay-Argentina): note e impressioni di Gina Lombroso Ferrero.* Milan: Fratelli Treves, 1908.

Lomonaco, Alfonso. *Al Brasile*. Milan: Società Editrice Libreria, 1889.

Looney, Dennis. *Freedom Readers: The African American Reception of Dante Alighieri and the Divine Comedy*. South Bend, IN: Notre Dame University Press, 2011.

Loveman, Mara. "Whiteness in Latin America: Measurement and Meaning in National Censuses." *Journal de La Société Des Américanistes* 95, no. 2 (2009): 207–34.

Luconi, Stefano. "Italian Immigrants, Whiteness, and Race: A Regional Perspective." *Italian American Review* 11, no. 1 (2021): 4–26.

Machado, António de Alcântara. *Cavaquinho e saxofone 1926–1935*. Rio de Janeiro: José Olympio Editora, 1940.

———. *Novelas paulistanas*. Rio de Janeiro: José Olympio Editora, 1961.

———. "O que eu disse a um comediógrafo nacional." *Novíssima*, December 1924.

Macola, Ferruccio. *L'Europa alla conquista dell'America Latina*. Venice: Ferdinando Ongania Editore, 1894.

Magalhães, Mário. *Marighella: O guerrilheiro que incendiou o mundo*. São Paulo: Companhia das Letras, 2012.

Malatian, Teresa. *O Cavaleiro Negro: Arlindo Veiga dos Santos e a Frente Negra Brasileira*. São Paulo: Alameda Editorial, 2015.

Marazzi, Martino. *Italexit: Saggi su risorgimento e disunione nazionale*. Florence: Franco Cesati Editore, 2019.

Marighella, Carlos. *Piccolo manuale della guerriglia urbana*. Florence: Passaggio al Bosco, 2022.

Matos, Maria Izilda de S. "Un sambista italiano a São Paulo: Adoniran Barbosa." In *Italiani in Brasile: Rotte migratorie e percorsi culturali*, edited by Vittorio Capelli and Alexandre Hecker, 73–88. Soveria Mannelli: Rubbettino Editore, 2010.

McGuire, Valerie. *Italy's Sea: Empire and Nation in the Mediterranean, 1895–1945*. Liverpool: Liverpool University Press, 2020.

Milazzo, Marzia. *Colorblind Tools: Global Technologies of Racial Power*. Evanston, IL: Northwestern University Press, 2022.

Miller, Francesca. "Anarquistas, Graças a Deus! 'Italy' in South America." In *Revisioning Italy: National Identity and Global Culture*, edited by Beverly Allen and Mary Russo, 213–32. Minneapolis: University of Minnesota Press, 1997.

Mills, C. Wright. *The Power Elite*. Oxford: Oxford University Press, 1968.

Mitchell, Michael. "Miguel Reale and the Impact of Conservative Modernization on Brazilian Race Relations." In *Racial Politics in Contemporary Brazil*, edited by Michael Hanchard, 116–37. Durham, NC: Duke University Press, 1999.

———. “Racial Consciousness and the Political Attitudes and Behavior of Blacks in São Paulo, Brazil.” PhD Dissertation. Indiana University, 1977.

Moe, Nelson J. *The View from Vesuvius: Italian Culture and the Southern Question*. Berkeley: University of California Press, 2002.

Monserrati, Michele. “A Victorian Taste of Italy: Situating the ‘Italian-Swiss Colony’ in California Wine Culture.” *Forum Italicum* 57 no. 2 (2023): 690–713.

Moriconi, Ubaldo A. *Nel paese de’ macacchi*. Turin: Roux Frassati, 1897.

Mugnaini, Marco. *L’America Latina e Mussolini: Brasile e Argentina nella politica estera dell’Italia (1919–1943)*. Milan: Franco Angeli, 2008.

Muscio, Giuliana. *Napoli/New York/Hollywood: Film between Italy and the United States*. New York: Fordham University Press, 2018.

Nathan, Vetri. “Mimic-Nation, Mimic-Men.” In *National Belongings: Hybridity in Italian Colonial and Postcolonial Cultures*, edited by Jacqueline Andall and Derek Duncan, 41–62. Bern: Peter Lang, 2010.

Negash, Tekeste. *Italian Colonialism in Eritrea 1882–1941: Policies, Praxis and Impact*. Uppsala: Uppsala University Press, 1987.

Neto, Odilon Caldeira. *Sob o signo do sigma: integralismo, neointegralismo, antissemitismo*. Maringá: Editora da Universidade Estadual de Maringá, 2014.

Njegosh, Tatiana Petrovich. “Gli italiani sono bianchi? Per una storia culturale della linea del colore in Italia.” In *Parlare di razza: la lingua del colore tra Italia e Stati Uniti*, edited by Tatiana Petrovich Njegosh and Anna Scacchi, 13–45. Verona: Ombre Corte, 2012.

———. “La finzione della razza: la linea del colore e il meticciato.” In *Il colore della nazione*, edited by Gaia Giuliani, 215–28. Florence: Le Monnier, 2015.

Nugent, Walter. *Crossings: The Great Transatlantic Migrations, 1870–1914*. Bloomington: Indiana University Press, 1992.

Nunes, Bendito. *A utopia antropofágica: a antropofagia ao alcance de todos*. São Paulo: Globo, 1990.

Nunes, Zita. *Cannibal Democracy in the Literature of the Americas*. Minneapolis: University of Minnesota Press, 2008.

Oliveira, Lúcia Lippi. *Nós e eles: relações culturais entre brasileiros e imigrantes*. São Paulo: FGV, 2006.

Ortiz, Renato. *Cultura brasileira e identidade nacional*. São Paulo: Brasiliense, 1985.

Pagano, Tullio. *Italy to Argentina: Travel Writing and Emigrant Colonialism*. Amherst, MA: Amherst College Press, 2023.

Parati, Graziella. *Migration Italy: The Art of Talking Back in a Destination Culture*. Toronto: University of Toronto Press, 2005.

Pareto, Vilfredo. *The Mind and Society*. Vol. 3. New York: Harcourt, Brace and Company, 1935.

Patriarca, Silvana. *Italian Vices: Nation and Character from the Risorgimento to the Republic*. Cambridge: Cambridge University Press, 2010.

Payne, Stanley G. *Fascism: Comparison and Definition*. Madison: University of Wisconsin Press, 1980.

Pecorelli, Joseph. "Constructing a Community: The Italian Press in São Paulo from 1880 to 1920." *Italica* 97, no. 2 (2020): 264–82.

Pesarini, Angelica. "'Blood Is Thicker than Water': The Materialisation of the Racial Body in Fascist East Africa." *Zapruder World: An International Journal for the History of Social Conflict*, no. 4 (2017). http://zapruderworld.org/journal/past-volumes/volume-4/blood-is-thicker-than-water-the-materialization-of-the-racial-body-in-fascist-east-africa/.

———. "When the Mediterranean Became Black: Diasporic Hopes and (Post)Colonial Traumas." In *The Black Mediterranean: Bodies, Borders, and Citizenship*, 31–55. London: Palgrave Macmillan, 2021.

Picchia, Menotti Del. "A Questão Racial." *Correio Paulistano*, May 10, 1921.

———. "Juca Mulato." Casa Menotti. Accessed February 14, 2020. https://www.casamenotti.com.br/.

Pinho, Patricia de Santana. "White but Not Quite: Tones and Overtones of Whiteness in Brazil." *Small Axe: A Caribbean Journal of Criticism* 13, no. 2 (2009): 39–56.

Pinto, Regina Pahim. *O movimento negro em São Paulo: luta e identidade*. Ponta Grossa: Editora UEPG, 2013.

Pisa, Beatrice. *Nazione e politica nella "Società Dante Alighieri."* Rome: Bonacci Editore, 1995.

Polezzi, Loredana. *Translating Travel: Contemporary Italian Travel Writing in English Translation*. London: Routledge, 2001.

Ponzanesi, Sandra. "The Color of Love: *Madamismo* and Interracial Relationships in the Italian Colonies." *Research in African Literatures* 43, no. 2 (2012): 155–72.

———. "The Postcolonial Turn in Italian Studies: European Perspectives." In *Postcolonial Italy*, edited by Cristina Lombardi-Diop and Caterina Romeo, 51–69. New York: Palgrave Macmillan, 2012.

Portelli, Alessandro. "The Problem of the Color Blind: Notes on the Discourse on Race in Italy." In *CrossRoutes: The Meaning of "Race" for the 21st Century*, edited by Paola Boi and Sabine Broeck, 29–39. Münster: Lit Verlag, 2003.

Prado, Antonio Arnoni. *Itinerário de uma falsa vanguarda: os dissidentes, a semana de 22 e o integralismo*. São Paulo: Editora 34, 2010.

Prado, Paulo. *Retrato do Brasil: ensaio sobre a tristeza brasileira*. São Paulo: Duprat-Mayença, 1928.

Pratt, Mary Louise. *Imperial Eyes: Travel Writing and Transculturation*. New York: Routledge, 2008.

Proglio, Gabriele, Camilla Hawthorne, Ida Danewid, P. Khalil Saucier, Giuseppe Grimaldi, Angelica Pesarini, Timothy Raeymaekers, Giulia Grechi, and Vivian Gerrand. *The Black Mediterranean: Bodies, Borders and Citizenship*. London: Palgrave MacMillan, 2021.

Rachum, Ilan. "Antropofagia against Verdeamarelo." *Latin American Literary Review* 4, no. 8 (1976): 67–81.

Raffa, Guy P. *Dante's Bones: How a Poet Invented Italy*. Cambridge, MA: Harvard University Press, 2020.

Re, Lucia. "Italians and the Invention of Race: The Poetics and Politics of Difference in the Struggle over Libya, 1890–1913." *California Italian Studies* 1, no. 1 (2010): 1–65.

Reale, Miguel. *Imperativos Da Revolução de Março*. São Paulo: Editora Martins, 1964.

———. *Memórias*. Vol. I: Destinos cruzados. 2 vols. São Paulo: Saraiva, 1987.

———. *Memórias*. Vol. II: A balança e a espada. 2 vols. São Paulo: Saraiva, 1987.

———. "Meu Dante." In *O Meu Dante*, edited by Maria Cecilia Casini. Cotia, SP: Ateliê Editorial, 2024.

———. *Obras políticas*. Vol. 1, 1931–1937. 2 vols. Brasília: Editora da Universidade de Brasília, 1983.

Reed, Adolph L., Jr. *The South: Jim Crow and Its Afterlives*. New York: Verso, 2022.

Riall, Lucy. "Men at War: Masculinity and Military Ideals in the Risorgimento." In *The Risorgimento Revisited*, edited by Silvana Patriarca and Lucy Riall, 152–70. London: Palgrave Macmillan, 2012.

Ricatti, Francesco. "Forum. Towards a Decolonial History of Italian Migration to Australia: Introduction." *AltreItalie* 59 (2019): 8–15.

Riccò, Giulia. "'Il segno di Menelik': Enrico Corradini, the *Protocolos*, and the Re-Staging of Adwa in São Paulo," *Italian Culture* 41, no. 1. (2023): 6–24.

———."Navigating between Italianità and Brasilidade: The Case of Menotti del Picchia," *Literatura da (i)migração no Brasil*, edited by Wail Hassan and Rogério Lima, 100–121. Rio de Janeiro: Edições Makunaima. 2020.

Ricupero, Rubens. "Introduzione." In *Notizie di São Paulo: racconti*, by Antônio de Alcântara Machado. Translated by Giuliano Macchi. Milan: All'insegna del pesce d'oro, 1981.

Rochat, Giorgio. "Adua: analisi di una sconfitta." In *Adua: le ragioni di una sconfitta*. Edited by A. del Boca. Bari: Laterza, 1997.

Roedinger, David R. *The Wages of Whiteness: Race and the Making of the American Working Class.* New York: Verso, 1999.

———. *Working Toward Whiteness: How America's Immigrants Became White: The Strange Journey from Ellis Island to the Suburbs.* New York: Basic Books, 2005.

Romani, Carlo. *Oreste ristori: vita avventurosa di un anarchico tra Toscana e Sudamerica.* Ghezzano: BFS Edizioni, 2015.

Romani, Carlo, and Bruno Corrêa de Sá e Benevides. "The Italian Anarchists' Network in São Paulo at the Beginning of the Twentieth Century." In *Transatlantic Radicalism: Socialist and Anarchist Exchanges in the 19th and 20th Centuries*, edited by Frank Jacob and Mario Keßler, 57–82. Liverpool: Liverpool University Press, 2021.

Romeo, Caterina. *Narrative tra due sponde: memoir d'italiane d'America.* Rome: Carrocci Editore, 2005.

———. "Racial Evaporations: Representing Blackness in African Italian Postcolonial Literature." In *Postcolonial Italy*, edited by Cristina Lombardi-Diop and Caterina Romeo, 221–38. New York: Palgrave Macmillan, 2012.

Roscilli, Rita Antonella. *Da palavra à imagem em* Anarquistas, graças a Deus *de Zélia Gattai.* Salvador: EDUFBA, 2011.

Rosoli, Gianfausto. "L'emigrazione italiana nel Rio Grande do Sul, Brasile Meridionale." *Altreitalie* 10, no. 2 (1993): 105–22.

Rossi, Adolfo. *Condizione dei coloni italiani nello stato di San Paolo (Brasile): relazione e diari.* Bollettino dell'Emigrazione, 1902.

Rossi, Gianni Scipione. *Mussolini e il diplomatico: la vita e i diari di Serafino Mazzolini, un monarchico a Salò.* Soveria Mannelli: Rubbettino Editore, 2005.

Rothberg, Michael. *Multidirectional Memory: Remembering the Holocaust in the Age of Decolonization.* Stanford, CA: Stanford University Press, 2009.

Rotondo, Francesco. "Reading a Travel Journal: The Melancholia of Gina Lombroso in Latin America." In *History of Law and Other Humanities*, edited by V. Ambrosi and V. M. Minale, 419–30. Madrid: Editorial Dykinson, 2019.

Ruberto, Laura E., and Joseph Sciorra. "Disrupted and Unsettled: An Introduction to Monuments, Memorials, and Italian Migrations." *Italian American Review* 12, no. 1 (2022): 1–35.

Ruíz Díaz, Matías. "Europa y América: Guglielmo Ferrero y Gina Lombroso En La Penitenciaría Nacional de Buenos Aires. 1907." *Anales del instituto de arte americano e investigaciones estéticas. Mario J. Buschiazzo* 46, no. 1 (June 2016): 77–90.

Salatini, Erica, Fernanda M. Cechinel, Ivair Carlos Castelan, and Sara Debenedetti. "A presença italiana nas revistas literarias brasileiras da primeira metade do século XX." In *A Literatura Italiana No Brasil e a Literatura Brasileira Na Itália: Sob o Olhar Da Tradução*, edited by Patricia Peterle, 81–100. Tubarão: Copiart, 2011.

Salgado, Plínio. *O estrangeiro*. Rio de Janeiro: José Olympio, 1972.

Salvatorelli, Luigi. *Nazionalfascismo*. Turin: Einaudi, 1977.

Salvetti, Patrizia. *Immagine nazionale ed emigrazione nella società "Dante Alighieri."* Rome: Bonacci Editore, 1995.

———. "Le scuole italiane all'estero." In *Storia dell'emigrazione italiana II: arrivi*, edited by Piero Bevilacqua, Andreina De Clementi, and Emilio Franzina, 535–50. Rome: Donzelli Editore, 2009.

Sanders, James. *The Vanguard of the Atlantic World: Creating Modernity, Nation, and Democracy in Nineteenth Century Latin America*. Durham, NC: Duke University Press, 2014.

Sansone, Livio. "Hiperbólicos italianos: as viagens dos integrantes da Escola Positiva de Antropologia da Itália pela América Meridional, 1907–1910." *História, Ciências, Saúde-Manguinhos* 27, no. 1 (2020): 265–74.

Santos, Carlos José Ferreira dos. *Nem tudo era italiano: São Paulo e pobreza (1890–1915)*. São Paulo: Annablume Editora, 1998.

Schnapp, Jeffrey T., and João Cezar de Castro Rocha. "Brazilian Velocities: On Marinetti's 1926 Trip to South America." *South Central Review* 13, no. 2/3, Futurism and Avant-Garde (1996): 105–56.

Schneider, Jane, ed. *Italy's "Southern Question": Orientalism in One Country*. New York: Routledge, 1998.

Schwarcz, Lilia Moritz. *Imagens da branquitude: a presença da ausência*. São Paulo: Companhia das Letras, 2024.

———*The Spectacles of the Races: Scientists, Institutions, and the Race Question in Brazil, 1870–1930*. Translated by Leland Guyer. New York: Hill and Wang, 1999.

Sciorra, Joseph. "'Italians Against Racism': The Murder of Yusuf Hawkins (R.I.P.) and My March on Bensonhurst." In *Are Italians White? How Race Is Made in America*, edited by Jennifer Guglielmo and Salvatore Salerno, 192–212. New York: Routledge, 2003.

Seigel, Micol. *Uneven Encounters: Making Race and Nation in Brazil and the United States*. Durham, NC: Duke University Press, 2009.

Seitenfus, Ricardo Silva. "Ideology and Diplomacy: Italian Fascism and Brazil (1935–1938)." *Hispanic American Historical Review* 64, no. 3 (1984): 503–34.

Serani, Ugo. "Nella letteratura brasiliana." In *Storia dell'emigrazione italiana II: arrivi*, edited by Piero Bevilacqua, Andreina De Clementi, and Emilio Franzina, 661–68. Rome: Donzelli Editore, 2009.

Sergi, Pantaleone. "Funzioni pedagogiche, etniche, e politiche della stampa italiana in Brasile." In *Italiani in Brasile: Rotte migratorie e percorsi culturali*, edited by Vittorio Cappelli and Alexandre Hecker, 9–30. Soveria Mannelli: Rubbettino Editore, 2010.

Shuchmacher, Nelson Endebo. "'A Invençó do Brasile': Juó Bananére and Non-Italian Literature." *California Italian Studies* 9, no. 1 (2019): 1–12.

Skidmore, Thomas. *Black into White: Race and Nationality in Brazilian Thought*. Durham, NC: Duke University Press, 1993.

Sorgoni, Barbara. "Diventare Antropologo: Alberto Pollera e l'etnografia Coloniale." *Quaderni Storici* 37 (February 1, 2002): 55–82.

Sottong, Heather. "'Hero of Two Worlds': The Equestrian Monument to Giuseppe Garibaldi in Buenos Aires, Argentina." *Italian American Review* 12, no. 1 (2022): 36–60.

Spackman, Barbara. *Accidental Orientalists: Modern Italian Travelers in Ottoman Lands*. Liverpool: Liverpool University Press, 2017.

———. *Fascist Virilities: Rhetoric, Ideology, and Social Fantasy in Italy*. Minneapolis: University of Minnesota Press, 1996.

Srivastava, Neelam. "Publishing the Resistance: Third-Worldist Writing in Cold War Italy." In *The Form of Ideology and the Ideology of Form: Cold War, Decolonization and Third World Print Cultures*, edited by Francesca Orsini, Neelam Srivastava, and Laetitia Zecchini, 137–76. Cambridge: Open Book Publishers, 2022.

Stewart-Steinberg, Suzanne. *The Pinocchio Effect: On Making Italians (1860–1920)*. Chicago: University of Chicago Press, 2007.

Tamburri, Anthony Julian. "Afterword: Rethinking Labels: The Italian Writer as Exemplar or Distinct Categories as Quixotic." In *New Italian Migrations to the United States: Vol. 2: Art and Culture Since 1945*, edited by Laura E. Ruberto and Joseph Sciorra, 193–202. Champaign: Illinois University Press, 2017.

Tintori, Guido. "The Transnational Political Practices of 'Latin American Italians.'" *International Migration* 49, no. 3 (2011): 168–88.

Totaro-Genevois, Mariella. *Cultural and Linguistic Policy Abroad: The Italian Experience*. Bristol: Multilingual Matters, 2005.

Trento, Angelo. "'Dovunque è un italiano, là è il tricolore': La penetrazione del fascismo tra gli immigrati in Brasile." In *Fascisti in Sud America*, edited by Eugenia Scarzanella, 3–54. Florence: Le Lettere, 2005.

———. "I Fasci in Brasile." In *Il fascismo e gli emigrati: la parabola dei fasci italiani all'estero*. Edited by Emilio Franzina and Matteo Sanfilippo. Bari: Laterza, 2003.

———. "In Brasile." In *Storia dell'emigrazione italiana II: arrivi*, edited by Piero Bevilacqua, Andreina De Clementi, and Emilio Franzina, 3–24. Rome: Donzelli Editore, 2009.

———. "Italianità in Brazil: A Disputed Object of Desire." In *The Columbus People: Perspectives in Italian Immigration to the Americas and Australia.* Edited by L. F. Tomasi, P. Gastaldo, and T. Row. New York: The Center for Migration Studies of New York, 1994.

———. *Là dov'è la raccolta del caffè: l'emigrazione italiana in Brasile, 1875–1940.* Padua: Editrice Antenore, 1984.

———. "'Wherever We Work, The Land Is Ours': The Italian Anarchist Press and Working-Class Solidarity." In *Italian Workers of the World: Labor Migration and the Formation of Multiethnic States*, edited by Donna R. Gabaccia and Fraser Ottanelli, 102–20. Champaign: University of Illinois Press, 2001.

Trindade, Helgio. *Integralismo: o fascismo brasileiro da década de 30.* São Paulo: Difel, 1974.

Truzzi, Oswaldo. *Italianidade no interior paulista: percurso e descaminhos de uma identidade étnica (1880–1950).* São Paulo: Editora UNESP, 2015.

———. *Syrian and Lebanese Patricios in São Paulo: From the Levant to Brazil.* Champaign: University of Illinois Press, 2018.

Ustra, Carlos Alberto Brilhante. *A verdade sufocada: a história que a esquerda não quer que o Brasil conheça.* São Paulo: Editora Ser, 2006.

Vangelista, Chiara. *Le braccia per la fazenda: immigrati e caipiras nella formazione del mercato del lavoro paulista (1850–1930).* Turin: Franco Angeli, 1982.

———. "Una viaggiatrice italiana di fine ottocento: Gemma Ferruggia in Amazzonia." *Fênix-Revista de História e Estudos Culturais* 13, no. 1 (2016): 1–13.

———. "Vita d'emigrante. Il colono nella piantagione di caffè paulista secondo l'interpretazione dei viaggiatori italiani (1880–1930)." In *Miscellanea di storia delle esplorazioni*, edited by F. Surdich, Vol. VII. Genoa: Bozzi Editore, 1982.

Varejão, Marcela. *Il positivismo dall'Italia al Brasile: sociologia del diritto, giuristi e legislazione (1822–1935).* Milan: Giuffrè Editore, 2005.

Vasconcelos, José Antônio. "Giovanni Rossi and His Anarchist Utopia in Nineteenth Century Brazil." *Anarchist Studies* 24, no. 2 (2016): 60–92.

Vellon, Peter G. *A Great Conspiracy against Our Race: Italian Immigrant Newspapers and the Construction of Whiteness in the Early 20th Century.* New York: New York University Press, 2017.

Veracini, Lorenzo. "Italian Colonialism through a Settler Colonial Studies Lens." *Journal of Colonialism and Colonial History* 19, no. 3 (2018).

Verdicchio, Pasquale. *Bound by Distance: Rethinking Nationalism through the Italian Diaspora.* New York: Bordighera Press, 2016.

Vezzosi, Elisabetta. "Radical Ethnic Brokers: Immigrant Socialist Leaders in the United States between Ethnic Community and Larger Society." In *Italian Workers of the World: Labor Migration and the Formation of Multiethnic States*, edited by Donna R. Gabaccia and Fraser Ottanelli, 121–38. Champaign: University of Illinois Press, 2001.

Viotti da Costa, Emília. *The Brazilian Empire: Myths and Histories.* Chicago: University of Chicago Press, 1985.

Viscusi, Robert. "The Future of Italianità: The Italian Commonwealth." In *The Columbus People: Perspectives in Italian Immigration to the Americas and Australia*, edited by Lydia F. Tomasi, Piero Gastaldo, and Thomas Row, 483–90. New York: Center for Migration Studies, 1994.

Weinstein, Barbara. *The Color of Modernity: São Paulo and the Making of Race and Nation in Brazil.* Durham, NC: Duke University Press, 2015.

Welch, Rhiannon Noel. *Vital Subjects: Race and Biopolitics in Italy.* Liverpool: Liverpool University Press, 2016.

Wong, A. *Race and the Nation in Liberal Italy, 1861–1911: Meridionalism, Empire, and Diaspora.* New York: Palgrave Macmillan, 2006.

Zanin, Valter. "O'Menelik eroe dei due mondi." *Il Manifesto*, March 25, 1996.

Zanoni, Elizabeth. *Migrant Marketplaces: Foods and Italians in North and South America.* Champaign: University of Illinois Press, 2018.

INDEX

GIULIA RICCÒ is an assistant professor of Italian at the University of Michigan, Ann Arbor.

Critical Studies in Italian Migrations

Nancy C. Carnevale and Laura E. Ruberto, *series editors*

Heather Renee Sottong, *Transnational Dante: Inventing Argentine Cultural Identity*

Giulia Riccò, *The Italian Colony of São Paulo: Race, Class, and Cultural Capital in Brazil*

Gaoheng Zhang, *Italian Dumplings and Chinese Pizzas: Transcultural Food Mobilities*

www.ingramcontent.com/pod-product-compliance
Lightning Source LLC
Chambersburg PA
CBHW020412110726
47899CB00006B/1957

* 9 7 8 1 5 3 1 5 1 2 2 5 5 *